Henry Clay Vedder

A History of the Baptists in the middle States

Henry Clay Vedder

A History of the Baptists in the middle States

ISBN/EAN: 9783337188085

Printed in Europe, USA, Canada, Australia, Japan

Cover: Foto ©ninafisch / pixelio.de

More available books at **www.hansebooks.com**

A HISTORY

OF THE

BAPTISTS IN THE MIDDLE STATES

BY

HENRY C. VEDDER

Professor of Church History in Crozer Theological Seminary
Author of "A Short History of the Baptists"
" The Dawn of Christianity"

"Different statements of truth, different forms of worship, an altered outward life, there may be; but the spiritual affections, the sense of duty, the charity, the penitent trust, the divine desire, the hatred of wrong, the faith in the unseen, which constitute true religion, belong to all generations."
S. L. CALDWELL, D. D.

PHILADELPHIA
AMERICAN BAPTIST PUBLICATION SOCIETY
1420 CHESTNUT STREET
1898

To
Henry Griggs Weston, D. D., LL. D.
for thirty years
President of Crozer Theological Seminary
and for more than fifty years
a maker of
Baptist History
But for whose encouragement and criticism
the story would be even less worthy of its theme
This book is affectionately dedicated

PREFACE

THIS history is founded on original sources. Second-hand authorities on the subject are few, incomplete, and untrustworthy, and there was nothing to do but seek and study the original documents. The task was the more difficult because the path was practically unbroken. There was from the first no lack of materials, but nobody had ever undertaken to sift and combine them. There were no successes of predecessors to emulate, no blunders to profit by; all had to be done for the first time. That it is done as it should be done, as it might be done, is not claimed. The author is sure of but one thing: that he has worked with diligence, and a faithful effort to tell the story truthfully, without so overloading it with details as to make it confusing or wearisome. Some one who shall undertake the task in future years, with documents in the meantime accumulated, will avoid the mistakes of this book and make a far better.

Probably every reader will note omissions, and among them things that he will think he had a right to look for in such a book. The chief reason for such omissions is lack of space. The author has examined many thousand volumes and files of documents, to say nothing of manuscripts and pamphlets amounting to many more thousands, and in few cases has he failed to find something germane to his subject, or to make note of some interesting fact or anecdote. Long before he began to write, he found himself in possession of material sufficient to make several volumes like this, and that without any " padding." It became at once a serious question what to include in such a sketch, and what might be excluded with least loss to the reader. This was a delicate problem; that it is correctly solved in all cases the writer does not flatter himself.

Those who compare this volume with the others of the series to which it belongs will find certain things related here that may be found in them, as well as other things that do not form part of the exclusive history of Baptists in the Middle States. From the nature of the case, this overlapping of narratives could not be avoided. The Baptists of the Middle States were not isolated from their brethren in other sections, and their story could not be told without frequent reference to things that are also part of the history of the New England and Western Baptists. But it is believed that, in every such case, the point of view in this book differs sufficiently from that of other writers, while also the grouping of facts and the coloring of the story have sufficient individuality to justify the retelling of an episode already recounted.

H. C. V.

CROZER SEMINARY, January, 1898.

CONTENTS

CHAPTER I
EARLY DAYS IN NEW YORK 9

CHAPTER II
THE EARLY DAYS IN NEW JERSEY 38

CHAPTER III
EARLY DAYS IN PENNSYLVANIA AND DELAWARE . . 56

CHAPTER IV
THE GROWTH OF ORGANIZATION 86

CHAPTER V
THE WESTERN MOVEMENT; ITS RESULTS AND SIGNIFICANCE 109

CHAPTER VI
EVANGELISM AND REVIVALS 149

CHAPTER VII
THE PERIOD OF CONTROVERSIES 175

CHAPTER VIII
BAPTISTS AND EDUCATION 207

CHAPTER IX
WORK FOR THE YOUNG—THE PUBLICATION SOCIETY . 255

CHAPTER X
BAPTISTS AND BIBLE WORK 286

CHAPTER XI
A COMPARATIVE STUDY OF PROGRESS 309

APPENDIXES
- A 333
- B 336
- C 339
- D 342
- E 346
- F 348

A HISTORY OF BAPTISTS

IN THE

MIDDLE STATES

CHAPTER I

EARLY DAYS IN NEW YORK

ON the 9th of September, 1609, Hendrick Hudson sailed into New York Bay in the "Half Moon" and cast anchor. His prophetic eye beheld the waters of this bay—then, as now, the most beautiful in the Western Hemisphere—filled with ships from every land and its shores occupied by teeming cities. He named the region New Netherland, and marked the isle of Manhattan as the site of a new colony. The Dutch were among the most enterprising colonizers of the seventeenth century, and the glowing reports brought back by Hudson stimulated them to make immediate trial of the possibilities of this new region, which promised profits as large as they had already obtained in their East Indian colonies. Private enterprise was first in the field. Merchants of

Amsterdam sent vessels to trade with the Indians in 1612, and the first settlement and fort was established on Manhattan Island, just below the present Bowling Green Park. Fort Nassau, near Albany, was also built at this time. In 1614 a charter, good for three years, was granted to certain Amsterdam merchants, and they named the young settlement New Amsterdam. After 1623 the Dutch West India Company assumed the control of the colony, and governed it through a director-general.

New England and Pennsylvania were settled by men whose dominating purpose in the planting of new colonies was that they might find freedom in the worship and service of God—freedom for themselves only being the Puritan ideal, freedom for others as well, the Quaker. New York and Virginia were settled by men whose dominant purpose was not religious; in the Southern colony love of adventure and the vague hope of sudden fortune were the impelling motives, while ordinary commercial thrift governed the Northern. The Dutch shrewdness in trade showed itself throughout the history of New Amsterdam, and is the key to much that would otherwise be perplexing. Still, though the settlers of Manhattan were inspired by the mercantile rather than the religious motive, they came of a race that was deeply and genuinely pious, though not of the Puritan type; they came of a people that had made great sacrifices to gain their liberty, both civil and religious, and had set an example of toleration to all Europe. Wherever the Dutch trader went, missionaries and churches followed closely in his wake. It had been so in the East Indies, and it was so in the New World colonization. There had been religious services for some years before the Rev. Jonas Michaelius arrived, in 1628, and became the first pastor in New Amsterdam. The faith of the settlers was that known as the Dutch Reformed; churches of that faith only were recognized as lawful from this time forth, and its ministers were maintained from the public revenues. But though this church may be called "established" in the colony, it was hardly established by law. The director-general was very much of an autocrat, with no check on his power but the orders of the company, and director-generals had a way of making laws to suit themselves, by proclamation—to be frequently overruled by the West India Company when the facts came to the knowledge of the directors.

It was not long before men of other religious beliefs were found in New Amsterdam. The policy of the government toward these colonists was not consistent. It changed with each director-general, since it depended rather upon his will and temper than on any written law. The Dutch people in general were favorably disposed toward religious freedom, as they understood it; that is to say, they alone of all the peoples of Europe had at this time risen to that plane where it seemed to them no longer to be a religious duty to burn or hang, or even to fine and imprison those who differed from them in matters of faith and practice. Nobody among them had arrived at the idea of complete religious freedom, a free Church in a free State, neither depending on the other, neither interfering with the other. They believed in a State Church, but they also believed in permitting dissent from such a church. They were in little danger, after suffering so greatly from Rome's persecutions while they were fighting the battle of religious liberty for all Europe, of becoming persecutors in their turn. But there were exceptions among them, and New Amsterdam was a long way off from the Netherlands.

While Wilhelm Kiefft was director-general (1637–1647) a liberal policy prevailed. Mrs. Anne Hutchinson, and others who had become obnoxious to the Puritans, were welcomed to the colony, and franchises were granted them by the terms of which they were allowed freedom to worship God in the manner that suited them best. With the advent of his successor, the able but choleric and tyrannical Peter Stuyvesant, there was a marked change. Stuyvesant, the son of a clergyman, was a consistent and uncompromising Calvinist, who believed that all wisdom was comprised in the decrees of the Synod of Dort, and had high notions of his own dignity and authority. He determined to enforce the laws he found regarding heresy, and to make such others as might be necessary in order to produce general conformity to the Reformed Church. He first turned his attention to the Lutherans, a considerable number of whom were by this time (1654) domiciled in the colony. For a time they attended the Reformed Church and submitted to its ordinances; but after a while, as their numbers increased, they naturally desired a church organization of their own. This was more than Stuyvesant could endure. He was a martinet if not a tyrant by nature, and believed above all things in obedience to established authority, especially when he was the executive of that authority; as to his own obedience to an established authority higher than his own, his views were a little hazy. When, therefore, a Lutheran or other dissenter from the Reformed Church persisted in his separate worship, in his eyes this was not only heresy, but obstinacy that deserved punishment. For a time he winked at private services in Lutheran houses; but on February 1, 1656, he and the council adopted an ordinance, which was posted in public places, forbidding all unauthorized conventicles and the preaching of unqualified persons. A penalty of one hundred pounds Flemish was prescribed for preaching in such a service, and twenty-five pounds for attending one. The ordinance disclaimed "any prejudice to any patent heretofore given, any lording over the conscience, or any prohibition of the reading of

God's holy word, and the domestic praying and worshiping of each one in his own family."[1] This outrage, it was piously added, was committed "to promote the glory of God, the increase of the Reformed religion, and the peace and harmony of the country."

This ordinance was no *brutum fulmen*; it was intended to be enforced, and it was enforced. Fines and imprisonments followed its infraction, for of course the Lutherans violated it; and then came appeals to the States-General. Persecution of this kind had been long unknown in Holland, and that it should be revived in her colony was fitly thought intolerable. Such a policy was not only unjust, but unwise, and none saw this more clearly than the directors of the West India Company. Such severity would hinder immigration to the new colony, which they were anxious by all means to encourage. Principle and profit both prompted rebuke of the hasty and irascible governor; but it must be admitted that the directors were very mild in their communication of June 14, 1656, in which they say:

We would also have been better pleased if you had not published the placat against the Lutherans, a copy of which you sent us, and committed them to prison, for it has always been our intention, to treat them quietly and leniently. Hereafter you will not publish such or

---

[1] "Laws and Ordinances of New Netherland," 1638–1674. Albany, 1868, p. 213.

similar placats without our knowledge, but you must pass it over quietly, and let them have free religious exercises in their houses.[1]

Stuyvesant, however, was not a man to be controlled by such mild measures, and he paid no attention whatever to the admonition of the directors. Before this action had become known to him, the Rev. John Ernest Goetwasser, a Lutheran minister, had arrived at New Amsterdam in the ship " Mill." The Reformed pastors at once petitioned the governor and council that " a stop be put to the work," and that the Lutheran pastor be sent home on the same ship in which he had come. Goetwasser's illness prevented this summary treatment; but May 20, 1658, he was sent back. The directors actually approved this proceeding, though they thought the governor might have proceeded " less vigorously." But vigor was Stuyvesant's great gift, and he next proceeded to exercise it against some Quakers who had invaded the colony, hoping doubtless to find a toleration denied them in Massachusetts. Robert Hodgson was arrested at Hempstead in the summer of 1658 while walking in a garden. He was detained in prison several weeks and treated with frightful barbarity, being several times whipped until his life was endangered—this without trial or accusation of any specific offense, his only crime

---

[1] O'Callaghan, "Documents Relating to the Colonial History of New York." Albany, 1856–1883, Vol. XIV., p. 351.

being that he was a Quaker.¹ Others were imprisoned and compelled to pay heavy fines. Finally Stuyvesant issued another proclamation against the preaching of any save the Reformed religion, by its authorized ministers, under penalty of fifty guilders fine on each and every person found in attendance thereon; and the same penalty was provided for every one who should harbor heretics.²

In the meantime (1661) the inconsistent policy of the colony received further illustration. The company caused to be circulated through the British kingdom, and apparently through the New England colonies, a proclamation of invitation to the "conditions and privileges" of the New Amsterdam colony. They especially offered "all Christian people of tender consciences, in England or elsewhere oppressed, full liberty to erect a colony in the West Indies between New England and Virginea in America, now within the jurisdiction of Peter Stivazent;" with "full liberty after they have planted their colony in case of difference with the aforesaid Peter Stivazant, to chuse a director or Cheife."³ This marks out a sufficiently liberal policy on the part of the company; their fault was that they did not more energetically and honestly seek to compel their agent to conform to it. Stuyvesant was doubtless a good servant in every other

---

[1] Lamb's "History of the City of New York," Vol. I., p. 184.
[2] O'Callaghan, "Documents," Vol. III., p. 37.
[3] "Laws and Ordinances," p. 428.

particular, and it would have been difficult for the company to put so good a man in his place; still, they cannot be relieved of responsibility for his persecutions.

The promise of their proclamation was never kept. Many who were persuaded by it to leave Massachusetts and settle on Long Island, found that they had only exchanged persecutors. Not a few of these Long Island settlers were of Baptist leanings, if they were not members of Baptist churches. John Bowne was a typical case. Of English birth, he had come to this country with his father, William Bowne, who settled in Salem, Mass., in 1635. Just before coming of age, in the year 1645, he removed to Gravesend. He was not yet a Baptist, so far as appears, but he was a dissenter from the established church in Massachusetts; and in his Long Island home he made himself obnoxious to the authorities by his kindness of heart toward the "abominable people called Quakers." He was arrested and fined, and on refusing to pay the fine he was banished in 1663. On his arrival in Holland, whither he had been sent, he appealed to the company, and so effectually that the directors administered another and more decided rebuke to Stuyvesant:

Although it is our cordial desire that similar and other sectarians may not be found there, yet as the contrary seems to be the fact, we doubt very much whether vigorous proceedings against them ought not to be dis-

B

continued; unless indeed you intend to check and destroy your population, which, in the youth of your existence, ought rather to be encouraged by all possible means. Wherefore it is our opinion that some connivance is useful, and that at least the consciences of men ought to remain free and unshackled. Let every man remain free, so long as he is modest, moderate, his political conduct irreproachable, and so long as he does not offend others or oppose the government. This maxim of moderation has always been the guide of our magistrates in this city, and the consequence has been that people have flocked from every land to this asylum. Tread thus in their steps, and we doubt not you will be blessed.[1]

Even this did not make the irrepressible Peter mend his ways much, and it was only the capture of the city by the English in 1664 that brought relief.

It does not appear that the above mentioned settlers at Gravesend, Jamaica, Newtown, Flushing, and adjacent places, had actually organized Baptist churches. A report made to the Classis of Amsterdam in 1657 by two Reformed clergymen, says: "At Gravesend are reported Mennonites; yea, they for the most part reject infant baptism, the Sabbath, the office of preacher and the teachers of God's word, saying that through these have come all sorts of contention into the world." The Dutch magistrates reported these settlements to be "tainted with Anabaptist sentiments," but the people were too scattered and probably remained on the island

---

[1] O'Callaghan, "Documents," Vol. XIV., p. 357.

too short a time to effect any formal organization.

The same report to the Classis contains an interesting item of information: "Last year a fomenter of evil came there. He was a cobbler from Rhode Island, in New England, and stated that he was commissioned by Christ. He began to preach at Flushing and then went with the people into the river and dipped them." This "cobbler," as we learn from other sources, was the Rev. William Wickenden. For the high crime and misdemeanor of daring "to explain and comment on God's holy word, and to administer the sacraments, though not called thereto by any civil or clerical authority," he was sentenced by the General Assembly of New Netherland to pay a fine of one hundred pounds Flemish, and be banished out of the province, to remain a prisoner until the fine and cost of the process was paid. It being represented to the Assembly that he was a poor man and unable to pay the fine, the sentence was modified on November 11, 1656, to immediate banishment, under condition that if ever again found in the province he should be imprisoned until fine and costs were paid in full.[1]

The capture of the colony by the British introduced a new era. Perfect religious liberty was not enjoyed, but there was great amelioration in the lot of Baptists and Quakers. The Church of England,

---

[1] O'Callaghan, "History of New Netherland," New York, 1848, Vol. II., p. 321.

of course, became the established religion, but other forms of worship were tolerated.[1] The "Duke's Laws," the first code drawn up by James, Duke of York, for the government of his colony, provided expressly, "nor shall any person be molested, fined, or imprisoned for differing in judgment in matters of religion who profess Christianity."[2] The first

---

[1] How very liberal the English were in their treatment of the conquered Dutch was set forth with pardonable pride by the Rev. Morgan Dix, D. D., rector of Trinity Church, New York, in his address at the Quarter Millennial Anniversary of the Reformed Church of New York: "New Amsterdam was taken; it became New York, and the Church of England was planted where the Classis of Amsterdam had been the supreme and only ecclesiastical authority. But observe how scrupulously the rights of your forefathers were respected. There is nothing like it in history; never did conquerors treat the conquered with such deference and consideration. As far as possible the old customs were preserved; private rights, contracts, inheritances, were scrupulously regarded; and as for the Reformed Dutch Church, it seems to have been treated as a sacred thing. It was more than protected; it was actually established by law by an English governor under English auspices. This was perhaps no more than a fair return for the good deeds done by your people. When your turn came to be under the yoke, it was said to you in substance: 'You shall still be free; not one of your old customs shall be changed until you change them yourselves; by us you shall not be meddled with; keep your places of worship, your flocks, and all you have, in peace.' And so to their old church of St. Nicholas, inside the fort, did your people continue to wend their way in absolute security, though English sentries were at the gates; and within the walls over which the standard of England waved did the good Dutch dominie speak his mind as freely as ever to his spiritual children; nor was it until they had finished their devotions and withdrawn that the English chaplain ventured within the same house of worship to read his office from the Book of Common Prayer." ("Proceedings," p. 63.)

[2] The brief reconquest of New Amsterdam in 1673 re-established the Reformed Dutch Church, but freedom of worship was

General Assembly, which met in 1603, adopted a "Charter of Liberties," in which it was declared:

> Thatt no person or persons, which proffesse ffaith in God by Jesus Christ shall, at any time, be any wayes molested, punished, disquieted, or called in question for any difference in opinion or matter of religious concernment, who do nott actually disturbe the civill peace of the province, butt thatt all and every such person or p'sons may, from time, and at all times freely have and fully enjoy his or her judgments or consciences in matters of religion throughout all the province, they behaving themselves peaceably and quietly, and nott using this liberty to Lycenciousnesse, nor to the civil injury or outward disturbance of others.[1]

This charter was signed by the duke; but after he became king, as James II., he repealed it, substituting therefor certain "instructions," of which the following is a significant part:

> 42. You shall permit all persons of what Religion soever quietly to inhabit within yor Government without giving them any disturbance or disquiet whatsoever for or by reason of their differing Opinions in matters of Religion, Provided they give noe disturbance to ye publick peace, nor doe molest or disquiet others in ye free Exercise of their Religion.[2]

From this time on there was no persecution for religion in the colony of New York, and after the

---

granted to all who asked for it. The Dutch had learned something. See O'Callaghan, "Documents," Vol. II., pp. 575–6, 581.
[1] O'Callaghan, "Documents," Vol. III., p. 331.
[2] O'Callaghan, "Documents," Vol. III., pp. 369–375.

passage of the Act of Toleration in 1688, the status of Baptists and other "sectaries" became a legal one, instead of depending on the whim of monarch or governor.

We find no certain trace of a Baptist church in the colony until after New York had been captured by the British. After that time Rev. William Wickenden frequently made visits to the city and preached, but it is not established by any record, or even handed down by tradition, that a church was founded. His death occurred in 1669, and for a period of fifty years we hear nothing more of Baptists in New York. The next positive record is, that about the year 1712 the Rev. Valentine Wightman, then pastor at Groton, Conn., was invited by Nicholas Eyres and others to come and preach to them. For some two years he continued to visit the city occasionally, and preached to the congregation gathered in the house of Mr. Eyres, and among those converted under his ministry was the master of the house, who until then had not been a Christian. Five women were baptized in the night by Mr. Wightman, for fear of disturbance by the mob, who had been very troublesome. The seven men among the converts, however, did not relish this stealthy method, and the next morning, headed by Eyres, they waited on Governor Hunter, stated their case, and claimed protection. This the governor promptly promised, and he was as good as his word, for he and a number of the gentry came to the waterside and for the first time in their lives witnessed a scriptural baptism. So impressed was the governor, that he was heard to say: "This was the ancient way of baptizing, and in my opinion much preferable to the practice of modern times."[1]

These baptisms occurred in 1714, and the following year the house of Mr. Eyres was registered "for an Anabaptist meeting-house." This fact we learn from a petition of his, preserved among the colonial records of the city of New York:

To his Excellency, William Burnet, Esq., Captain-General and Governor-in-Chief of the Province of New York and New Jersey, and the Territories depending on them in America, and Vice-Admiral of the same.

The humble petition of Nicholas Eyers, brewer, a Baptist teacher in the city of New York:

Sheweth unto your excellency that on the first Tuesday of February, 1715, at a general quarter sessions of the peace, held at the city of New York, the hired house of your petitioner, situated in the broad street of this city, between the houses of John Michel Eyers and Mr. John Spratt, was registered for an Anabaptist meeting-house within this city; that the petitioner has

---

[1] This story is told as it has been handed down by tradition and repeated by all Baptist historians in their turn, with one correction. As it has been hitherto told, Governor Burnet has been named as the man who gave the protection and made the remark quoted. This must be an error, as Robert Hunter was governor from 1710 to 1720 and William Burnet from 1720 to 1732. With this change of name the story is at least consistent with the facts of record, and there is no reason to question its substantial truth.

it certified under the hands of sixteen inhabitants, of good faith and credit, that he had been a public teacher to a Baptist congregation within this city for four years, and some of them for less; that [he] has it certified by the Hon. Rip Van Dam, Esq., one of his Majesty's council for the province of New York, to have hired a house in this city from him, January, 1720, only to be a pub-. lic house for the Baptists, which he still keeps; and as he has obtained from the Mayor and Recorder of this city an ample certificate of his good behavior and innocent conversation, he therefore humbly prays:

May it please your Excellency,

To grant and permit this petitioner to execute the ministerial function of a minister within this city to a Baptist congregation, and to give him protection therein, according to his Majesty's gracious indulgence extended towards the Protestants dissenting from the Established Church, he being willing to comply with all that is required by the Act of Toleration from dissenters of that persuasion in Great Britain, and being owned for a reverend brother by other Baptist teachers.

As in duty bound the petitioner will ever pray.

NICHOLAS EYERS.[1]

In pursuance of this petition, Mr. Eyres was in 1721 duly licensed by Governor Burnet to preach; and in the document he is described as "Mr. Nich. Eyers, brewer, a freeman and inhabitant of ye city of New York, pretending to be at present a teacher or preacher of a congregation of Anabaptists, which has had its beginning about five years ago within this city and so has continued hitherto." It would ap-

---

[1] O'Callaghan, "Documentary History of New York," Albany, 1850–1, Vol. III., pp. 480–482.

pear from this, as well as from his own words in his petition, that Mr. Eyres was already recognized as the head of this congregation, but he was not ordained to the ministry, nor was the church formally constituted, until September, 1724.

Nicholas Eyres was born in Wiltshire, England, in 1691, and came to this country about 1711. He was, as the above extract proves, a brewer by occupation, a business in which Christian men in that day did not scruple to engage for their own profit and the glory of God. He was a man of some substance and more ability. Under his ministry the church prospered to such an extent that soon no private house would accommodate the congregation. Accordingly they bought a lot on Golden Hill, and built a house of worship in what is now Cliff Street, near John; and some time in the year 1728 the first Baptist meeting-house in New York City was opened for divine service. Mr. Eyres resigned his pastorate in 1731, and in the following year the church disbanded, having lost its house of worship by the action of one of the trustees who is said to have sold it without the knowledge or consent of the congregation.

The contemporary testimony is unanimous that this church was Arminian in theology, but the trustworthiness of this testimony is impugned by David Benedict, in the second edition of his "History of the Baptists." "We must bear in mind," he says, "that all were then set down as Arminians who did not come up to the highest point of hyper-Calvinism. Our old ministers in this region half a century since, would have denounced as unsound in the faith the great mass of our community of the present day, both in Europe and America, Fuller and Hall among the rest." Without disputing this assertion of Benedict, one cannot shut his eyes to certain facts that amply corroborate the contemporary accounts. William Wickenden, to whose labors the establishment of the church was primarily due, was the most active elder of the Six Principle or Arminian wing of the First Church in Providence. Rev. Valentine Wightman was the most eminent Arminian Baptist preacher of his generation. The Second Church, Newport, to which Mr. Eyres went as associate pastor of Rev. Daniel Wightman, in 1731, and where he labored until his death in 1759, was established as a Six Principle church in 1656, and had not yet become Calvinistic in sentiment. Without reasonable doubt, this first church in New York was what was in those days called Arminian; what it would be called in these days is quite another question.

The second Baptist church established in the colony of New York was that at Oyster Bay, Long Island. Baptist colonists from Rhode Island settled here toward the close of the seventeenth century, reinforcing some who had fled thither to escape persecution in Massachusetts. As early as 1700, one William Rhodes, an unordained preacher, fled to Oyster Bay because of persecutions elsewhere, and under his preaching several persons were converted, among them Robert Feeks. When a Baptist church was organized is not precisely known, but Robert Feeks was ordained in 1724, and since that time the church has had an unbroken history.[1] In 1741 we find Mr. Feeks writing to brethren in Newport: " God has begun a good work among us, which I hope he will carry on. There have been seventeen added to our little band in about three months." So far as numerical growth is concerned, this hope was doomed to disappointment. For some reason, Long Island, outside of Brooklyn and its suburbs, has always been sterile soil for Baptists. The Oyster Bay Church has never numbered more than fifty members, and a century passed before another Baptist church was organized on Long Island, the First Church, Brooklyn, having been formed in 1823.

Somewhere about the year 1740—the exact date being unknown—a company of Baptists from New York settled in the region now known as Dutchess County. The first church organized by them was in Fishkill, and for a time it prospered under the pastoral care of a Mr. Halstead, but after a while ceased to exist. A member of this church, Jeremiah Dodge,

---

[1] Benedict, "History of the Baptist Denomination in America," p. 580, N. Y., 1848. It is extremely probable that this was an Arminian church in the beginning; when it became Calvinistic is not definitely known.

whose great-grandfather was one of the original settlers on Block Island and whose family were all stanch Baptists, a shipbuilder by trade, came to New York about 1745 and began to hold prayer meetings in his house. Some of the former members of the now extinct Arminian church met with other brethren here. After a few years their numbers increased to thirteen, and in 1753 they joined themselves to the Baptist church at Scotch Plains, N. J., which had been organized in 1747, whose pastor, Elder Benjamin Miller, preached and broke bread for them once in three months. The congregation became too large to meet in a private house, and they hired a loft in Cart and Horse Lane, now William Street.[1] A sale of the building made it necessary for the church again to meet for a time in private houses, but they soon purchased a lot on Gold Street just south of Fulton, and built there a small stone meeting-house, which was opened for worship March 14, 1760. Three years later it was enlarged to fifty-two by forty-two feet, to accommodate the growing congregation; and soon after other lots on Gold Street were bought for the building of a parsonage, thus enlarging the church plot to one hundred and twenty-five by one hundred feet.

Soon after the building of their house of worship, the number of members had grown to twenty-seven,

---

[1] "Jubilee Discourse," by Rev. William Parkinson, 1813. Compare memorial address by Roger H. Lyon, Esq., at the laying of the corner-stone of the present edifice, September 25, 1891.

and, obtaining letters of dismission from the church at Scotch Plains, they were constituted a church June 19, 1762. They adopted as their articles of faith the Confession of English Baptists in 1688, and Rev. John Gano became their first pastor. He was a native of Hopewell, N. J., born in 1727, and was of French descent, the family name having been originally Gerneaux. He had been ordained in 1754 and already had considerable experience in the ministry. Crowds flocked to hear him from the first, and by the testimony of many contemporaries he was a preacher of exceptional powers. Still, in 1763 the church numbered only forty members, and was so little known in the city that Morgan Edwards had difficulty in finding it. Wandering up and down in search of the place of meeting, he saw an old man on the porch of a respectable looking house and accosted him. "Good-morning, sir; can you tell me where any Baptists live in this city?" "Baptists! Baptists!" said the old man, musing as if ransacking all the corners of his memory; "Baptists, I really don't know as I ever heard of anybody of that occupation in these parts." A few years later Mr. Edwards would probably have had less difficulty, for before the outbreak of the Revolutionary War the church had grown to two hundred members, and their house of worship had to be again enlarged.

Mr. Gano's nominal pastorate of twenty-six years was seriously interrupted by the war of the Revolution and the British occupation of New York. He was a patriot as well as a preacher. Most of his male parishioners became soldiers in the American army and he himself became a chaplain. In more than one action he was under fire, and his fearless bearing won the commendation of the officers and held the men to their duty. Washington is reported to have said that " Baptist chaplains were the most prominent and useful in the army," and if there were many like John Gano they well deserved the compliment. When the conclusion of peace was celebrated at Washington's headquarters, near Newburg, April 19, 1783, he was called on to offer the prayer of thanksgiving on that joyous and memorable occasion.

When the pastor returned to his flock in New York he could find but thirty-seven of the former members of his church. There had not been a baptism from April, 1776, to September, 1784. The meeting-house had been used as a stable by the British cavalry. Soon after his resumption of pastoral labors there was a gracious revival in the church that encouraged their hearts and added largely to their numbers; and in two years the membership had again grown to two hundred. Mr. Gano's labors continued with great acceptance and success until his resignation, in May, 1788. The pastorate was not without its difficulties and disturbances, however. In the early part of his labors the peace of the church was several times broken by preachers from England, who successively tried, though in vain, to propagate peculiar notions and foment strife. A more serious trouble arose toward the latter part of the pastorate. The custom among them had been from the first, as in other Baptist churches of that day, to have the hymns "lined" in public worship. In 1770 they purchased hymn books; but some of the brethren could not abide this new-fangled notion, and accordingly went forth to found the Second Church, which a few years later took the name of Bethel. A division arose in this body in 1791, which resulted in the establishment of the Fayette Church, later known as the Oliver Street, and now as the Baptist Church of the Epiphany.

Mr. Gano's resignation was a painful surprise to his people. It would appear from his own account of the matter, though he does not say this in so many words, that the church had not been over liberal in providing for his support. He was considerably in debt and saw no way of relief but by selling his house and lot, which would defray his debts and leave him some surplus. At this juncture he received an urgent call to a new church in Kentucky, that needed an experienced minister, with "flattering temporal prospects for the support of my [his] family." He called a church meeting and informed them of his intention. "They treated it as a chimera," he says, "and thought they could stop me by raising my salary. They, with all possible coolness, left me to determine for myself. I immediately determined to go, and desired them to look out for a supply. This aroused them, and they very affectionately urged me to tarry. I told them if they had desired me to stay before I had put it out of my own power, I should then have given it up." [1] During his pastorate, Mr. Gano had baptized two hundred and ninety-seven persons into the fellowship of the church. He removed to Kentucky, encountering many difficulties on the way, and continued to labor there with marked success until his death in 1804. Though he did not enjoy a liberal education, he was a man of acute and trained mind, very energetic, eloquent of speech, and spiritually minded. He was, indeed, one of the first Baptists of his day, and left an indelible imprint on the Baptist cause in New York City. Rev. Benjamin Foster, of Rhode Island, succeeded him as pastor,

---

[1] "Biographical Memoirs of the late Rev. John Gano, of Frankfort (Kentucky), formerly of the city of New York. Written principally by himself." New York, 1806, pp. 118, 119. Mr. Gano was not only an eloquent preacher, but had a vein of dry humor, that crops out occasionally in his "Memoirs," and probably sometimes enlivened his preaching. In the narrative of his first visit to South Carolina, soon after his ordination, he tells this story: "On my way to Mars-bluff, on the Pedee, I lodged at the ferryman's house. He observed that he believed I was a minister, and wished me to tell him of the best and shortest way to heaven. I told him that Christ was the best way; and that he must be experimentally acquainted with him, and believe in him, which was the hope of glory. That after he had obtained this, the shortest way that I knew, would be to place himself in the front of some army in an engagement." This was spoken in the midst of the French wars, not long before the disastrous Braddock campaign.

and labored with fidelity and success until he died of yellow fever in 1798.

The Baptist settlement in Fishkill, to which brief allusion has already been made, had a very important influence on the history of the Baptist churches of New York. Though the organization first formed soon ceased to exist, other churches were founded a few years later, one of which, the Kent and Fishkill (1782), is still a flourishing body. The growth of Baptists in this region was much promoted by the progress of the great Whitefield revival. Many of the converts, reading the Bible for themselves, were not able to join Pedobaptist churches. In the decade between 1750 and 1760 four churches that are still members of the Dutchess Association were organized: the North East, of Millerton (1751), the First Stamford, of Bangalls, and the First Pawling, of Holmes (1755), and the First Dover Furnace (1757). Other churches founded prior to 1780 and still existing, that owe their origin to this settlement, are, the Carmel, the Bottskill, of Greenwich (both 1765), the Pleasant Valley, of Crum Elbow (1770), and the White Creek (1779).

Perhaps the most remarkable movement in New York State, and that which had the most far-reaching results, is directly traceable to the organization of the Warwick Church, in the village of that name, in Orange County. This church was established in 1766, by the labors of the Rev. James

Benedict, who came from Ridgefield, Conn., a distant relative of Dr. David Benedict, the Baptist historian. In a few years it had increased to two hundred members, and a number of neighboring churches were set off from it. In the year 1773 Ebenezer Knap and Increase Thurstin, members of this church, moved with their families into what was then described as "the wilderness of the far West," settling at a place soon known as the Butternuts,[1] on Butternut Creek, about twenty miles southwest of the headwaters of the Susquehanna. There was no settlement westward nearer than Fort Niagara (some two hundred miles), and not a house nearer than sixteen miles. At this earliest outpost in the wilderness, religious meetings were held from the beginning by these Baptists, at first by their own families only. A daughter of Ebenezer Knap was married to Benjamin Lull, Jr., and the first meetings were held with this household. During February of their first winter here, Mrs. Elizabeth Lull awoke in the night in great distress of mind, because of her sins, and the mind of her sister Martha was greatly affected by this circumstance. Their only instructor was their mother, the father being absent from home, but they both found peace in believing in the following April. Seven other families moved into the settlement the

---

[1] So called because three patents cornered here, at a spot marked by three butternut trees. "A view of the Rise and Increase of the Churches Comprising the Otsego Baptist Association," by A. Hosmer and J. Lawton. Whitestown, 1800.

following summer, and the wife of Increase Thurstin, with others, was brought to rejoice in the Lord. The prospects of a flourishing Baptist church were excellent; but just then the tide of war rolled that way and the Butternuts settlement was the prey of the Indians. None of the settlers lost their lives, but some were made prisoners for a time, all were driven from their homes, and their houses were pillaged and burned. With the establishment of peace four families returned, and from 1787 they enjoyed the occasional preaching of the word, under which a number of converts were made. In August, 1793, the elder of the church in Greenfield, Saratoga County, together with some members of the same church, met with them and gave them formal recognition as a church of gospel order. In those days in the wilderness, a council of recognition or ordination not infrequently consisted of the pastor and delegate members of a single church. The body so recognized still lives and flourishes as the Morris Church of the Otsego Association.

Successive immigrations to this tract increased the number of Baptist churches rapidly throughout Central New York. The church at Wellsburg, now in the Chemung Association, was organized soon after peace was concluded (1789), and in the last decade of the century there was a remarkable expansion throughout this region. Seven churches were constituted in the Otsego district, three each in the Cayuga and Madison, two each in the Franklin, Oneida, and Ontario, and one each in the Seneca and the Broome and Tioga. During the same period there was also a considerable advance in the southern counties, especially in what is now the Union Association, four churches being formed there besides one in the Dutchess district. The above enumeration includes only churches that are now existent, though some of them are no longer strong. A considerable number of churches organized at this time long ago became extinct, and the very names of some are not remembered. Dr. Benedict does not exaggerate when he says of this Otsego settlement that it "laid the foundations for the immense growth of the denomination in the State."

The single exception to this remark relates to the northeastern part of the State. There another quite distinct movement was going on, that had nearly as great an influence on the denominational growth. This was a rapid increase of Baptist churches in Rensselaerville, Saratoga, and Washington counties, which owed its impulse, not to Southern or Central New York, but to Vermont. Baptists had begun to settle in the southern part of Vermont about the beginning of the Revolution. Many of them were Separatists, or New Lights, of the Congregational body, former dwellers in Massachusetts, who had been converted during the Whitefield revivals and came to adopt Baptist views regarding the church and its ordinances. The beginnings of most of the churches in this part of New York may be traced to the Shaftsbury region of Vermont, and some of them were members of the Shaftsbury Association for many years. During the last fifteen years of the eighteenth century a numerous body of Baptist churches sprang into being in this region. In the Saratoga district alone twelve churches still existing were organized; in the Stephentown and the Washington four each, and three in the Rensselaerville. The influence of this movement spread farther north, for in 1796 the Chester Church, in the Lake George district, was formed.

By the year 1800, therefore, the Baptist cause was firmly established in New York State, and awaited only a favorable opportunity to make an advance of phenomenal rapidity. How that opportunity arose and what came of it will be told in a later chapter. So far as appears, with the exception already noted of the Oyster Bay Church, these churches were all Calvinistic in theology. Doubtless there were individual members, possibly a minister or two, of more or less pronounced Arminian views; but they exerted no appreciable influence on the churches. In New England, on the contrary, the Arminian influence during this period was decidedly in the ascendant, and in Pennsylvania and New Jersey it was by no means settled which type of doctrine was ultimately to prevail among the Baptist churches until well on toward the end of the eighteenth century.

CHAPTER II

THE EARLY DAYS IN NEW JERSEY

THAT tract of land now known as New Jersey was by a royal grant, in 1664, ceded to James, Duke of York. His Majesty Charles II. was notoriously generous to his favorites; but he was especially prodigal of that which cost him little or was not his own. New Jersey was not his to give; both the Dutch and the Swedes had better claims to the tract than the English, the former by right of discovery, the latter by right of purchase from the natives. The Duke of York, however, was not one to question the legality of a title vested in him, and soon after he sold all his rights to Lord Berkeley and Sir George Carteret. Neither Holland nor Sweden being in a position to contest the title, New Jersey became an English colony, and remained such until the Revolution.

One of the first acts of the new proprietors was to issue certain " Concessions and agreements of the Lords Proprietors of New Jersey to and with all and every of the adventurers and all such as shall settle and plant there." This document, which bears date February 10, 1664–5, assures liberty of conscience to all becoming subjects of England and swearing allegiance to the king and fidelity to the lords proprietors. It 'distinctly provides :

That no person qualified as aforesaid within the said Province at any time shall be anyways molested, punished, disquieted, or called in question, for any difference in opinion or practice in matters of religious concernment, who do not actually disturb the civil peace of the said Province; but that all and every such person and persons may, from time to time, and at all times, freely and fully have and enjoy his and their judgments and consciences in matters of religion throughout the said Province.[1]

Nevertheless, churches were to be established by law, and the Assembly of the Province was authorized to appoint as many ministers as should be thought proper, and to provide for their maintenance.[2] Evidently referring to this document, Benedict says : "As the first bill of rights under the administration of Lord Berkeley and Sir George Carteret established a full liberty of conscience to all religious sects that should behave well, this favorable feature of the government of this new colony induced many men of different opinions to flee from the oppressions of other regions to enjoy the mild shade of religious toleration which, in the good old Jerseys, had always been enjoyed."

This first bill of rights took effect in 1665, when

[1] Whitehead, "New Jersey under the Proprietors," p. 27. See also the volume of "Grants and Concessions."
[2] Winsor's "Narrative and Critical History of the United States," Vol. III., pp. 423, 424.

Philip Carteret came over to act as governor of the colony. It will be observed, however, that these "concessions" were in form a toleration, not the granting of equal religious rights to all, and that they were made by favor of the rulers of the country under the royal grant, not conferred as an inherent right. A similar measure of toleration was promulgated by Lord Baltimore in Maryland, though he was by royal charter invested "with all and singular the like, and as ample rights, jurisdictions, privileges, prerogatives, . . . as any bishop of Durham, in our kingdom of England, hath at any time heretofore had, held, used, or enjoyed."[1]

The first country in which equal religious liberty was secured by law was the colony of Rhode Island. In the original compact of the settlers, made in 1636, they promised obedience to laws and magistrates "only in civil things." This was confirmed by the royal charter of 1663, in which Charles II. thought fit to publish:

That our royal will and pleasure is, that no person within the said colony, at any time hereafter, shall be in any wise molested, punished, disquieted, or called in question, for any differences in opinion in matters of religion, and do not actually disturb the civil peace of our said colony; but that all and every person and persons may, from time to time, and at all times hereafter, freely and fully have and enjoy his and their own judgments and consciences in matters of religious con-

---

[1] "Maryland Charter," 1632. See Preston's "Documents Illustrative of American History," pp. 62-77, especially p. 65.

cernments throughout the tract of land hereafter mentioned, they behaving themselves peaceably and quietly, and not using this liberty to licentiousness or profaneness, nor to the civil injury or outward disturbance of others.[1]

As a matter of fact, the measure of religious liberty in New Jersey was not greatly exceeded in Rhode Island. Though the "concessions" of the proprietors might have been withdrawn, they never were withdrawn; though they promised only toleration, they really gave liberty. Not only was there never any persecution in the colony, but the power of the Assembly to create and maintain an established church was never used. In some towns, however, local statutes of doubtful legality were enacted, disfranchising all but the members of some sect that chanced to be predominant in that locality. The old records of Newark are said to contain the following:

None shall be admitted freemen or free burgesses, within our town upon Passaick River in the Province of New Jersey, but such planters as are members of some or other of the Congregational churches; nor shall any but such be chosen to magistracy . . . or to any chief military trust or office. Nor shall any but such church-members have any vote in any such elections.[2]

---
[1] Preston's "Documents," p. 113.
[2] Celebration of the Twenty-fifth Anniversary of the First Baptist Church of Bloomfield, N. J., p. 57, address by Rev. Henry F. Smith, D. D.

42 BIBLE SOCIETIES AND THE BAPTISTS

Among the first to be drawn toward this colony by these promises were Baptists who had suffered from persecution in other parts. As early as 1660, according to Morgan Edwards, a few Baptist settlers had found refuge here; but it was not until 1688 that a church was formed. This was the Middletown Church, composed of such men as Richard Stout, James Grover, Jonathan Brown, Obadiah Holmes, John Holmes, and John Bowne. The last-named member[1] gave the lot on which the first meeting-house was built, and was the first preacher, though he was never ordained to the work of the ministry. Rev. John Ashton was the first ordained pastor, and he served the church acceptably for more than twenty years, during which time its membership increased to nearly a hundred.

The most celebrated among the early pastors was the Rev. Abel Morgan, " the great, the incomparable Abel Morgan," as Dr. Samuel Jones called him. He was a native of the Welsh Tract, being born in 1713, and received a good academic education. He was converted and baptized when about twenty years of age, and not long after was ordained. From 1739 he was pastor of this church until his death in 1785. He had a great reputation throughout all the region roundabout as a scholarly divine and an able debater. Several times he was drawn into the public defense

---

[1] Benedict persistently and incorrectly prints his name Brown. We have seen what were his trials under Stuyvesant's government in New York.

of distinctive Baptist principles, and, according to contemporary testimony, never failed to gain a signal victory—doubtless the Pedobaptist traditions of the time, if any survive, are different. One of his treatises, called "Anti-Pædo Rantism," in reply to a tract of Rev. Samuel Finley's, is a prize to the collector nowadays, being cheap at twelve dollars, a price probably exceeding the value of the entire edition when published. This divine was an eminent patriot during the revolutionary struggle, and his outspoken preaching was a tower of strength to the Continentals in New Jersey. Morgan Edwards, who by no means agreed with him in politics, writes of him this high praise: "Mr. Morgan's life and ministry were such, that his people speak of him with veneration and regret to this day. He was not a *custom-divine*, nor a *leading-string-divine*, but a *bible-divine*. In his last sickness he sent for the elders of the church to anoint him with oil, according to the precept (Jam. v. 14, 15): elder Crawford attended: but elder Mott was hindered by sickness; and the healing rite was deferred for want of *elders*, in the plural."[1] In spite of his eccentricities, Mr.

---

[1] The reader of Edwards will not fail to note that he strongly favors ideas and practices that would certainly be pronounced "cranky" in these days. This anointing of the sick with oil is only one case of several. Another is the practice of feet-washing as an ordinance of the church, after the custom of the Tunkers, which Edwards believed to be scriptural, as will be seen from the following in his New Jersey "Materials": "During the ministration of rev. David Sutton there was a considerable stir in the [Kingwood] church relative to the rite of washing feet;

Morgan well deserved the inscription that his loving people placed over his grave : " His life was blameless, his ministry was powerful ; he was a burning and a shining light, and his memory is dear to the saints." [1]

The peaceful growth of this church was interrupted toward the end of the century by a quarrel that continued for years and at one time threatened its total extinction. The members were divided into two factions, that mutually excommunicated each other and voted each to silence the other's minister. A council of the other churches finally helped them to make peace, and though a minority remained recalcitrant they disappear from history. By this contention the church was reduced to forty-two members; but learning wisdom by this costly experience, they thereafter kept the unity of the Spirit in the bond of peace and continued to prosper.

The year following the organization of the Middletown Church probably saw the formation of the Piscataqua (now Piscataway) Church, though this date is by no means certain.[2] These people had an

---

but could not be established in a general way; neither will it prevail until Christians be converted and become as little children, who do as the father bid them without remonstrance" (p. 57).

[1] "Materials," Vol. II., p. 19.

[2] Edwards very candidly says: "The history of this church from the beginning to the present time, is not easy of acquisition; nor will be altogether certain when acquired; the reason is, their records have been destroyed in the late war" ("Mate-

interesting, not to say romantic, origin. A settlement of this name formerly existed in New Hampshire, at what is now Dover, and from 1638 to 1641 Hanserd Knollys was pastor of a church there. Knollys was not an avowed Baptist until several years later (he was ordained pastor of a Baptist church in London in 1645), but it is probable that he had already substantially become a Baptist. We know certainly, on the testimony of an Episcopalian visitor to Dover during his pastorate, that there was a hot controversy between him and a fellow-minister about baptizing children, and that the church was divided on this question. It would seem, therefore, that this was not a Baptist church, but that there were Baptists in it.[1] In order to escape persecution, these Baptists moved to Long Island, which proved to be much like jumping out of the frying-pan into the fire, so they sought a third asylum in New Jersey and named their settlement New Piscataqua, after their first New Hampshire home. Several years before the organization of this church members of a Baptist church in Tipperary, Ireland, had made a settlement at Cohansey. Being joined by some Baptists from England, and certain others baptized by Rev. Elias Keach, they formed a Baptist church there,

---

rials," Vol. II., p. 21). Tradition attributes this destruction to the clerk, who was a Tory. The existing records begin in August, 1781.

[1] See Burrage, "History of the Baptists in New England," p. 65.

in 1691 probably.[1] "These three churches," says Benedict, "were among the first constituted members of the Philadelphia Association, and it is pleasing to reflect that, amidst all the changes of time, the dilapidations of churches, and the inroads of heresy and fanaticism in other communities which once appeared fair and strong, these bodies have maintained a regular standing, and each of them is now sound in the faith, respectable in size, and in a flourishing condition."[2] After the lapse of another half-century, these words still hold good of the only three Baptist churches established in New Jersey during the seventeenth century.

One of the churches formed early in the eighteenth century—the Hopewell, in 1715—did not have this good fortune. Though still existing, it cannot be called sound in the faith, respectable in size, or flourishing. Its early history was remarkable. "Jonathan Stout and family," says Edwards, "were the seed of Hopewell Church, and the beginning of the Hopewell settlement, and that of the fifteen which constituted the church, nine were Stouts: the church was constituted at the house of a Stout: and the meetings were held chiefly at the dwellings of the Stouts for forty-one years. In 1790 the two deacons and four elders were of this name." This church continued to be a strong and

---

[1] Asplund's date. The New Jersey Convention Minutes give 1690. The early records of the church were burned.
[2] "History of the Baptists," p. 584.

flourishing body until the early part of the present century; then it adopted anti-mission sentiments and allied itself with those churches popularly known as "Old School" or Primitive Baptists. From this time its decline in numerical and spiritual strength was steady.[1]

The Hopewell Church deserves to be gratefully remembered among the New Jersey Baptists as the mother of several distinguished preachers. John Gano was first licensed to preach by this church, and it was seemingly through his labors that Hezekiah Smith was converted and baptized into a branch of the Hopewell Church. At this time young Smith was living near Morristown, N. J., where Gano was acting as supply and preaching in surrounding towns. "The appearances of success," he tells us, "were such as induced me to repeat my visits as often as possible, and almost beyond what my health would admit of. At one of these places there was a happy instance of a promising youth (by name Hezekiah Smith), who professed to be

---

[1] The Hopewell Church withdrew from the Central New Jersey Association about 1826, and with other churches joined in forming the Delaware River Association of Old School Baptists. Though before this time the church had maintained a Sunday-school and been active in missionary enterprises, it now abandoned these, as well as prayer meetings and evangelistic efforts. The church has now (1897) no pastor. Many families for miles around Hopewell are sympathizers with the church and its doctrines, and its congregation in favorable weather will generally be larger than the membership. It is probably the strongest Old School Baptist church in the Middle States. It has a fine church property, including a parsonage and farm.

converted, and joined the church, who appeared to have an inclination for education, to which his parents objected. His eldest brother joined me in soliciting his father, who finally consented to his receiving an education. He went through a collegiate education at Prince Town College, and came out a zealous preacher, and to appearances a useful one." This church is also remarkable for another thing: its first pastor, the Rev. Isaac Eaton (1748-1772), was the first Baptist to establish an academy in these parts; and by so doing became a pioneer in the movement that resulted in the founding of Brown University, as will be told later.

One of the most eminent Baptists of Revolutionary days was a lay member of the Hopewell Church. John Hart was born in the village early in the eighteenth century. When he became a member of the Baptist church is not definitely known, but he was for many years one of its firmest supporters and gave the land on which the house of worship (still standing) was built. Mr. Hart was a man of great abilities, though modest to a fault; and in spite of the fact that he had no taste for public life, the times brought him to the front and kept him there. He was a member of the Continental Congress, of the New Jersey Provincial Congress, a signer of the Declaration of Independence, a member of the Committee of Safety, and Speaker of the Assembly. For months he was a fugitive in the mountains, pursued by the Hessians, but he was an unflinching patriot to the end. The State of New Jersey honored itself as well as John Hart by erecting a granite shaft to his memory near the Hopewell meeting-house, which was dedicated by Governor Joel Parker, July 4, 1865.[1]

Several other churches of New Jersey belong, as to time of origin, with the Hopewell. The Cape May Church was formed three years earlier, and still lives and prospers. The churches at Scotch Plains and Morristown are offshoots of the Piscataway Church. There were Baptists in the last-named town as early as 1717, but for a time they continued to be members of the Hopewell Church, and the Morristown Church was not constituted until 1752. For some years, as we have seen, in the lack of a regular pastor, the Rev. John Gano ministered there. The Scotch Plains Church was organized September 8, 1747. Edwards tells the story in his usual quaint way: "Theretofore all Baptists in this part of the country were members of Piscataqua Church; but, growing numerous, and distance considerable, the mother church detached from the old hive, a swarm, and formed them into a distinct society."[2] The first pastor of this church, the Rev. Benjamin Miller, was a close friend of John Gano. The two agreed that whichever survived should preach the other's funeral sermon, and it fell to the lot of Mr.

---

[1] "History of the Hart Family," by W. W. H. Davis. Privately printed at Doylestown, Pa., 1867.
[2] "Materials," Vol. II., p. 69.

Gano to fulfill this pledge.[1] "Never did I esteem a ministering brother so much as I did Mr. Miller," he said, "nor feel so sensibly a like bereavement as I sustained by his death." One is a little surprised, after this testimony, that Edwards can find nothing better to say of such a man than this : "Mr. Miller's character is hard to be delineated for want of originality ; all that hath been said of a good, laborious, and successful minister, will apply to him."[2] This may be candor, but it seems like something less creditable.

Unusual interest attaches to the organization of a church at Wantage, as narrated by Edwards. It traces its origin to Mansfield, where about the beginning of 1750 there was a church of Separates, or New Lights, who emigrated in a body to Newtown, N. J.

They had not been long in their new settlement before some (who had scruples about infant baptism at Mansfield) declared openly for the baptism of believers. But now the same question puzzled them which had puzzled others in both the Englands and Germany, etc., viz., "Whether baptism administered by an unbaptized person be valid?" for they considered infant baptism as a nullity : however, they resolved the question in the affirmative from the consideration of necessity : accordingly mr. Marsh was baptized by mr. Elkana Fuller, and then Elkana Fuller by mr. Marsh : this was in the winter of 1752 ; for it is remembered that the ice was broken

---

[1] Gano's "Biographical Memoirs," pp. 80, 81.
[2] "Materials," Vol. II., p. 71.

for the purpose in the form of a grave. Next year were baptized by mr. Marsh, Joshua Cole, cap. Roe, Daniel Roberts, Hezekiah Smith (yet alive) and wife, and Rudolphus Fuller : these 8 persons were, Nov. 14, 1756, formed into a Baptist church, by a new covenant which is still extant.[1]

According to Edwards, "Mixed communion continued in this church after it became Baptist, which the Baptists excused from the consideration of necessity."[2]

In all, twenty-two of the existing Baptist churches of New Jersey were constituted before the close of the eighteenth century.[3] Edwards gives (1792) the following summary of facts: churches, twenty-four; members, two thousand nine hundred and ninety-four; ministers, sixteen; meeting-houses, thirty-one—a goodly foundation for nineteenth century Baptists to build upon.[4]

This, it should be understood, includes none but such as are now called "regular" Baptists. There were several other sorts of Baptists represented in the colony. The most important of these were

---

[1] "Materials," Vol. II., p. 88.   [2] *Ibid.*, p. 89.

[3] Besides those mentioned in the text, there were the Mannahawkin (1777) and Pemberton (1764) in the Camden Association; Flemington (1798) in the Central; Mount Bethel (1767), Lyons Farms (1769), and South Plainfield (1792) in the East; Mount Olive (1753), Deckertown (1778), Northfield (1786), and Hamburg (1796), in the North; Hightstown (1745), Imlaystown (1766), and Jacobstown (1785) in the Trenton; Salem First (1755), Dividing Creek (1761), and Pittsgrove (1771) in the West. Dates from the New Jersey Convention's Minutes.

[4] "Materials," Vol. II., p. 128.

those known as Seventh-day Baptists, whose first church was formed at Piscataway "in the fourth month, 1707," composed of about seventeen persons, mostly seceders from the First-day church of that place. For thirty years this church stood alone. In 1753 there was a schism between the Calvinists and the Arminians, which continued for four years, when they reunited. The Shiloh Church, of Cohansey (1737), and the Squan (1745) were constituted of Baptists from Rhode Island and Connecticut. These were, in the time of Edwards, the only churches of this order in the State; and he gives their numbers as two hundred and forty-nine, with three meeting-houses and five ordained ministers.[1]

There was also a Tunker church at Amwell, constituted in 1733, of emigrants from Schwardzenau. Edwards tells us that it celebrated the ordinances at no set time, "but as often as a brother finds himself disposed to give the feast of charity; then the church is invited to meet at his house (for they have no meeting-house): and when washing feet is over, and the right hand of fellowship and the kiss of charity given, the Lord's Supper is administered, with the usual elements, and singing of hymns."[2] This church had forty-six members. So far as is known, it was the only church of this order in New

---

[1] "Materials," Vol. II., p. 143.
[2] *Ibid.*, p. 145. Edwards speaks of this as "the only church which statedly uses the eight Christian rites," but does not further define what is meant by this.

Jersey before 1800; but there were in Pennsylvania fifteen Tunker churches, besides seven in Maryland, and ten in the more Southern States.

In this sketch of early Baptists in New Jersey one should not overlook the curious Rogerine Baptists, a variety of the Seventh-day Baptists, mainly confined to the family and relatives of one John Rogers, of New London, Conn. Among the tenets of this body were such as these: All days are alike since the death of Christ; no medicines should be used nor doctors or surgeons employed; no grace should be said at meals; no vocal prayer should be offered, save when the Spirit compels the use of the voice; all unscriptural parts of worship are idols. Among the idols Rogers included the observance of the first day of the week and infant baptism. The Rogerines sometimes worshiped with other Baptists, when they created scandal by insisting on their right to take work into the meeting-house, the women knitting and the men making splints for baskets.[1] Twenty-one souls of this peculiar folk emigrated to New Jersey in 1734, and settled on Schooley's Mountain. They were nearly extinct when Edwards wrote, and not long afterward disappeared altogether.

It is not possible to determine, with any approach to exactness, whether Arminians or Calvinists predominated in these early New Jersey churches. The

---

[1] "Materials," Vol. II., p. 147, *seq.*

Hopewell and Middletown churches seem to have been decidedly Calvinistic from the beginning. There is room for suspicion, at least, that the Piscataway and Cohansey churches were partly composed of Arminians. There was an Arminian church at Cohansey, when formed is not known,[2] composed of the Rev. Timothy Brooks and others from the Second Church of Swansea, Mass. This body united with the Cohansey Church, whose organization in 1680 has already been narrated. Since it maintained a separate existence for some years, there must have been a reason for so doing; and what reason could there be but that the other church was too Calvinistic for the Swansea Baptists to find a comfortable home in it? It is more than probable that the majority in these churches were Calvinists and the minority Arminians. The Rev. Thomas Killingworth, who came from Norwich, England, and was probably a member of a well-known General Baptist family there, was instrumental in organizing the Cohansey Church, became its first pastor, and was influential in all that region until his death in 1708. There is no evidence, however, that these differences of doctrine were pressed by either party, and there is no trace of divisions being caused on account of controversies on such matters, unless the trouble in the Middle-

---

[2] Dr. Whitsitt gives 1687 as the date, but this is evidently conjectural, because it is not certain that the Second Swansea Church was formed before 1793. (See Backus, Vol. I., p. 450.)

town Church, already mentioned, may have been caused by a theological controversy. No particulars have, however, been preserved. By the time Morgan Edwards began his researches the churches must have been substantially Calvinistic or he would not have failed to inform us to the contrary.

CHAPTER III

EARLY DAYS IN PENNSYLVANIA AND DELAWARE

PENNSYLVANIA'S annals were never smirched by the record of such religious persecutions as mark the early history of most of the colonies. This was not for lack of persecuting laws in its earliest history, before Penn received his charter. Then it was under the authority of James, Duke of York, and was governed by a code of laws enacted by him and published as of general authority "at a general meeting at Hemsted upon Longe Island," March 1, 1664 (O. S.).[1] By this code the Church of England was established by law; all ministers must present certificates of episcopal ordination, and were to be paid out of the common treasury. It does not appear that these laws were ever carried into effect. William Penn, the real founder of the State, was a member of the Society of Friends, or Quakers, who had close affiliations with the English Baptists, and were opponents on principle of church establishments and persecution for the sake of religion. Nevertheless, even Pennsylvania did not embody in her laws the spirit of true and complete soul liberty. The original charter of Penn, from Charles

[1] "Charter and Laws of the Province of Pennsylvania," 1682-1700. (Official.) Harrisburg, 1879, pp. 3-77.

II., bearing date January 27, 1682 (O. S.), and the frame of government or constitution that Penn proclaimed in accordance with the charter, are both absolutely silent on this most important subject.[1]

The first Assembly under this constitution, held "at Chester alias Upland, the 7th day of the 10th month, called December, 1682" (O. S.), enacted what is known as "The Great Law," a code consisting of sixty-one chapters, fundamental and miscellaneous laws. Chapter I., recognizing God as the only Lord of conscience, provides:

> That no person, now, or at any time hereafter, Living in this Province, who shall confess and acknowledge one Almighty God to be the Creator, Upholder, and Ruler of the world, and who confesses, him, or herself Obliged in Conscience to Live peaceably and quietly under the civil government, shall in any case be molested or prejudiced for his or her Conscientious persuasion or practice. Nor shall hee or shee at any time be compelled to frequent or Maintain anie religious worship, place, or Ministry whatever, Contrary to his, or her mind, but shall fully and freely enjoy his or her Christian Liberty in that respect, without any interruption or reflection. And if any person shall abuse or deride any other, for his, or her, different persuasion and practice in matters of religion, such person shall be looked upon as a Disturber of the peace, and be punished accordingly.[2]

On the other hand, it is provided in Chapter II. :

---

[1] "Charter and Laws of the Province of Pennsylvania," 1682–1700. (Official.) Harrisburg, 1879, pp. 81–99.
[2] *Ibid.*, p. 107.

That all officers and persons Commissionated and employed in the service of the government in this Province, and all Members and Deputies elected to serve in the Assembly thereof, and all that have a Right to elect such Deputies, shall be such as profess and declare they believe in Jesus Christ to be the Son of God, the Saviour of the world, And that are not Convicted of ill-fame, or unsober and dishonest Conversation, and that are of twenty-one years of age at Least.[1]

That is to say, all Israelites and unbelievers in Christ were disfranchised, though no physical pains and penalties were visited upon them. Even this was, however, a remarkable thing in its day, and we are rather to admire Penn's new State for going so far than condemn it for not going farther.

On June 1, 1696, the Assembly passed a Petition of Right, addressed to Governor Benjamin Fletcher, which re-enacted both these provisions. In 1696, William Markham being governor, a new Frame of Government was enacted, in which a property qualification for electors and deputies was substituted for the religious, and the guarantee of freedom of conscience was omitted. From this *resumé* of the early laws of Pennsylvania, it will soon be seen that they came considerably short of the religious liberty granted from the first in the colony established by Roger Williams.

The mention of this name recalls the fact that the

---

[1] "Charter and Laws of the Province of Pennsylvania," 1682-1700. (Official.) Harrisburg, 1879, p. 108.

first Baptists to settle in Pennsylvania were from Rhode Island. Thomas Dungan, a Baptist preacher of Ireland, fled to Newport to escape the bitter persecutions which Baptists were subjected to during the reign of Charles II. In 1684 he went to the new colony of Penn and settled at Cold Spring, where he soon gathered a number of Baptist families about him and organized a church. Keach calls Dungan "an ancient disciple and teacher among Baptists;" he must, therefore, have been well on in years when he planted this new church in the wilderness. It disbanded in 1702, and barely a trace of its meeting-house now remains. When Morgan Edwards wrote (1770) there was still a graveyard to be seen adjoining the site, on the stones of which were carved the names of many of the members of this church; and the first Baptist pastor of Pennsylvania then lived in a progeny of between six and seven hundred.[1] Besides these descendants after the flesh, Thomas Dungan left behind him a son in the faith, Rev. Elias Keach, the son of one of the most famous of English Baptist writers and preachers of the seventeenth century.

Thereby hangs a curious tale. Elias Keach was born in England, in 1667, and at the age of nineteen came to Philadelphia. It is related of him that at this time he was "a very wild spark," and on his landing in this country he undertook to pass

---

[1] "Materials Towards a History of the Baptists," by Morgan Edwards. Philadelphia, 1770. Vol. I., p. 10.

himself off as a clergyman, dressing in black and wearing a band. The supposed young London divine was welcomed as he had anticipated, and soon was invited to give a sample of his talents. "He performed well enough till he had advanced pretty far in the sermon, then stopping short, he looked like a man astonished. The audience concluded he had been seized with a sudden disorder; but on asking what the matter was, received from him a confession of the imposture, with tears in his eyes and much trembling. Great was his distress, though it ended happily; from this time he dated his conversion."[1] Learning that there was a Baptist minister at Cold Spring, he sought out Mr. Dungan and was by him instructed in righteousness and baptized.

In the meantime a company of Baptists who had settled at Pennepek, or Lower Dublin (now in the twenty-third ward of Philadelphia), were desirous of forming a Baptist church, which Mr. Keach assisted them to do. The constituent members were John Eaton, George Eaton, and his wife Jane, Sarah Eaton, and Samuel Jones, all of whom had been members of a Baptist church in Wales; John Baker, a Baptist from Kilkenny, Ireland; and Samuel Vaus, from England; Joseph Ashton, and his wife Jane, William Fisher, and John Watts, the four last named having been baptized by Mr. Keach the preceding year. Samuel Vaus was chosen deacon,

---
[1] Edwards, Vol. I., p. 9.

and was "with lying on of hande ordained" by Mr. Keach, who, says the record, "was accepted and received for our pastor, and we sat down in communion at the Lord's table."[1] This was in January, 1688. By its zeal and faithfulness, joined to the evangelistic labors of its pastor, the little one became a thousand. Mr. Keach toiled with unsurpassed energy and effectiveness, and we are told that "he was considered the chief apostle of the Baptists in these parts of America." He preached in many adjacent settlements and towns, especially in Burlington, Cohansey, Chester, and Philadelphia, in all of which mission stations were established that soon became flourishing churches. For some time these missions continued their connection with the parent church, the ordinances being administered quarterly at each of them.

All of these churches were from the first, in faith and order, substantially what they now are;[2] but

---

[1] MS. records of the Pennepek Church. See an interesting historical sketch of this church by the late Horatio Gates Jones, in the "Minutes of the Philadelphia Association" for 1882.

[2] The church at Pennepek had a number of customs that have since fallen into disuse among Baptists. For some years they practised the rite of confirmation, or the laying on of hands on members after baptism. At a later time they regarded the rite as a matter of indifference and gradually discontinued it. They also had for many years ruling elders, founding the practice on 1 Tim. 5 : 17, "Let the elders that rule well be counted worthy of double honour, especially who labour in the word and doctrine." They held, as do the Presbyterians still, that this makes a distinction between elders who teach and lay elders who only rule. The Minutes of the church contain the following entries:

some years after their organization they were joined by immigrants from sundry churches in Europe, who brought a rich and varied assortment of notions with them. The result was, in nearly every church, a period of interminable controversy about absolute predestination, laying on of hands, singing psalms, and Sabbath versus Lord's-day worship. In some cases these controversies led to the formation of new churches; but in other cases, the majority it would appear, the brethren agreed to dwell together in unity if not in exact agreement.

Mr. Keach returned to England in 1692, and John Watts, a member of the church, was chosen his successor. The Pennepek Church has had twenty pastors since its organization and has sent forth twenty-two preachers of the gospel. Many neighboring churches owe their origin to her, including the First Church of Philadelphia, which has had an existence from 1698, though for a good many years it was probably no more than a branch of the

---

1715. June 19. A proposal was made for having ruling elders in ye church; left to consideration till next quarterly meeting.

1726. June 17. At the same time ye church called forth brother John Holme to take upon him the office of a ruling elder, to which he answered he thought himself not fitly qualified for a place of charge and weight yt yt place did require.

1747. June 18. Brother Vansandt was caled to the office of ruling elder by prayer and laying on of hands.

These appear to be the only elders elected by this church, save William Marshal, whose name is mentioned as a ruling elder in the records in 1763, which is the last allusion to the office that is found in them. The First Church, Philadelphia, also had ruling elders for a time. The first three were elected May 10, 1766, and ordained the following June 14. (See Spencer's " Early Baptists of Philadelphia," Philadelphia, 1877, p. 94.)

Pennepek Church, since one pastor ministered to both. A few Baptists had settled in Philadelphia at an early date, one John Holmes being the first to come, in 1686. They were joined in due time by other English Baptists, and the congregation thus gathered enjoyed the frequent ministrations of the Rev. Elias Keach. On the second Sunday in December, according to Morgan Edwards, they "did coalesce into a church for the communion of saints, having Rev. John Watts to their assistance."[1] From the fact that John Watts was then pastor of the Pennepek Church, it has been inferred that it was not the intention of the Philadelphia brethren to constitute themselves an independent church. The relations between the two churches were so hazy, up to 1746, that in that year a serious question arose as to the property rights of the Philadelphia church; and to set all doubts at rest this body was formally organized as an independent church on May 15 of that year and chose Jenkins Jones as their pastor—the first they had had whose service were given wholly to them. During the pastorate of this able and laborious minister the church grew in numbers and spiritual strength. The title to their house of worship, which had been clouded by an unauthorized conveyance of the premises to the Episcopal church, was confirmed to the church, mainly through the efforts of Mr. Jones. He also built for them a parsonage, partly at his own charge.

---

[1] "Materials," etc., Vol. I., p. 43.

In thus tracing the history of the Pennepek Church and its more distinguished daughter, we have passed by events in the early history of Pennsylvania Baptists, to which we must now return. Shortly after the formation of the Pennepek Church there arose a division among the Quakers. George Keith taught a doctrine of salvation that bore closer resemblance to orthodox theology than to the teachings of Fox and Barclay. These maintained the "inner light," the sufficiency of what every spiritually minded man has within himself for his own salvation. Keith magnified the external word and the authority of Christ to such an extent as to be regarded as a heretic by some of the Friends, and in 1631 this produced a schism. The opponents of the "Keithians," as the new body was called, attempted to suppress them by suits at law, the Quakers being willing to give the lie to all their past professions if they might overcome these new heretics. To the honor of John Holmes, before mentioned, and now a magistrate of Philadelphia, he refused to entertain such suits, declaring the matter to be a religious dispute and therefore not fit for a court to decide. He also protested against the acts of his Quaker fellow-magistrates, and condemned their zeal in persecuting the Keithians. Keith himself became an Episcopalian, and many of his followers returned to the orthodox Friends, but some, taking the written word for their guide, found that water baptism was plainly commanded.

On January 28, 1697, Abel Nobel, a Seventh-day Baptist minister from England, baptized a Friend named Thomas Martin in Ridley Creek, and afterward baptized sixteen more, who organized themselves into a church October 12, 1697. Thomas Martin was chosen their minister by lot, and administered the Lord's Supper to them for the first time. In 1700 they were much troubled by a controversy touching the Sabbath, and finally became a Seventh-day church. Those who adhered to the Lord's Day were scattered for a time, until Mr. Abel Morgan gathered fifteen of them and organized them into the Brandywine Church in 1715. Several other societies of Keithian Quakers also became Baptists in whole or in part. About half of them observed the Seventh-day, and all of them retained for a time some of the Quaker peculiarities; they made a point of distinguishing days and months numerically, instead of by the conventional "heathenish" names, while in simplicity of speech and plainness of dress they were an exact copy of the Quakers, who in turn had copied these peculiarities from the Anabaptists. In the day of Morgan Edwards these peculiarities had disappeared, and these Baptists were fully conformed to the manners and customs generally obtaining among Baptist churches.

Very influential among the Baptists of this early period was the church of the Welsh Tract. In June, 1700, sixteen Welsh Baptists embarked at

Milford for the new world, and in the following September eight of them landed at Philadelphia. They first settled in Pennepek; but not finding themselves in close agreement with the church there, they bought a tract of thirty thousand acres in Northern Delaware, which they named Welsh Tract. Their first pastor was Thomas Griffiths, and they throve greatly in their new location. For some time they were in continual controversy with the Pennepek Church, which they had left, principally about the "laying on of hands" after baptism— the Pennepek Church having abandoned this rite. Finally they held a conference at which they reached an amicable agreement, whose terms were: "(1) That members of either church might transiently commune with the other, but not be received into membership. (2) That the votaries of the rite might freely converse on the subject, and that the rest would hear." The result was that "some ministers and about fifty-five private persons" were convinced by the arguments of their Welsh Tract[1] brethren and submitted to this as to an ordinance of the Lord.

These Baptists of the Welsh Tract held firmly to other peculiarities which were shared by churches of similar origin. Notable among these peculiar practices was the anointing of the sick with oil, which they considered to be not merely authorized but commanded in the Scriptures. One of the pas-

---

[1] Edwards, Vol. I., p. 20.

tors of the Welsh Tract Church, the Rev. Owen Thomas, left behind him this remarkable note: "I have been called upon three times to anoint the sick with oil for recovery. The effect was surprising in every case; but in none more so than in that of our brother, Reynallt Howell. He was so sore with the bruises of the wagon when he was anointed that he could not bear to be turned in bed otherwise than with the sheet; the next day he was so well that he went to meeting." Morgan Edwards, who records this case, adds on his own account: "I have often wondered that this rite is so much neglected as the precept is so plain and the effects have been so salutary." Mr. Edwards also records the following in another connection: Some years before the death of the Rev. Hugh Davis, which occurred in 1753, "he had a severe pain in his arm which gradually wasted the limb and made life a burden. After trying many remedies, he sent for the elders of the church to anoint him with oil, according to James 5 : 14–17. The effect was perfect cure so far that the pain never returned. One of the elders concerned (from whom I had this relation) is yet alive and succeeds Mr. Hugh Davis in the ministry, viz., Rev. John Davis." [1]

Prior to the Revolution, no Baptist churches were organized in Pennsylvania outside of what may be

---
[1] "Materials," etc., Vol. I., p. 28. See also Appendix, p. 115, seq., in which he gives a long account of the healing of a lame girl.

called the Philadelphia region; but in addition to those already mentioned in that district, several others deserve a brief account. The Great Valley Church was constituted April 22, 1711, by sixteen persons from Wales, including the Rev. Hugh Davis, who became their first pastor. Elder Elisha Thomas, then pastor of the Welsh Tract Church, was present and conducted the services. In the same year this church was admitted to the Philadelphia Association, being the first to join that body after its organization. For some time the members met in the house of Richard Miles, in Radnor; but in 1722 they built a house of worship, twenty-eight feet square, " with seats, gallery, and *stove*," as contemporary record triumphantly observes, the last being by no means a common adjunct of worship in the Baptist churches of that day. As has been observed by some of their admirers, those old-time Baptists believed in putting the stove in the pulpit, and it kept the whole church warm. There was a secession of Seventh-day brethren from this church in 1726, and up to 1841 eight neighboring churches had been formed from it.[1]

The Montgomery Church was organized June 20, 1719, of ten Welsh Baptists, with the approval and assistance of Abel Morgan. No name is more frequently found than his in these early annals, and he is always found doing that which promised to be for

---

[1] See the history of this church in the "Minutes of the Philadelphia Association" for 1883.

the best interests of the denomination that he so heartily loved and served. Like many other Baptist churches of the time, this church had a stormy time of it at intervals. Brethren could not always agree, and were often self-willed and obstinate about their differences. In 1754, in consequence of theological disputations relating to the doctrine of the person of Christ, they divided, and a part of them formed the New Britain Church. The Southampton Church was organized in 1746, its constituents being the remains of an old Keithian society that had existed there for half a century and certain members of the Pennepek Church. In 1781 another division in the Montgomery Church resulted in the dismission of fifty-four persons to form the Hilltown Church.

In 1789 were formed the churches at Marcus Hook and Roxborough. There had been Baptists and preaching in both these places for some years before, but no formal organization. The Marcus Hook Baptists built a house of worship of brick, a house twenty-five feet square, and its cost —£164 16s. 6d., a large sum for those days—was paid before the church was organized. The Roxborough Church was composed mainly of persons who had been previously members of the First Church, Philadelphia, thirty-two having been dismissed for that purpose. If there are any other Regular Baptist churches still existing in proximity to Philadelphia, that were formed before the beginning of the present century, they have escaped the author's search.[1]

A very interesting immigration of German Baptists into Pennsylvania occurred in the fall of 1719. They settled at Germantown and adjacent places, and were joined by others in 1722 and again in 1729. These immigrants were the originators of the body known as Tunkers or Dunkards or German Baptists, a body now numbering about seventy-five thousand communicants in the United States. They had all been members of a single church in Germany, which was constituted at Schwardzenau in 1708 with eight members. Those who formed it had all been bred Lutherans or Presbyterians, and did not know that there was in the world such a people as the Baptists. Through their own study of the Scriptures they came to see that believer's baptism only is taught in the New Testament, and that the apostolic churches were congregational in polity. They resolved to follow the Scriptures. One of their number was appointed to administer baptism, and he immersed the others in the river Eder. Persecution soon scattered them, and they migrated to America by way of various European countries. In their new home they increased with great rapidity for a time and have maintained a steady growth up to the present, having spread from Pennsylvania into many of the other States.

---

[1] The histories of these churches are given in the Philadelphia Association's "Minutes" for 1888 and 1889.

A part of these Tunkers separated from the main body on the question of Sabbath worship, resolving to observe the seventh day. Under the leadership of Conrad Beissel they established the town known as Ephrata, near Lancaster, about 1730.[1] Here, on a tract of land including about one hundred and fifty-five acres, between thirty and forty buildings were built in the next forty years. Morgan Edwards, who visited them and formed impressions on the spot when the society was most flourishing, tells us that this was a communistic town. At first the members of the community were very austere; they slept on board couches with blocks for pillows, but after a time they came to sleep on beds like other folk. "The brethren," he tells us, "have adopted the dress of the white friers (*sic*) with some alterations; and the sisters that of the nuns; and both, like them, have taken the vow of celibacy." Mr. Edwards bears eloquent testimony to the virtues of the community: "From the uncouth dress, the recluse and ascetic life of these people, sour aspects and rough manners might be expected; but on the contrary, a smiling innocence and meekness grace their countenances, and a softness of tone and accent adorn their conversation, and make their deportment gentle and obliging. Their singing is charming, partly owing to the pleasantness of their

---

[1] The early records of the body have been translated and published under the title of "Chronicon Ephratense." Lancaster, Pa., 1889.

voices, the variety of parts they carry on together, and the devout manner of their performance." There were at this time forty families in the community, and about one hundred and thirty-five persons all told, only fourteen of whom were single brethren and twenty-eight single sisters. The village was then enclosed with a very large ditch, and fortified with posts and rails and quicksets, precautions by no means needless at that time.[1] A few years after the visit of Mr. Edwards the community began to decline, and though it still exists, but little is left of it. While they flourished, the Ephrata community were remarkable for their intelligence and progressiveness. They had a printing press, and long before the day of Sunday-schools they had a Sunday class for the instruction of children in the Scriptures that continued for more than thirty years.

The general body of Tunkers did not and does not differ from Baptists in any essential matter of belief or practice. In theology they incline toward the Arminian type and would find themselves in full harmony with the General Baptists of England. They are commonly said to believe in an uneducated and unpaid ministry, but it would be more just to say that they do not regard education as essential to a minister, and that a minister should have no salary, though his people may give and he

---

[1] This account of the Tunkers is almost wholly drawn from the "Materials" of Morgan Edwards, who collected the facts with great labor. See Vol. I., pp. 67-77 especially.

may receive anything in the way of voluntary contribution. Their method of choosing ministers is thus described by Edwards: "Every brother is allowed to stand up in the congregation to speak in a way of exhortation or expounding; and when by these means they find a man eminent for knowledge and aptness to teach, they choose him to be a minister, and ordain him with imposition of hands, attended by fasting and prayer and giving the right hand of fellowship."[1] The Tunkers practise trine immersion, the candidate kneeling and being baptized forward, and continuing on his knees until after prayer and the imposition of hands. They practise feet washing as a religious ordinance, and at the conclusion of their meetings give one another the holy kiss of charity. The wearing of beards while not a religious ordinance, is generally practised by the men, and is greatly encouraged, especially among the ministers. These are all superficial peculiarities, unless the trine immersion be excepted; they do not touch the fundamental unity of Baptists and Tunkers regarding the nature of the church and the subjects of baptism. And all of us might well admire and imitate the meek and pious Christian lives of these people, which long ago gained for them the title of "the harmless Tunkers."

Soon after the close of the Revolutionary War,

---

[1] "Materials," etc., Vol. I., p. 67.

Ebenezer Green and others from the Warwick Church, New York, emigrated to the Susquehanna region and settled on a tract of land then known as "the Wyoming country." Rev. Roswell Goff visited and preached among them and finally helped them to organize the Chemung Church, in 1791. Their second pastor was Rev. Thomas Smiley, whose pastorate was terminated in a very summary manner. The ownership of this tract was long in dispute and serious troubles arose in 1800. Mr. Smiley had some governmental papers in his study, and he was visited at dead of night by a band of "Wild Yankees," who seem to have been very like the "White Caps" of our own day. Their faces were blackened and they were otherwise disguised. They dragged Mr. Smiley out of bed, compelled him to burn his papers, and then tarred and feathered him. As, even after this treatment, he continued a steadfast adherent of the Pennsylvania side of the dispute, the "Wild Yankees" threatened his life, and he fled for safety to the White Deer Valley, now in the county of Northumberland, where he organized another Baptist church in 1808, and continued to be its pastor for many years. The Chemung Church was not long alone in the Wyoming region, for by 1796 there were four other Baptist churches not far away; but the exact order of their organization is not known.

It is difficult to obtain any satisfactory statistical information regarding these early churches. Their records are lost or incomplete, and there was no systematic attempt to collect and record the facts until long after. Morgan Edwards, from the result of careful inquiry, gives the following as the approximate condition of Baptist affairs in 1770: Churches, ten; ministers, eleven; members, six hundred and sixty-eight. These are of "regular" Baptists only; his totals, including Tunkers and others, are: Churches, forty-two; ministers, thirty-five; members, two thousand nine hundred and twenty.[1] From the best and most accurate information now obtainable it appears that in all only fourteen "regular" Baptist churches were organized in Pennsylvania before 1800.[2] The growth of Baptists in Central and Western New York was more rapid than that of their brethren in Pennsylvania, doubtless owing to the fact that the first great wave of emigration westward after the Revolution surged through the fertile valleys of what was thereafter to be the Empire State.

---

[1] Edwards was always careful and judicious, but many collectors of religious statistics then, as now, were wild to a laughable degree. For example, Rev. Dr. Smith, an Episcopal clergyman, wrote to Archbishop Secker, in 1759, an account of the religious state of Pennsylvania, in which he estimates the number of English Anabaptists at 5,000, and of German Anabaptists, or Mennonites, and other Quietist sects, 30,000. (O'Callaghan, "Documents," Vol. VII., p. 407.)

[2] There is no such record kept by Pennsylvania Baptists, as to the date of the organization of their churches and Associations, as appears in the Minutes of the New York and New Jersey State Conventions. Dr. Benedict's figures are trustworthy as far as they go, but incomplete.

These early Pennsylvania churches were rich in the possession of an able and consecrated ministry. A few of the men who laid foundations, on which others have built an imposing denominational structure, have been named in the progress of the preceding narrative. There were others, however, not inferior in character or services or devotedness to those who founded the first churches. The Lower Dublin or Pennepek Church had a succession of ministers second to none of their time, of whom John Watts, Evan Morgan, and Samuel Jones were the most eminent. These would have been men of mark in any generation and in any community. Dr. Samuel Jones, in particular, was a notable man. Born in Wales, in 1735, but coming to this country in infancy, he was educated at the college of Philadelphia, where he was graduated in 1762. The following year he was ordained, and until his death in 1814 he remained pastor of the Lower Dublin Church. To remain in one pulpit for over fifty years with no diminution of influence, and to do the work of pastor and preacher so that the church constantly grew in numbers and strength ; to take a leading place among the men of his day as preacher, scholar, and man of affairs ; to win the esteem, respect, and honor of those of other communions, as well as those of his own brethren—the man who can do such things must be held to possess unusual gifts of mind and graces of character. In addition to his other work, Dr. Jones for some thirty years maintained an academy, at his own risk, in which many were trained not only for the ministry but for other professions. No name occurs more frequently or in a more honorable way in contemporary Baptist records than that of Samuel Jones. When his brethren wished for a man to perform some special public service in a way to reflect credit on the denomination, they turned as a thing of course to him. Thus, it was he who, at the request of the Association, prepared its treatise on discipline in 1798; he was appointed to preach the centenary sermon in 1807; and when Dr. Manning died, he was the first choice for the presidency of the Rhode Island College. He preferred to any other the work to which he felt himself called, that of preaching the gospel, and nothing could persuade him to leave his beloved church.

Equally fortunate in its pastors was the Philadelphia church, with such leaders as Morgan Edwards, William Rogers, and William Staughton. The first named was one of the most remarkable Baptist ministers of colonial times—as eccentric as he was able, and as obstinate as he was conscientious. A native of Wales, ordained to the ministry in Ireland, and called in middle life to the pastorate of the Philadelphia church while still laboring successfully in the mother country, he came hither in 1761. He had not been long enough in America to become Americanized when the Revolution began, and it is not cause for surprise to find that he was a stiff Tory—the only one, it is said, on record among the Baptist ministers of the colonies. The state of his feelings, so late as 1792, may be inferred from this outburst, *apropos* of the loss of a large part of its property by the church at Scotch Plains during the Revolution:

"Oh, thou robber of churches, and of the fatherless and widows, what hast thou to answer for! Can an end gained by such means prosper? The widow Micah cursed him that robbed her (Judg. 17 : 2); but when it was restored, she blessed. And cannot a certain revolution do as much to reverse a curse into the blessing of the widow and fatherless and churches?"[1]

This may be taken to prove that Mr. Edwards acted under virtual compulsion when he signed the following recantation, dated August 7, 1775, and that his use of "rash and imprudent expressions" was not thoroughly cured:

Whereas, I have some time since frequently made use of rash and imprudent expressions with respect to the conduct of my fellow-countrymen, who are now engaged in a noble and patriotic struggle for the liberties of America, against the arbitrary measures of the British ministry; which conduct has justly raised their resentment against me, I now confess that I have spoken wrong, for which I am sorry and ask the forgiveness of the public. And I do promise that for the future I will conduct myself in such a manner as to avoid giving offense, and at the same time, in justice to myself, de-

[1] "Materials," Vol. II., p. 70.

clare that I am a friend to the present measures pursued by the friends to American liberty, and do hereby approve of them, and, as far as in my power, will endeavor to promote them.

We may pardon at this late day a loyalty to his king and a courage in avowing his sentiments that his contemporaries found trying. To us of this generation such pardon is not difficult, because of the eminent services of Edwards. It is easy to see, however, why his conduct should have so irritated his co-laborers in the Baptist pulpit, for he was more loyal to King George than the Baptists of England, if we may trust Dr. Rippon. In a letter to President Manning, written in 1784, this eminent English Baptist divine says :

I believe all our Baptist ministers in town except two, and most of our brethren in the country, were on the side of the Americans in the late dispute. . . We wept when the thirsty plains drank the blood of your departed heroes, and the shout of a king was amongst us when your well-fought battles were crowned with victory. And to this hour we believe that the independence of America will for a while secure the liberty of this country ; but if that continent had been secured, Britain would not long have been free.[1]

It is a fact beyond question that Baptists, and particularly Baptist ministers, were patriots almost to a man during the Revolution. They had little cause to love some of the colonial governments, it is

---

[1] Guild, "Manning and Brown University," p. 314.

true. They had been persecuted in Massachusetts and Virginia, to mention no other colonies, with a relentless bitterness that might well have rankled in their souls and made them say, "Fight this battle for yourselves; as for us, we have no part nor lot with you." But they did not take this attitude. They saw clearly enough that they had a larger stake in the contest than any others, for if the colonies obtained their political liberties in that struggle, and especially if they obtained these liberties by the aid of Baptists, it could not be long before complete civil and religious liberty must be conceded to those who had suffered so long and so bitterly. And though the Baptists of New York, New Jersey, and Pennsylvania had themselves felt less than most others the sting of persecution, their sympathies were keenly stirred for their less fortunate brethren elsewhere. They accordingly took advantage of the meeting of the first Continental Congress to petition that body for relief from persecution.[1] Dr. Samuel Jones, in his centenary sermon before the Philadelphia Association, in 1807, said:

> On the assembling of the first Continental Congress I was one of the Committee, under appointment of your body, in company with the late Rev. Isaac Backus, of Massachusetts, and met the delegates in Congress from that State in yonder State House, to see if we could not

---

[1] See the address of Dr. Cathcart on "Baptists and the Revolution," in the "Minutes of the Philadelphia Association" for 1875, for much interesting and valuable matter on this subject.

obtain some security for that liberty for which we were then fighting and bleeding at their side. It seemed unreasonable to us that we should be called upon to stand up in defense of liberty, if, after all, it was to be liberty for one party to oppress another.

But to return to Edwards: he was virtually the founder of Rhode Island College, as we shall see in a later chapter, and almost the sole reference to himself that he makes in his books is concluded with these words: "He labored hard to settle a baptist college in Rhodeisland government and to raise money to endow it; which he deems the greatest service he has ever done or hopes to do for the honor of the baptist interest."[1] Baptists of all coming time will owe him an immeasurable debt of gratitude for his pioneer labors in the cause of higher education. He is entitled to almost equal gratitude and honor for his labors as a historian. At great expense of time and labor, he traveled among the churches of Pennsylvania and New Jersey, collecting facts from original records now lost and from the recollections of men long since dead. These digested facts form the "Materials Towards the History of the Baptists," from which so many quotations have been made in these chapters.

As Delaware had no existence apart from Pennsylvania until 1776, the story of the formation of

---

[1] On the title pages of his books he describes himself as "Morgan Edwards, A. M., Felow of Rhodeisland College, and overseer of the Baptist Church in Philadelphia."

the Welsh Tract Church has properly been told in another connection. This was the only Baptist church in Delaware for more than three-quarters of a century—unless we except a church that Edwards says was formed near the Iron Hill, Newcastle County, as early as the spring of 1703, of which nothing more seems to be known. In 1778 the Rev. Elijah Baker came from Virginia into Delaware, followed at no long interval by the Rev. Philip Hughes, and together they labored as evangelists for about a year, baptizing many converts, some of whom were gathered into churches. Twenty-one churches in Delaware, Maryland, and Virginia are said to owe their origin to these evangelistic labors. Mr. Baker at least had suffered persecution for his religious principles in Virginia; but in Delaware the spirit of Penn prevailed, and no law interfered with the preaching of the gospel or the worship of God.

In 1779 the second Baptist church in Delaware was formed at the Sounds, in Sussex county. It was constituted, with the aid of Messrs. Baker and Hughes, of twenty-five members, and for a time met in the homes of its members, having in 1791 no place of meeting. It never became a strong body, and at length ceased to exist. The Broad Creek Church, in the same county, was formed in 1781 with forty-seven members, and in the same year were organized the Cowmarsh and Bryn Zion churches. Four other churches were formed before the end of the century: Mispillion (1783), Gravelly Branch (1785), Bethel (1786), and First Wilmington.

The last named is the most important and historically the most interesting. There were a few scattered Baptists in Wilmington from 1748 onward, members of the Welsh Tract, Brandywine, and Philadelphia churches having removed thither at various times. It was not until 1782, when the Rev. Philip Hughes preached for a time in the town, that any design was seriously entertained of organizing a church, and it was not finally accomplished until October 8, 1785. Nine of the converts baptized by Mr. Hughes had united with the Welsh Tract Church, and obtaining letters of dismission they were joined by six others in constituting the new church, which was received into the Philadelphia Association the next year. About this time Mr. Hughes printed a pamphlet on baptism in Wilmington in answer to a Virginia clergyman; and this, together with the formation of the new church, roused considerable feeling against the Baptists. Some ministers preached against them and their doctrines, but the pastor of the Presbyterian church, "Father McKannan," as he was affectionately called, invited Mr. Hughes to preach for him, and as Edwards says, "taught his people to love their neighbors as themselves." In the same year they were organized this church built a brick house of worship, thirty-five by forty feet;

and a recent historian of Wilmington Baptists pithily remarks, " The house still stands and the church stands still." The church has had great vicissitudes of fortune, and at times has not been in fellowship with its sister churches, but is now a member of a Delaware Association which calls itself an Old School Baptist body.

This Association was formed October 24, 1795, by the five churches whose origin has been related above, and another, Queen Anne's, which was probably located across the Maryland border. For nearly half a century thereafter, until the formation of the Second Wilmington Church, the history of the Baptists of Delaware is a painful story. No church was organized in all these years, several of those named became extinct, and the rest fell into a state of coldness and declension that has made the few survivors a feeble and uninfluential folk. The historical records of the early history of this Association and the churches composing it show that as Baptists they at first belonged to the oldest school of all, that of the apostles. It is they and not the denomination at large that have changed in this regard. They were missionary churches at first, as indeed they could not well fail to be, since they owed their very being to missionary labors. Missionary sermons and missionary collections were regular features of their church life at the beginning of this century, and they approved the earliest plans for ministerial education and foreign missions.

In short, up to about 1816, these churches were, so far as the records show, in entire sympathy with their sister churches in the great educational and missionary enterprises then being undertaken; and at that time the Welsh Tract Church numbered one hundred and ninety, while the Wilmington Church had grown to two hundred and eight members. Anti-missionary principles were not openly avowed until about 1830, though they appear to have been pretty faithfully practised for a good while before. After that avowal the declension of the churches was steady and even rapid; but the further history of this matter belongs to a later chapter.

In 1791, when Morgan Edwards finished compiling his "Materials Toward a History of the Baptists in Delaware," there were in the State eight Baptist churches, with three hundred and eighty members, nine ministers, three licentiates, and four meeting-houses. There was then no reason apparent why the Baptists of Delaware should not prosper and increase like their brethren in the other Middle States.

CHAPTER IV

THE GROWTH OF ORGANIZATION

FERTILE in generalizations after his kind, a German historian has first pointed out the significant feature in the history of American Baptists, the fact that their rapid growth is exactly conterminous and contemporary with the development of the idea of association of their churches.[1] This is certainly more than a coincidence, though it would be easy to exaggerate the effect of mere organization. The great progress of the denomination after the Revolution was manifestly due in the first instance to the impulse received by the churches, in common with all other American Christians, from the great spiritual movement that marked the closing years of the eighteenth century.[2] It was no doubt a marked piece of good fortune, or rather a signal proof of the providential guidance of the early Baptists of America, that when such a spiritual rousing came and the religious life of the churches was elevated and intensified, an instrument was ready to their hands. The associational organiza-

---
[1] Nippold, "*Handbuch der neuesten Kirchengeschichte,*" Vol. IV., p. 61.
[2] For an account of these revivals, which were general throughout the United States, see Dorchester's "Christianity in the United States," pp. 363–380.

tion thus became a chief means of advancement in evangelizing the new regions opened up for settlement in the first years of peace.

It has sometimes been conjectured that Baptists borrowed their idea of association from the Yearly Meetings of the Friends. These yearly meetings, or some of them, clearly antedate the Baptist Associations of this country, having been established in New England in 1661, in Philadelphia in 1683, and in New York in 1695. This Quaker institution has, however, only a superficial resemblance to a Baptist Association; what it really resembles is a Presbyterian Synod. It is a body in which supreme law-making and disciplinary powers are vested, the highest member of a system of gatherings by which the local societies are ruled, and its decisions are binding on every Friend. This system of government is every whit as rigid and precise as that of the Presbyterian Church, with this difference, that the meetings are in theory quite democratic in their composition. One need not argue that this is a thing entirely different from the theory and practice governing Associations of Baptist churches.

If any connection is traceable between the Yearly Meeting and the Association, the Friends were the borrowers of the idea. The Particular Baptists of Somerset, England, formed the first Association of Baptist churches in 1653;[1] and by the end of the

---

[1] Manuscript records of this body still exist, beginning with a meeting held at Wells November 8 and 9 of that year. (See "Con-

century these Associations were common among all branches of Baptists in England. The first Yearly Meeting of the Friends was held, according to the best authority,[1] in London, November 6, 1668 ; but it was not until 1683 that Fox succeeded in fully introducing his system of discipline and made the Yearly Meeting a permanent institution. The intimate connection between the early Friends and the Baptists is well known, and Fox may have derived his suggestion of the Yearly Meeting from this source.

American Baptists do not appear to have been influenced by this movement among their brethren in England, of which they were more than likely in complete ignorance, nor yet by the example of their neighbors, the Friends in this country. We can trace exactly the history of the first Association among American Baptists, and the circumstances point clearly to an origin by evolution, not by imitation.

Soon after the organization of the Pennepek Church, and the preaching of the gospel in adjacent towns of Pennsylvania and New Jersey, small companies of Baptists were gathered at Salem, Cohansey, Burlington, and other places. For some time they had no pastors, even no separate church organ-

---

fessions of Faith," in the publications of the Hanserd Knollys Society, Introductory Notice, p. 11. Compare Goadby's "Bye-Paths in Baptist History," pp. 182-185.)

[1] Barclay, "Religious Life of the Societies of the Commonwealth," p. 394.

izations. For the convenience of these brethren and their comfort and edification in the faith, "General Meetings" were held with them from time to time. These date back as far as 1688. At first held only once a year, they were soon made semi-annual gatherings, in the months of May and September.[1] These meetings were held for many years simply for the ministry of the word and the ministration of gospel ordinances, and were exactly what their name implied, general meetings, not the sessions of a representative or delegated body. The records of the Pennepek Church inform us exactly of the time when the character of these meetings underwent the change that transformed them from mass meetings into an Association:

---

[1] Edwards, "Materials," Vol. I., p. 8. Compare MS. records of Pennepek Church, quoted by Jones, "Minutes of Philadelphia Association" for 1882, p. 57. These records read as follows: "But, however, when Elias Keach was with us we commonly acted as a particular Church, and at the general meetings of the Brethren from all parts of the Provinces, were desired generally to come together to hear the word, etc., and to communicate at the Lord's Table. These general meetings were appointed twice in the year; once in the spring, about the third month [May], and one time in the fall, about the eighth month [October]. In the spring at Salem and in the fall at Dublin or Burlington. But it is to be noted that in these times of beginning we had not opportunity to be formed into particular Churches for want of persons fitly qualified to oversee a Church or to carry on the work of the ministry." Thus, as Edwards puts it, "They were all one church and Pennepek the centre of union." But church business was transacted at any of these meetings; as for example, at Salem, N. J., in May, 1688, Joseph Ashton was chosen a deacon, and was ordained by Elias Keach with laying on of hands.

Before our generall meeting held at Philadelphia in the 7th month [September], 1707, it was concluded by the severall congregations of our Judgment, to make choyse of some particular Brethren such as they thought most capable in every congregation and those to meet at the yearly Meeting, to consult about such things as were wanting in the Church, and set them in order, and those brethren met at the said yearly meeting, which began the 27th of the 7th month on the 7th day of the week, agreed that the said meeting should be continued till the third day of the week, in the work of the publick ministry and by whom the publick ministry of the word should be carried on.[1]

Five churches thus appointed delegates that year, viz., Pennepek, Middletown, Piscataqua, Cohansey, and Welsh Tract; and the history of the Philadelphia Association is properly dated from that meeting. The early Minutes of this body do not appear to have been preserved, and the earliest copy of the printed Minutes known to be now in existence bears date 1769. In that year the Association contained thirty-four churches, with thirty-four pastors, and two thousand three hundred and sixty-six members; and sixty-eight baptisms were reported. At that time the body included churches in New Jersey and Southern New York. The First Church of New York City was then a member, having been received into the Association October 12, 1763,[2] at

---
[1] Edwards, "Materials," Vol. I., p. 121. Compare Dr. Jones' history as above.
[2] "Minutes of the Philadelphia Association," edited by A. D. Gillette, p. 89. These records prior to 1760, were kept by Benjamin Griffith, after that by Morgan Edwards.

that time numbering forty-three members. In the Minutes of 1769 it reports one hundred and forty members, and its pastor, the Rev. John Gano, was its delegate to the Association. Mr. Gano was held in deserved honor by this body, for the file of Minutes shows that he was chosen moderator in 1773 and again in 1775, besides being called upon for his full share of service in various ways at other meetings. Another delegate whose name is worthy of special note was the Rev. Hezekiah Smith; and the Minutes show how strong was the solicitude felt at this time by Messrs. Gano and Smith for the infant Rhode Island College.

Before its printed records thus give us full knowledge of its work, the Association had done two things that entitle it to grateful and perpetual remembrance. The first of these was the adoption, in September, 1742,[1] of the Articles of Faith since known as the Philadelphia Confession. This is substantially identical with the Confession put forth in 1689 by the English Baptists, which in turn was little more than a revision of the Westminster Confession. The London document consisted of thirty-two articles, and an appendix—which latter was, however, never regarded, even in England, as part of the articles. The Philadelphia Confession adds

---

[1] Gillette, "Minutes," p. 46. This may have been only a re-adoption, since there is an entry under date of 1724 to the effect that the Confession was at that time accepted by the Association. The record is not known to be based on an original document, and cannot be regarded as conclusive.

two articles—one treating of singing in public worship, the other of the laying on of hands after baptism—and substitutes a different appendix, in large part identical with a London publication of 1697, by the Rev. Elias Keach, styled "The glory and ornament of a true gospel-constituted church," Not only was the London appendix incontinently thrown aside, but a new article definitely rejected its doctrine of compromise, and arrayed the Philadelphia Association once for all on the side of strict communion. "We believe," says this article, "that laying on of hands with prayer, upon baptized believers, as such, is an ordinance of Christ, and ought to be submitted unto by all persons that are admitted to partake of the Lord's Supper." This Confession of Faith has served as the basis of probably the majority of the Baptist churches of this country; and it is still, with the omission of the article on the laying on of hands and revisions here and there in no wise affecting its substance, the Confession that generally obtains in the Baptist churches of the Southern and Southwestern States.

The historic importance of this action is very great, for it is plain that the adoption of this strongly Calvinistic Confession was the turning point in the early history of American Baptists, and fixed the character of the denomination for all time. Up to 1742 the Arminian Baptists had decidedly the advantage in numbers and enterprise, and seemed likely to become the dominating

THE GROWTH OF ORGANIZATION 93

party. The turning of the tide may be noted in the formation of the Welsh Tract Church, and the increase of its influence in the Philadelphia Association. The Baptists who came from Wales really determined the character of the Baptist denomination in America, and finally overcame the strong Arminian influence of New England. From 1742 the influence of the Philadelphia Association was paramount. Its missionary zeal was great; men closely connected with this body, and fully believing its Confession, became preachers of the gospel in New England, New York, and the Carolinas. By the close of the century, the Calvinistic party was in the ascendency everywhere; it had completed its triumphs by the capture of the stronghold of Arminianism, the First Baptist Church of Providence, thanks to the Rhode Island College and President Manning.

Another thing that proved of the greatest service to American Baptists through all after years was, the definite settlement by this body, in accordance with scriptural principles, of associational constitutions. Our first Baptist historian says:

> Some motions were made in 1766 and afterward which (if admitted one way) would have brought in, by way of appeal, matters that had been determined in particular churches; but an effectual opposition was made to the motions from an apprehension that as soon as the Association starts from its present firm basis of an advisory council so soon will it become contemptible for

want of power; or, having power, become tyrannical, as all assemblies of the kind have proved.[1]

How wise this decision was is shown by the history of Associations among the General Baptists of England. From the first, these bodies assumed functions incompatible with the independence of the churches. They undertook the reform of inconsistent or immoral conduct in ministers and even among private Christians, to suppress heresy, to reconcile differences between individuals and churches, and to give advice in difficult cases both to individuals and churches— in short, they assumed all the functions of a synod. This was Presbyterianism in Baptist churches, and when a celebrated heresy case came up for adjudication, it split the General Baptist churches in twain. It was well, therefore, from mere considerations of worldly prudence, independent of the teaching of the New Testament in the matter, which is equally unmistakable, that the Philadelphia Association

[1] Edwards, "Materials," Vol. I., pp. 123, 124. Compare, Gillette, "Minutes," pp. 99, 101, 105. The first decision of the question, "Whether an appeal from any member of the associated churches, or from one excommunicated from any of said churches may be made to the Association?" was "That in some cases they may, as every church may sometimes suspend their prerogatives, of which every church is to judge for itself." This was in 1767. The decision was so misunderstood and roused so much opposition, that in 1768 it was voted "that the word *appeal* was not quite proper, as the Association claims no jurisdiction, nor a power to repeal anything settled by any church; but if, before settlement, parties agree to refer matters to the Association, then to give their advice." That settled once for all the question of the relations of the churches to Associations, and *vice versa*.

firmly opposed every proposal to interfere with the discipline and internal affairs of the churches composing it. American Baptists have been very generally and very justly jealous of anything that looks like usurpation of power over the churches by any other body. Associations and missionary organizations are the creation of the churches and should be their servants.

For nearly half a century the Philadelphia Association continued to be the only organization of this kind among Baptist churches. The next to be formed was in South Carolina, where, in 1751, four churches formed the Charleston Association. This organization is directly traceable to the Philadelphia body, Mr. Hart, then pastor of the Charleston Church, "having seen in the Philadelphia Association the happy consequences of union and stated intercourse among churches maintaining the same faith and order."[1] Four years after its organization, this Association, taking into consideration the destitute condition of many settlements in the interior, recommended the churches to make contributions for the support of a missionary. Mr. Hart was authorized to engage a suitable person, visited the Philadelphia Association, and prevailed on the Rev. John Gano to undertake this work. Resulting missionary tours among these settlements were very fruitful, and this was the beginning of that work of evangelization to which the subsequent

[1] Benedict, p. 707.

rapid progress of Baptists was due. In 1771 the Congaree Association was organized (becoming the Bethel in 1789), a fact that is in itself a testimony to the worth of Gano's work.

It is less easy to trace a connection between the Philadelphia Association and the next development of associational organization in the neighboring State of North Carolina;[1] yet that the connection exists hardly admits of a doubt. The founder of the Sandy Creek Association, the oldest body of the kind in the State, was the Rev. Shubal Stearns, a native of Boston, converted during the Great Awakening, and from the first one of the New Lights, or Separates. He was for a time a resident of Upper Virginia, whither he had gone from New England in consequence of a deep conviction that God had a great work for him to do in these new regions; but about 1755 he removed to North Carolina and settled at Sandy Creek. He was a man of great energy and devotion, and wonderful tales are still told of his power in the pulpit. A remarkable work of grace followed his settlement at Sandy Creek, the church being in a little while increased from sixteen to six hundred and six. In his Northern residence it is hardly possible that Mr. Stearns should not have

---

[1] It may seem that here, as in the two following paragraphs, one is trespassing upon the ground of other contributors to this series. The justification of the brief outline given of associational development is, first, its relations to the parent Association; and, secondly, its relations to the larger societies that arose as a natural consequence.

heard about the Philadelphia Association and gained some acquaintance with its work. Several churches having been constituted in his neighborhood, as a consequence of the revival in all the region, he visited every congregation and persuaded each to send delegates to his meeting-house in January, 1758, and an Association was then and there formed.[1] The Kehukee Association was formed in 1765, but seems to have owed its origin to the Charleston body, with which several of its constituent churches were previously united.

The next marked advance of the associational idea was in New England. The Warren Association took its name from the Rhode Island church that was the leader in its organization; but the three other churches that in 1767 united to form this body—the Bellingham, Second Middleborough, and Haverhill—were in Massachusetts. By 1772 there were twenty-one churches, the majority of them in Massachusetts, affiliated with this Association, and it was not until 1811 that some of these churches left the "Old Warren" to form the Boston Association. In the meantime other New England Baptist churches had taken up the idea and Associations were formed in all their States. The most notable development of the associational idea was in Vermont, where no fewer than four Associations were

---

[1] Benedict, pp. 683, 685. So also Morgan Edwards, in his MS. "Materials" on North Carolina Baptists. Semple, however, gives the date as 1760: "History of Virginia Baptists" (Beale's edition), p. 18. In this he follows Backus, Vol. II., p. 530.

organized by 1796. This was due to the zealous labors of the Separates in that State, as a result of which thirty-two Baptist churches were there organized in the single decade between 1780 and 1790.

Simultaneous with this advance in New England was a great development in the Middle South, beginning in Virginia, where the Ketockton Association was formed in 1768. This was a union of the Regular Baptist churches, as they were called, the old-fashioned High Calvinists, who would have none of the new-fangled notions introduced by the converts of Whitefield. The New Lights, or Separates, began about this time to establish churches of their faith, and for some years those in Virginia were affiliated with the Sandy Creek Association, across the border of North Carolina. South Carolina Separates were also affiliated with this body until 1770, when, it having become unwieldy and inharmonious, it was, by mutual consent, divided into three Associations. One retained the old name and the North Carolina churches, while the South Carolina churches organized the Congaree Association, and the fourteen Virginia churches were set off to form the Rapidan or General Association of Separate Baptists.[1] Before any further advance occurred in Virginia itself, there was growth in the regions beyond. Baptists from the Old Dominion who settled in Tennessee

---

[1] The distinction between Regulars and Separates disappeared after 1787, a union having been effected between them in that year under the title of the "United Baptist Churches of Virginia." Semple, pp. 99–101.

and there planted churches, organized the Holston Association in 1781, and in 1885 four Associations were formed in Kentucky, in which State Baptists were among the pioneer settlers and the first to preach the gospel and plant churches in this wilderness. In Maryland also two Associations were organized, in 1782 and 1792 respectively; and in Virginia six other Associations came into existence before the end of the century, owing to the labors of the Separates, from whom "originated the great mass of the churches which, with such overwhelming rapidity, spread over most of Eastern Virginia in the course of about a quarter of a century."[1]

By the year 1800, forty-eight Associations had been organized among the Baptist churches of the United States,[2] most of which were in a flourishing

---

[1] Benedict, p. 646.

[2] These Associations, with the dates of their organization, are as follows: PHILADELPHIA (1707); CHARLESTON (1751); SANDY CREEK, N. C. (1758); Kehukee, N. C. (1765); Ketocton, Va. (1766); WARREN, R. I. (1767); Rapidan, Va. (1770); Congaree, S. C. (1771; in 1789 reorganized as the Bethel); STONINGTON, Conn. (1772); Redstone, Pa., and STRAWBERRY, Va. (1776); SHAFTESBURY, Vt. (1780); HOLSTON, Tenn. (1781); Salisbury, Md. (1782); WOODSTOCK, Vt., DOVER, Va., MIDDLE DISTRICT, Va. (1783); GEORGIA (1784); New Hampshire (1785, though 1776 is also given as a date. This body afterward became the YORK, Me.); Vermont, ELKHORN, Ky., SOUTH KENTUCKY, and SALEM, Ky. (1785); BOWDOINHAM, Me. (1787); ROANOKE, Va. (1788); PORTSMOUTH, Va., and YADKIN, S. C. (1790); NEW YORK and Warwick, N. Y. (1791); Baltimore, GOSHEN, Va., and SHILOH, Va. (1792); NEW RIVER, Va., and TATES CREEK, Ky., (1793); HEPZIBAH, Ga., and Neuse, N. C. (1794); OTSEGO, N. Y. (1795); RENSSELAERVILLE, N. Y., New District, Tenn., Chemung, Pa., and Fairfield, Vt. (1796); Miami, O. (1797); Delaware (exact date not known, but before 1798); Mayo, N. C., Mountain, N. C., SAREPTA, Ga., GREEN

condition, active in evangelization, and powerfully promoting the unity, piety, and mutual acquaintance of the churches, systematizing their efforts and provoking one another to good works. They had proceeded, as we have seen, from a single center, the Philadelphia Association being the mother of them all. They had a common principle, a common form of organization, and similar aims. Their mutual relations were friendly, harmonious even, but not close. A local bond of unity had now been provided for the churches; Baptists who were near enough together to meet conveniently once a year were drawn in closer bonds of love and of common service than ever before. What was further needed was something that would bind together all the churches of like faith and practice, whether they were contiguous or widely scattered—something that would bring about a consciousness of oneness, develop an *esprit de corps*, unite them in a single evangelizing enterprise. Up to this time there had been Baptist churches; in the providence of God there was soon to be a Baptist denomination.

In September, 1813, some Baptists of Boston

RIVER, Ky., and CUMBERLAND RIVER, Ky. (1799). These dates are those of Benedict, which the author has found correct in every case where verification has been possible, and he therefore assumes their correctness in the other instances. The Associations in small capitals still exist as Associations of regular Baptists under the same name; those in italics have become Old School or Primitive Baptists. Most of the others have been divided and reorganized, and still exist under other names. Only one or two have become extinct.

were waited upon by the Rev. Luther Rice, a missionary to India, whose relations with the American Board had just been severed. They received from him a particular account of what had previously become known to them—how he, the Rev. Adoniram Judson, and Mrs. Ann Hasseltine Judson, had during their voyage from America to India, by independent study of the Scriptures, come to see that the only baptism of the New Testament is the immersion of believers. They had accordingly been immersed on profession of faith by the English Baptist missionaries at Calcutta. Having thus, in obedience to what they believed to be the command of Christ, separated themselves from the Congregational churches that had sent them forth, they threw themselves and their new mission[1] upon the Baptist churches of their native land. They did not appeal in vain. By the advice of the Boston brethren, Mr. Rice made a tour among the Baptist churches throughout the country. Many who read these words have heard from the lips of eye-witnesses of the high tide of missionary enthusiasm that followed this tour. For the first time the Baptists of this country had a common cause and a consciousness of brotherhood. They were no longer scattered units, but one body; obedience to the Great Commission, as it produced the Christian

---

[1] They had already been compelled by the intolerance of the East India Company to seek a field of labor in Burma, and established themselves at Rangoon, July 14, 1813.

Church in the days of the apostles, now welded the churches of like faith into what we call the denomination.

This changed feeling quickly found an organic expression. Delegates were appointed by the churches to meet in council over this matter, and on May 18, 1814, they assembled in the meeting-house of the First Baptist Church of Philadelphia, and organized "The General Convention of the Baptist Denomination in the United States for Foreign Missions." In the constitution adopted it was clearly stated that the object of the organization was to direct "the energies of the whole denomination in one sacred effort for sending the glad tidings of salvation to the heathen, and to nations destitute of pure gospel light." These words remained unaltered for more than thirty years, notwithstanding the constitution was several times amended so as to make them no longer descriptive of the document.

For several years Mr. Rice continued his work among the churches, organizing some seventy auxiliary missionary societies, and collecting what was for those times a very respectable sum of money. He reported at the next meeting of the convention, 1817, that he had traveled seven thousand eight hundred miles and raised three thousand seven hundred dollars. To measure the worth of this service, as well as the difficulty of its accomplishment, we must realize the poverty of the Baptist churches of that time and the primitive means of travel that were at his command.

These results were not achieved without opposition; in fact, this new missionary enterprise split the churches of the United States into two parties, the Mission and the Anti-Mission. Prejudice against missions was strongest in the South, where although the names of Regulars and Separates had measurably disappeared, the distinction of doctrine and spirit between the two classes of churches still remained. The new line of cleavage followed, in the main, this old division—the former Separates being heartily in favor of the new missionary enterprise, while the old Regulars were either hostile toward it or coldly indifferent. In the Northern States there was, on the whole, less division of sentiment; but in some of the older communities the feeling became intense. Dr. Benedict, the historian, relates that there was a newspaper war in Rhode Island to discourage missions. The people said, as some of them say now, that the efforts of good men were needed at home; that the evangelization of the heathen should wait until America is evangelized. An editor of the day said, "I think it my duty to crush this rising missionary spirit." Whereupon Dr. Benedict responded, "If it is your duty, I think you will die without performing it."[1] And so it proved; for the missionary cause steadily gained in the favor of the Baptist churches, and

---

[1] "The Missionary Jubilee," p. 16.

wherever it was stubbornly opposed and condemned, the piety of the churches declined and their membership wasted away, until the Anti-Mission Baptists have come to be little more than a name in the Middle States, though remnants still exist.[1]

At its meeting in 1817, the Convention so amended its constitution as to give its Board power "to appropriate a portion of the funds to Domestic missionary purposes." By this time there was an unexpended balance of twenty-one thousand five hundred dollars in the treasury, and the policy of the body underwent an important change. Instead of waiting for candidates to offer themselves for missionary service, committees were appointed for the three sections of the country to discover and examine applicants for missionary appointment. Three foreign missionaries were almost immediately sent out as a result of this policy, and men were appointed to labor among "the aborigines on the Wabash" and among the Cherokees. At the second triennial meeting, in 1820, the constitution was still further amended, the name being enlarged by the addition of the clause, "and other important objects relating to the Redeemer's Kingdom." In consequence of this enlargement of its scope, the Convention for a number of years engaged zealously in an educational project, the history of which will be told in another chapter; but the consequences were

---

[1] For a further history of the anti-mission movement, see Chapter VII.

so disastrous to the missionary cause that in 1826 the Convention returned to its original name and purpose, devoting itself exclusively to the promulgation of the gospel among the heathen. Under this constitution it continued to do efficient service down to the year 1845.

The missionary fervor aroused by the visit of Luther Rice did not expend itself wholly on the foreign field. The need of additional missionary agencies on the home field, and of a more effective bond of local union in the States, was strongly felt. Here too the Baptists of the Middle States were among the first to move. As early as 1807 the Baptists of Central New York had become much exercised regarding domestic missions, and a call was issued for a meeting to consider the propriety of organizing a society "for the prosecution of the missionary enterprise in the destitute regions around." The meeting was duly held at Pompey and the "Lake Baptist Missionary Society" was formed, which two years later took the name of the "Hamilton Missionary Society"—the second large organization of the kind, the first being the Massachusetts Domestic Missionary Society, organized in 1802. The need was more and more felt of a society that should enlist in its work all the churches of the State; and as a result of much consultation and prayer a meeting was held, November 21, 1821, at Mentz, Cayuga county, N. Y., and an organization was effected of "The Baptist Domestic Missionary

Convention of the State of New York and its Vicinity." The object of the body was defined in its constitution to be "to promote domestic missions." Among the notable men present at this meeting were Elon Galusha, Sylvanus Haynes, and A. M. Beebe.[1] The Hon. S. Monroe, of the Cayuga Association, was the first president of the convention. When the body met the following year at Whitesboro, the name was changed to "The Baptist Convention of the State of New York and Vicinity." The first treasurer's report appears in the Minutes of 1827.[2] It acknowledges receipts of one thousand sixty-one dollars and seventy-three cents and records disbursements of three hundred twenty-eight dollars and ninety-one cents, from which some idea of the Convention's scale of operations in the early days may be obtained.

The Baptists of Pennsylvania were not far behind their New York brethren in this matter. At the meeting-house in Sansom Street, Philadelphia, December 7, 1825, they met "for the purpose of combining the efforts of societies which at present exist

---

[1] Among the names of those printed in the Minutes of 1826 as life-members by the payment of $10 each are: William Colgate, Elon Galusha, A. M. Beebe, Charles G. Somers, Alfred Bennett, John Peck, Archibald Maclay, N. Kendrick, and Daniel Hascall —all men of mark then or subsequently in the history of New York Baptists.

[2] It may be of interest to some Baptists to know that the Minutes of 1830 to 1839 bear the imprint of Bennett & Bright, Utica, while those of 1848 and 1849 were from the press of A. Strong & Co., of Rochester.

or which may hereafter be formed for missionary purposes, foreign or domestic." They organized "The Pennsylvania Baptist Missionary Society," whose object was declared to be " to aid the General Convention of the Baptist denomination in the United States of America." For some reason not very clear, this organization did not command the sympathy and co-operation of the churches, and a second attempt was made to organize a State Convention on July 4, 1827, at the Blockley Church. "The Baptist General Association of Pennsylvania for Missionary Purposes" was there formed. The second article of its constitution read, "It shall be the object of this society to spread the gospel in Pennsylvania, and to extend its operations to other States, as its funds may allow." At its meeting in Philadelphia in 1837 the body was reorganized as "The Pennsylvania Baptist Convention," which name was afterward changed to " The Pennsylvania Baptist State Mission Society," which it still (1897) bears.

From this beginning, State Conventions—or General Associations, as some of the States preferred to call them—rapidly came into existence throughout the denomination.[1] They were organized on

---

[1] By the year 1832 there were fourteen such State organizations, as follows: New York and South Carolina, 1821; Virginia and Georgia, 1822; Connecticut and Alabama, 1823; Massachusetts, Vermont, and Maine, 1824; New Hampshire and Rhode Island, 1825; New Jersey and North Carolina, 1830. Many of these State organizations have a history like those of New York and

two quite different plans. One model is that of New York, where the work is wholly local, the Convention raising no money and attempting no work, except for what may be called State missions. Another type is that furnished by the first and abortive constitution of the Pennsylvania Convention, which, however, has since that time been successfully put into operation and maintained in many States—the Convention or Association regarding itself not merely as a local evangelizing body but as the auxiliary and agent of the larger missionary organizations. In such Conventions, there are State Boards for home missions and foreign missions, and these take charge of the work of collecting money for the national societies. Both methods of organization have their ardent defenders and their keen critics; each has special excellencies and defects.

It would be difficult to exaggerate the effect that these State organizations have had in unifying the churches and promoting missionary effort. To tell in part the story of their evangelizing labors will be the subject of the next chapter.

Massachusetts, and were the direct outgrowth of other organizations of earlier origin but more circumscribed in area and object. No account has been taken, for obvious reasons, of the Six Principle Association of New England, though it is older than the Warren. Had Professor Newman's studies of "Delegated bodies in connection with Baptist Churches" appeared before the chapter was electrotyped, more weight might possibly have been assigned to the influence on American Baptists of the Welsh Associations.

CHAPTER V

THE WESTERN MOVEMENT: ITS RESULTS AND SIGNIFICANCE

AT the time of the adoption of the Federal Constitution Western New York was an unbroken wilderness. A small settlement at Fort Niagara was probably the only spot at which a white face could have been seen by the first adventurous explorer. The advance line of emigration and settlement had reached the Seneca and Cayuga lakes, and turned southward toward the region of Elmira. The fertile valleys of the Hudson and of Central New York were rapidly filling up with hardy and thrifty settlers, a considerable proportion of whom were Baptists. A rapid growth of Baptist churches followed in these regions, and particularly in the valley lying west of the Hudson between the Adirondacks and the Catskills and stretching away to the central lakes.

The centers of this remarkable development were two: the first, that settlement of Baptists in Butternuts, in the Otsego district, whose early history has been told in a previous chapter; and the second an independent settlement near Lake Cayuga. In the Otsego district the Baptists increased rapidly from the close of the Revolutionary struggle, and by the year 1795 twelve other churches had been organized, as follows : Springfield (1789) ; Franklin (1792) ; Kortright, Charlestown (1793) ; Burlington, Edmeston, Richfield, First Otsego, Fairfield and Palatine, New Berlin (1794) ; Hartwick, Otego (1795).

In the year 1789 Elder William Furman, then about forty years of age, moved to the new town of Springfield and was instrumental in organizing the Baptist church of that place. In the spring of 1794, eleven churches having been formed by that time, he proposed to them that they meet in conference and consider the propriety of uniting in an Association. Representatives of seven churches met in Burlington, at the house of William Goff, September 4, 1794. Elders Peter Worden, Joseph Cornell, and Joseph Craw, from the Shaftsbury Association, were present and participated in the deliberations. They adjourned to meet again January 8, when delegates from nine churches were present. A plan for the organization of an Association was unanimously agreed to, and referred to the churches, with the request that they appoint delegates to meet in Springfield in the following September. On the second day of that month the meeting was accordingly held, and after a sermon by Elder Ashbel Hosmer, the Association was organized with a membership of thirteen churches, reporting four hundred and twenty-four members and five ministers.¹ The five were William Furman, Ashbel Hosmer, John Hammond, Elijah Herrick, and Joel Butler. To the incessant and devoted labors of these men was mainly due the rapid progress of the Baptists of the Otsego region. These five were speedily joined by such other ministers as Peter P. Root, James Bacon, and John Lawton, all of whom were abundant in labors and successful in founding many of the churches that are still strongest in Central New York.

An interesting review of the labors of these worthy Baptist pioneers says of them:

An extensive circuit became the lot of each of these men; especially of the first three, who, being the earliest laborers in this uncultivated country, were counted as leaders in this glorious enterprise, and were regarded as fathers by the younger men. The frequent calls, "Come over and help us," from the little clusters of saints here

---

[1] "This being the first interview of the kind ever enjoyed in the wilderness, it was one of intense interest. The presence of the great Jehovah was deeply felt, and the souls of his people expanded with joy. Some, who came to the meeting with a resolution to oppose the forming of an Association, were constrained to acknowledge that God was there; their opposition ceased, and their souls melted in the pleasure occasioned by the union of their infant churches. Indeed, it was a delightful scene to behold these little flocks scattered throughout this extensive region, coming up out of the wilderness, evidently led by the Good Shepherd to associate together in this capacity, and thereby exhibit what the Lord had done, and what he was still to do, in this once howling desert. Thus in weakness, with much fear and trembling, and amid trials of the most distressing character, was the foundation laid on which a glorious superstructure has been raised in Western New York" (Hosmer and Lawton's "History of the Otsego Association," pp. 11, 12).

and there in the wilderness, subjected them to frequent journeys, in which they had to encounter many obstacles and endure many hardships and various sufferings. They toiled in the cold and in the heat, by day and by night, traversing the wilderness from one solitary dwelling to another, by marked trees and half-made roads, fording dangerous rivers and rapid streams, often without a guide, and at the hazard of their lives. They suffered much from hunger and thirst, and frequently had to pursue their journeys through bleak winds and storms both of rain and snow, to meet their appointments and administer to the perishing the bread of life. The afflictions of some of them were greatly increased and their tenderest sympathies often excited by the privations and sufferings in respect even to the necessities of life to which their families were subjected. Sometimes, in their journeys, on sitting down at the tables of their brethren, to enjoy their hospitality, a recollection of the sufferings of their families at home would destroy their appetite and fill them with grief. They could receive but little earthly reward, the country being new, the churches small, and the people hardly able to support themselves, much less to expend a large amount on the preachers. Added to these discouragements was another of greater magnitude, which arose from the frequent intrusion of men of corrupt principles and practice. These, imagining that the state of the country was favorable to their sinister views, not only journeyed, but in some instances actually removed and settled in the vicinity of some of the small churches. Through their means divisions and contentions arose, which called for councils, which, whatever might be the conduct of other brethren, the preacher must attend; and when he had discharged his duty by hearing testimony against their evil conduct, heavy reflections from them and their partisans were the consequences. Yet amid all these discouragements they continued their exertions, relying on Israel's God. Jehovah crowned their labors with abundant success, and comforted their souls by pouring out his Holy Spirit. Those who had been long professors of religion were induced to unite in church relation, backsliders were reclaimed, and sinners converted to the knowledge of the truth. Thus the wilderness and solitary place were made glad for them and the desert began to rejoice and blossom as the rose.[1]

This picture of things as they existed among the early Baptist churches of New York may be commended to those who are forever lauding the fathers and their days as the best that ever were or will be. The golden age of Baptists seems to be in the past, because we commonly see the past through a haze of ignorance or a glamor of romance that hides from us all the small and mean and sordid things in it, and gilds with sentiment much from which we should recoil in disgust if it were actually before us. Something more than the efforts of a handful of ministers, however faithful and arduous, is needed to account for the rapid growth of Baptists in this region. The immigration into this district was not by way of New York and the Hudson so much as from New England. Massachusetts and Connecticut furnished the greater part of these new settlers. The extent of this movement of population may be

---

[1] "An Historical Sketch of the Baptist Missionary Convention of the State of New York," by John Peck and John Lawton. Utica: Bennett & Bright, 1837, p. 25.

measured by the facts that in the first census of 1790 Massachusetts stood fourth among the States in point of population, while New York was fifth; in the census of 1800 New York had risen to third place, while Massachusetts had fallen to fifth. In addition to the motives that led other men from New England into this wilderness, Baptists had an additional reason for immigration. In 1786 Baptists had been deprived of the protection, such as it was, afforded to them by the Exemption Act of 1729,[1] by the passage of a statute consolidating the civil and ecclesiastical taxes. Out of the common tax fund a majority of the voters might appropriate "such sums of money as they shall judge necessary for the settlement, maintenance, and support of the ministry, schools, etc."[2] Of course this meant that Congregational ministers, the choice of the majority, were to be supported from the public treasury, and that the minority must contribute through their ordinary taxes to the support of ministers selected

---

[1] This act exempted "persons commonly called Anabaptists and those called Quakers" from paying taxes for the support of ministers of the "standing order." By a later act the assessors were required to make lists of Anabaptists entitled to such exemption, subject to correction by "two principal members of that persuasion," but no penalty was provided for the failure of assessors to perform their duty, and in consequence Baptists were often subject to much trouble and expense to obtain their lawful exemption. See Backus, Vol. I., p. 517, *seq.*

[2] For the protests aroused by this and similar legislation, see Backus, Vol. II., p. 329, *seq.* Compare also Newman's "History of the Baptist Churches of the United States," pp. 347-364; Burrage, "History of the Baptists in New England," Chap. VI.

by the majority. To escape annoyances of this kind, New England Separates in considerable numbers sought homes in Central New York. Some of these remained faithful to their former church principles and organized Congregational churches in their new homes, but many of them soon found that their true affinity was with the Baptists and contributed to swell the numbers of the newly organized churches.

One of these bands of immigrants from New England settled in 1795 at the headwaters of the Chenango, about one hundred miles west of Albany. One of the leading spirits among them was Samuel Payne, already a Baptist, and his brother Elisha accompanied him. The little clearing in the wilderness was first known as Payne's Settlement, and later as Hamilton. Religious meetings were held from the first in this community, which was soon joined by the Olmsteads, Pierces, and Osgoods, men and women of like character and religious convictions. June 24, 1796, they met in conference in the house of Samuel Payne, related their experiences to each other, and then or soon after formally constituted themselves a Baptist church. On October 10 following, a council consisting of the Fairfield and Palatine, Second and Third Burlington, and First Litchfield churches received them into fellowship as a church in gospel order. At this time they had twelve members. At the third session of the Otsego Association, held at Fairfield, September

6, 1797, the Hamilton Church, together with seven others, was received into membership. This meant much in those days, for admission was by no means a mere form. Great pains were taken to insure the soundness in the faith of all churches and ministers. The standing rule of the Otsego Association at this period, and for long thereafter, was : "Churches who offer themselves to join with us shall be thus examined in the presence of the Association by a person whom they shall appoint: 1. When did you embody as a church? 2. What church gave fellowship (as a church of gospel order), and when? 3. What are the doctrines you believe? 4. What practice do you pursue? 5. Have you a minister?"

Toward the end of the year 1798 a Baptist preacher named Price visited Hamilton and a remarkable revival followed. One conversion was specially impressive—that of a Deist who delighted in Paine's "Age of Reason" and despised the Bible. Daniel Hatch, for such was his name, became as ardent a Christian as he had been bitter scoffer, was long a pillar of the Eaton Church, a leader in all good works, and has left behind him a fragrant memory. This revival, the precursor of many others, greatly strengthened the Hamilton Church and prepared it for the leading part it was to take in a few years in promoting denominational growth in the State.

It is obviously impossible, within the limits of such a volume as this, to go much into detail in recording the progress of the denomination, unless some special significance attaches to the history of a particular church. The only practicable method has seemed to be to trace the line and rate of progress by groups of churches as organized into Associations. When first formed the Otsego Association covered quite an extensive area of one hundred and forty miles from east to west, and sixty miles from north to south, no two ministers living nearer to each other than twenty-five miles. Its methods were as primitive as the life of the people. The second meeting is said to have been held in the woods, and the third in a barn—there were few or no church edifices in those days. By 1800 the Otsego Association had increased to thirty-seven churches, fifteen ministers, and one thousand seven hundred and sixty-four members. In 1807 the number of churches had risen to fifty-five, and the membership to three thousand two hundred and sixty-five, a rate of growth that is probably unsurpassed in any locality or period in the history of Baptists. In the following year fourteen of these churches were dismissed to form the Madison Association, which in time became the mother of the Cortland (1832) and Chenango (1833). From the Otsego afterward were formed, in large part at least, the Franklin (1871), Worcester (1830), and Mohawk (1840). The Oneida was formed in 1820, about equally from the Otsego and its eldest daughter, the Madison. By these successive partitions of its territory and numbers, the Otsego Association became less important in the State, but in the fruitfulness of its labors is second to none, and it should be held in the high honor which it deserves because of this useful past.

The other center of increase in this part of the State was the Cayuga district. The Cayuga Association was formed in 1801, its organization having been preceded for several years by a less formal annual meeting of several churches in "The Scipio Conference." The original territory of this Association was quite as large as that of the Otsego, and it was barely second to that body in fruitfulness. We may trace to it the origin of the Ontario (1813), Steuben (1817), Seneca (1832), Wayne (1835), and Yates (1843). Then Steuben in turn became the mother of the Canisteo River (1834) and Cattaraugus (1836), and in connection with the Seneca was also the origin of the Chemung River (1842).

It was not possible to begin the subjugation of the wilderness prior to the Revolution. Beyond the central districts the Indians were still powerful. Even in the central districts the dangers and sufferings of the early settlers were great, and further advance was out of the question. The defeat of the Six Nations by General Sullivan, in 1779, avenged the Wyoming massacre, broke the power of the confederated tribes that had held undisputed possession of Western New York, and opened this region to comparatively safe settlement. So late as 1800, however, the process had only begun. In that year the first settlement was planted on the site of the present city of Buffalo. The city of Pittsburg had already begun to grow up around the old Fort Duquesne, but in both New York and Pennsylvania there was a great intervening wilderness between eastern and western inhabitants during the first decade of the century. It was not until 1815 that the westward movement could be called well-established and general.

The name of Robert Morris, gratefully remembered by all patriots, is closely connected with this new westward movement. In 1791 he purchased from the State of Massachusetts (which at that time claimed title to this region, a claim afterward relinquished), a tract of three million acres. He in turn sold to the Holland Land Company in 1792–3 all of this tract west of the meridian of Washington. By treaty with the Indians at Genesco, in 1797, Morris secured a relinquishment of their title to the land, except certain "reservations." This tract was long known as the Holland Purchase, and it was the enterprise and liberality of this company, under the guidance of their chief surveyor and engineer, Joseph Elliott, that led to the rapid settlement of this part of the State. A perfect mania for western emigration and speculation in western lands seized the people farther east, and amusing records of it are found in the newspapers of the day. The disease that was named "terraphobia," became distressingly prevalent; companies were organized that purchased land by the thousand acres and laid out towns (on paper), and people sold farms and corner lots that they had never seen to people who knew still less about them. Fortunes were made by some and others lost all they had in the world, but the net result was a great stimulus to the progress of emigration and settlement.

Baptist churches, as was the case elsewhere, sprang into existence almost as rapidly as new settlements, but the first organization of Baptists in this region—other than local churches—was the Holland Purchase Conference, which was constituted in 1811. At its first anniversary, in Sheldon, Wyoming County, ten churches were represented. This body, long ago extinct, still lives in the vigorous Associations of this region that owe to it their life. The first offshoot was the Genesee, organized in 1818 at Sweden, Monroe County; the Niagara was formed in 1822; the Monroe separated from the Genesee in 1827; from the Monroe and Niagara the Orleans was formed in 1843; while the mother of them all gave place to the Buffalo in 1845.

Probably no other agency was so influential in promoting the progress of Baptists in Western New York as the Hamilton Missionary Society.

Hamilton was very nearly the geographical center of the region in which Baptists were strongest during the first decade of the present century, both in active churches and in consecrated ministers. In 1807 several faithful Baptist ministers were laboring between Cayuga Lake and the Genesee, but there was at that time no Baptist church or settled minister in all that district. The spiritual destitution was great and keenly felt, and the Baptists of the central part of the State were not unmindful of their obligations to the regions beyond. It was this sense of duty that led a few zealous men to meet, August 27th, 1807, at the house of Elder Nathan Baker, in Pompey, Onandaga County, to consider the propriety of forming a missionary society to evangelize the destitute parts of the State, especially in the west. Because of this projected field of operations the organization was at first named the Lake Missionary Society. A constitution was adopted, twenty gave in their names as members, and the society began its work with twenty dollars in the treasury.

On October 28, a second meeting was held in Hamilton, and the organization was completed by the election of officers. Elder Ashbel Hosmer was the first president, and Elder Salmon Morton was the first missionary commissioned and sent out. He made a missionary tour of eight weeks, traveling as far west as the Holland Purchase, and in his first report makes touching mention of the gratitude of the people whom he visited and to whom he ministered. He was received, he said, "with great satisfaction by the inhabitants; and many of the people of God were made to rejoice in the privilege of hearing the preaching of the gospel in their destitute situation, while many blessings were bestowed on the society, and ardent prayers addressed to God for its prosperity." He adds: "It was enough to move a heart of stone to witness the expressions of joy made by the people on the occasion. But the parting scenes were peculiarly interesting. Nor could I witness without emotion the tears that were shed, and their earnest solicitations for a continuance of like favors, when giving the parting hand and exclaiming, with tears in their eyes, 'Do come again. Tell the society of our destitute situation, and request them to remember us.'"

The salary of the missionary at this time was four dollars a week, and at the end of the first year the society was able to report all obligations met and a balance of one hundred and seventy-one dollars. This encouraging state of the funds continued during the early years of the society's operations, and at the meeting of 1812 a communication was received that promised further effective help:

To the Directors of the Hamilton Baptist Missionary Society:

BRETHREN: Being sensible of the lost situation into which the human family have plunged themselves by the fall, and that the only way of their recovery is through faith in the Redeemer, and that it has pleased God by the foolishness of preaching to save them that believe, and that faith comes by hearing, and hearing by the word of God, and being instructed that they that preach the gospel shall live of the gospel, we have thought it our duty to assist you in your laudable efforts to disseminate the gospel among the destitute; for which purpose we present you with twenty yards of fulled cloth, and wish you to receive it, and dispose of it for the above purpose. And may the great Head of the church increase our zeal, and bless your endeavors for the advancement of his kingdom.

By order, and in behalf, of the Hamilton Female Baptist Missionary Society,

FREEDOM OLMSTEAD,
BETSEY PAYNE.[1]

Like auxiliary societies of women were formed in Cazenovia, Fabius, and other adjacent towns; and in February, 1814, these societies were able to present to the Hamilton Board articles of their own manufacture valued at one hundred and forty-eight dollars.

Among the earliest missionaries of this society were John Peck, Alfred Bennett, Nathan Baker, John Lawton, Ashbel Hosmer, and John Upfold. These were all men of might, but the two first named stand forth pre-eminent above all their fellows in those days. John Peck was a native of Dutchess County, where he was born in 1780. He was converted and baptized in his eighteenth year,

---
[1] History of the Convention, pp. 35, 36.

and June 11, 1806, was ordained pastor of the church in Cazenovia, where he remained for nine years. His work as a missionary was incidental, being performed at intervals when he could obtain leave of absence from his church. As pastor and preacher he was indefatigable and wonderfully blessed. Frequent revivals accompanied his ministry, and six neighboring churches were organized during his Cazenovia pastorate, mainly of members dismissed from his church. Fifteen young men from the church were ordained to the ministry during the same period. In 1824 the Baptist State Convention having absorbed the Hamilton Missionary Society, Mr. Peck was appointed general agent, and began his labors January 1, 1825. It was the great trial of his life to break the bonds that bound him to his church, but he felt that the providence of God as well as the choice of his brethren called him to this larger work, and he obeyed. He remained in the service of the Convention for fifteen years, and contributed more than any single man to its marked success as an evangelizing agency throughout the first quarter century of its existence. From May, 1839, he was also general agent of the Home Mission Society, and in 1847 he made the following summary of his labors:

> I have been enabled, by the blessing of God, to travel in eighteen of the United States; mostly in the Northern; have delivered one thousand four hundred and forty-one sermons and public addresses, and collected

for the Home Mission Society thirty-two thousand four hundred and seventy-eight dollars and twenty-seven cents; also for the New York State Convention, four thousand one hundred and fifty-eight dollars and seventeen cents; in all, for Home Mission and Convention, thirty-six thousand six hundred and thirty-six dollars and forty-four cents. . . I have also, besides the special duties of my agency, been called, in various parts of the country, to the performance of missionary and pastoral labors, in visiting the sick and afflicted, settling difficulties and healing divisions among the churches and individual brethren, and assisting pastors in revivals of religion.

Never of robust physique, and worn out by these arduous labors, he died in 1849, leaving behind a record of faithful and laborious service unsurpassed in the history of American Baptists. It is doubtful, however, if in all his career he did a work of greater necessity and blessedness than in his early missionary tours in the Western part of the State. Nothing will so give an adequate idea both of the value of this service, and of the religious condition of Western New York at this time, as the report he made on returning from one of these tours:

To the President and Directors of the Hamilton Missionary Society:

DEAR BRETHREN : Agreeably to the appointment I received from you, I left my family, and the dear people of my charge, June 5, 1810, and set out on my tour to the west. I preached at different places until I arrived at Eld. Irish's, in Aurelius, where I preached in the evening, and received much instruction, both as to the country and people where I was going. Next day rode to Phelps, and the next day, being Lord's Day, preached to a crowded and solemn assembly. On Monday I designed to pursue my journey, but by the request of Eld. Wisner and the church I staid and attended the ordination of Br. William Roe, one of their members. I preached in the vicinity daily until the council met. Thursday, June 14, the ordination of Br. William Roe was attended in the following manner: I tried to preach on the occasion, from Ps. 126 : 6; Eld. Jeremiah Irons offered the ordaining prayer, and laid on hands with Elds. Wisner and Shays; Eld. Solomon Goodell gave the charge; Eld. Samuel Messenger the hand of fellowship; Eld. Daniel Irons made the concluding prayer. The exercises appeared to be attended with the smiles of Heaven.

From thence I pursued my journey and preached in Gorham, Palmyra, Bloomfield, and Livonia. In Avon I called on Eld. Wm. Furman, that aged father in the gospel, and the season was agreeable to me. He still appears to be engaged in the service of his Divine Master, and though he has been called to pass through a scene of trials, yet he appears to be worshiping, leaning on the top of his staff. I parted with him, and rode to Batavia—preached in the evening at the court house. Next morning visited the prisoners : some of them were confined for passing counterfeit money, and one for murder. I gave as good advice as I was able; I tried to demonstrate, from the confinement they here justly suffered, the prison mankind are in by nature, and to show that Christ is the only door to liberty ; and as they expected to have their trial shortly, so they, with all mankind, must be tried at the bar of God; and if not prepared by grace, they must sink beneath the grave, into that prison where there is no hope of reprieve. After this conversation I tried to pray with them; some of them appeared much affected. After receiving their thanks for my visit I parted with them.

I then calculated to go directly to Buffalo, and rode thirteen miles. As I got through the eight mile woods, I came out to a little settlement of three families, and by their request I preached a sermon to them; and I believe the Lord was present. I had the whole settlement together and one traveler, which made ten souls, and they all seemed to listen as for eternity. I then rode five miles, and providentially put up with a Baptist brother for the night; and by request preached the next morning to a solemn assembly. I thought then to pursue my journey, and took leave of the family, leaving them in tears, and went half a mile to take some refreshment. Here a number of the neighbors had collected together, and solicited me to tarry longer. Of the number, two women desired to go forward in the ordinance of baptism. I thought, truly, the Lord had more work for me here. I consented to spend the next Lord's Day with them, and to preach to them on Saturday, at ten o'clock; then rode six miles to a new settlement, and found two brethren and a few sisters. They had agreed to meet each Lord's Day for the worship of God; they seemed to rejoice to see me come to visit them in their lonely situation; there had been but one sermon preached in the place by a Baptist, and that by old Eld. Niles, of Sempronius. The next day the settlement came together, and I tried to preach to them, and think it was a comfortable season to my soul; and it appeared to be to others. The next day returned to the aforementioned appointment, and preached at ten o'clock, A. M., to a crowded assembly. After the meeting closed, the two women before mentioned, and a young man, came forward, and related what the Lord had done for their souls. After this I requested that if any one had anything on their minds to communicate, they would embrace the opportunity. I think there were upwards of a dozen that spoke, the most of them being Baptist professors. The season was glorious; and it seemed that the Lord was there in very deed.

Lord's Day, June 24, I preached to the people assembled in a grove, there being no house sufficiently large to hold them. At the close I baptized three persons, the first that were baptized in this part of the country. It was a solemn scene, and saints and sinners seemed alike affected.

June 25, rode to Buffalo, and, at the desire of the people, preached in the court-house. Next day rode to Eighteen Mile Creek, and preached in different places five times; and as the attention and wish of the people appeared so urgent, I agreed to spend three days with them the next week. I returned to Buffalo, and on Lord's Day I delivered two sermons in the court-house. The people gave good attention, and appeared to be thankful for the visit. On Monday returned to Eighteen Mile Creek, and preached to the people, who had assembled in the grove. We then repaired to the water-side, and after singing a hymn, and solemn prayer to God, I baptized a woman. The Lord evidently graced his ordinance at this time with his divine presence. After this I preached three times before I left the neighborhood, and every meeting appeared to be attended with some token of divine approbation. The people, notwithstanding the busy season of the year, and the roughness of the roads, would travel some even ten miles on foot, to hear the word of God proclaimed by such a feeble instrument. On Thursday returned to Buffalo, and preached to a solemn assembly; then rode to Clarence, and on Saturday, as I had agreed, met with the brethren in conference. I advised them, when here before, to meet in conference, and gain acquaintance as to their standing, ideas of doctrine, practice, &c., and try to maintain the worship of God. They met at 1 o'clock P. M.; the meeting being opened, they related their Christian experience, conversed on articles of faith, practice, and a covenant; and there was a happy agreement. Then five persons came forward, and related what the Lord had done for their souls, and wished to be baptized. It was a joyful time.

Lord's Day, July 8, I preached to a crowded assembly, some of whom came from a distance of twenty miles. One man came forty miles for the purpose of attending the meeting. In the afternoon I preached to the youth; and a more solemn attention I never witnessed. At the close we repaired to the water, three miles distant, where I baptized five persons, three males and two females. It was a continued scene of solemnity. On Monday I thought of setting out for home, but duty called me to stay another day. At 10 o'clock A. M., I met the brethren and sisters in conference, and we had an agreeable interview. Twenty-one brethren and sisters covenanted together to maintain the worship of God. What a beautiful sight in this wilderness! At 2 o'clock in the afternoon the people assembled for public worship, and I preached to them. I was now called to pass through a solemn scene. I had formed a short but an agreeable acquaintance, but now we must part. I took an affectionate leave of them, not expecting to see them again. Many tears were shed. Oh! how my soul felt to leave them!—a little handful of brethren and sisters, like sheep without a shepherd in this wilderness; some of them living ten miles apart, and no one to go before them as an under-shepherd. This passage of truth, however, comforted me : "He shall feed his flock like a shepherd, he shall gather the lambs with his arm, and carry them in his bosom." I thought I could leave them in the hand of Him that said, "I will never leave thee nor forsake thee." Next day I set out for home, and on Saturday, July 14, returned safely to my family, and, through the goodness of God, found them in good health.

From the time when I left home, until my return, was five weeks and four days, in which time I traveled about five hundred and fifty miles, attended one council, one ordination, four conferences, baptized nine persons, and tried to preach thirty-six times. I have been blessed with health, and think I have enjoyed some small share of that peace which the world cannot give nor take away ; and, though I traveled alone, the way did not seem long, nor the time disagreeable.

I subscribe myself, through the grace of God,
your unworthy brother and servant in the Lord,
JOHN PECK.[1]

Alfred Bennett was a man of like character and fervor and superior ability. Born in 1780, at Mansfield, Conn., and converted in his eighteenth year, he was baptized in 1800 into the fellowship of the Hampton Church. Having married in 1802, in the following year he sought a new home in New York, and settled in the town of Homer, Cortland County. Here he began life as a farmer, in a log house, surrounded by an almost unbroken forest. In a short time a little Baptist church was formed, of which he and his wife were constituent members. They

---

[1] History of the Convention, pp. 38-42.

rarely enjoyed the visit of a minister, and this seems first to have suggested to Bennett the idea of preaching. It was several years before he could be prevailed on by his brethren to devote himself to this work, so great was his sense of unfitness for it because of his meagre education; but he was at length ordained pastor of the church, and continued in its service from 1807 to 1832.

During this time there were numerous revivals of religion in the community, and he baptized more than seven hundred and seventy persons. The church increased in numbers and spiritual power until it was one of the strongest in Central New York. Several colonies were sent forth to found other churches in the vicinity, the original church finally locating at Cortland, where it is now the largest in its Association and twice the size of the mother church. In addition to his pastoral labors, which were constant and untiring, Father Bennett—as he is still called in all that region—found time to do a large amount of missionary service in the employ of the Hamilton Missionary Society and its successor. He made more than one tour in the "Holland Purchase," preaching and baptizing converts; and in Tioga, Steuben, and Alleghany Counties he made many missionary visits to weak churches and to churchless communities. To such earnest, continuous, self-sacrificing labors, unpaid for the most part except in the blessings and prayers of those to whom he and his fellows ministered, was very largely due the rapid growth of Baptist churches in New York during the early part of the present century.

Perhaps the greatest service of Father Bennett's busy and useful life was that which he rendered, from 1832 till his death in 1851, as district agent for foreign missions, first of the Triennial Convention, and afterward of the Missionary Union. All the energies of a very energetic nature he devoted to urging upon the Baptist churches of his day their duty to the heathen, in fulfillment of the Great Commission. The Baptists of that time were a missionary folk, as they showed by their zeal in the work of home evangelization; and they were by no means unmindful of the duty of sending the gospel to the heathen, but responded nobly to the appeals of such men as Bennett. The results of his labors are still apparent in all the region over which he traveled and preached so tirelessly. Though not a liberally educated man, Father Bennett was well read, intelligent, an instructive preacher, and withal a man of much shrewd sense. A lover of peace, but tenacious of his own convictions, he did much to increase a healthful and enlightened denominational sentiment among New York Baptists. His memory is blessed.[1]

After the Hamilton Missionary Society had been in existence ten years, the Baptists of the State

---

[1] Many interesting anecdotes have been preserved of Elder Bennett; one of these will be found in Appendix E.

numbered twenty-eight thousand, in three hundred and ten churches, served by two hundred and thirty ministers—a marvelous growth, in which this organization had had a very considerable share.

The two most important churches formed in this region in these years were the First Rochester and First Buffalo, not so much because of their superior age as for the influence they have had on Baptist growth in Western New York. The First Church of Rochester was organized in 1818, in that part of the settlement known as Brighton. It consisted at first of twelve members, and for some years was a feeble body. It made its first real advance under the ministry of Rev. Eleazer Savage, through whose labors it increased from thirty-five to eighty-five members. There was a great revival in 1831, in which one hundred and fifty were added to the church by baptism, and from that time onward it became the strong and influential body it has ever since remained. The First Church of Buffalo was not organized until January 1, 1822, though there had been a number of baptized believers living in the place for several years, and they had enjoyed the occasional ministrations of itinerant Baptist ministers. Shortly after the formal organization, Rev. Elon Galusha came to the town in the employ of the Baptist Missionary Convention of the State of New York. His preaching was effective in awakening a new religious spirit in the community, and especially in inspiring the infant church with hope and courage. Nineteen were baptized by Mr. Galusha during his three months' labors here, and in September the Convention assisted the church to settle a pastor, the Rev. J. Newton Brown—a name well known and highly honored among Baptists for the learning, piety, and good works of him who bore it. This church has the distinction of having enjoyed the labors of the first missionary, and of the first missionary pastor, employed by the Convention. It was not until the year 1833 that the church (the name of which had been changed in 1832 to the Washington Street) was able to dispense with such assistance, but to her great honor she has ever been a firm friend and supporter of the body to which she owes so much.

The westward movement of population in Pennsylvania was even more marked than in New York. Between 1790 and 1800 New York added one hundred and forty-eight thousand nine hundred and thirty-one to her population, while Pennsylvania added one hundred and eighty-nine thousand nine hundred and ninety-two and retained her place as the second State of the Union—Virginia being still the first, though relatively losing ground, her gain for the same period being only one hundred and thirty-two thousand five hundred and ninety. No large proportion of Baptists seem to have been among those who settled in this State, and the relative progress of the denomination was slower than in New York, where growth of the churches was so powerfully helped by immigration.

The first traces of Baptist growth outside of the Philadelphia district are found in the Minutes of the Philadelphia Association. At the meeting of 1774, "letters from well-disposed people, requesting supplies, were read . . . from Tolbert, in Northumberland, in the province of Pennsylvania," and from other places. The requests were favorably considered, for we read that "Brother David Sutton, William Worth, and Elkana Holmes are to visit the inhabitants of Tolbert township, at time to be fixed by themselves." From this time on the Association took a very active interest in the progress of these inchoate Baptist churches and engaged in active missionary work among them. In 1775 supplies were granted to Tolbert, "Baltimore town," and six other points. In 1778 it was voted to raise a fund "for the particular and express purpose of preaching the gospel among the back settlements."

The war of the Revolution and the occupation of Philadelphia by the British necessarily and seriously retarded the progress of this work. For some years the churches composing the Association were barely able to preserve their existence and union, and it is not until 1792 that we find evidence of further vigorous prosecution of this missionary enterprise. Then we read that "Elders Patton, Clingan, and Vaughn agree to travel for three months in the ensuing year, about Juniata and the West Branch of the Susquehanna, to preach the gospel to the destitute." A direct result of these labors was the organization of the Shamokin Church, June 21, 1794, by Elders Patton and Clingan, Elder Patton becoming its pastor. In 1796 this church was received into the Philadelphia Association, the original nine members having become fifty. The White Deer Church was formed, with ten members, in 1808, and the Little Muncy (now Madison), with fourteen members, in 1817. These two churches at first joined the Chemung Association, mainly composed of churches across the New York border, but in 1821 they united with the Shamokin Church in forming the Northumberland Association.[1]

The facts just narrated illustrate a characteristic feature in the history of many Pennsylvania churches and Associations—their close connection with the Baptists of New York. The history of the Abington Association is another striking instance. From 1807 onward, missionaries from the Massachusetts Baptist Missionary Society occasionally visited this region, but this was soon recognized as the proper field of the Hamilton Missionary Society. Rev. John Lawton traveled and preached extensively in 1811 and following years. Rev. Peter P. Root[2] had preceded him along the

---

[1] The history of this Association has been marked by really wonderful revivals. In the second decade (1831–41) there were over 700 baptisms; and in the fifth decade (1861–71) 2,000 baptisms were reported.

[2] Peter Philanthropos Root was the son of a Congregational

Susquehanna in a like evangelistic tour. The first church in this region was the Palmyra, in Wayne County, organized in 1792 by William Purdy and other settlers who came from Orange County, N. Y. The next church to be formed was of New England origin. Baptists from Plainfield, Conn., among whom was William Clark, removed to Abington, Luzerne County, in 1800, and the following year Jonathan Dean and others from Rhode Island joined them. A church was constituted in May, 1803. As early as 1791 some Connecticut Baptists settled at Mt. Pleasant, Wayne County. They were probably of the Arminian wing, and in 1796 they united in forming a free communion church— the only one of the kind in Pennsylvania. In September, 1807, six members of this church obtained letters of dismission and organized a strict communion church, which was duly recognized by the Abington and Palmyra Churches; and in the following December these three united in the Abington Association.[1] These churches were situated about thirty miles apart, separated by a wilderness traversed only by bridle paths marked by "blazed" trees. For this reason they probably felt more keenly than churches in a settled community the need of mutual counsel and encouragement.

minister of Connecticut, a graduate of Dartmouth, in 1789, but united with the First Baptist Church of Boston in May, 1793. During most of his remaining years (he died in 1828) he was an itinerant preacher in seventeen of the States and in Canada.

[1] Sermon by Rev. E. L. Bailey at the fifty-fifth anniversary, August 27, 1862, at Benton Center.

The growth of Associations in Northern and Western Pennsylvania was somewhat later than in New York. But three, the Philadelphia, the Redstone, and the Chemung, were organized in the State prior to 1800, and during the first quarter of the present century but three more were added to the number, the Abington (1801), the Beaver (1809), and the Susquehanna (1818). The Beaver was long the strongest body in the western part of the State. It was originally constituted by seven churches represented by eighteen delegates, two of them ministers. In 1819 all the churches in Pennsylvania west of the Allegheny River, also all the churches in Ohio east of Wooster and as far north as the lake, were included in this body. In that year the Mahoning (Northeastern Ohio) and Mohegan (Southeastern Ohio) were formed, leaving Beaver twelve churches, three hundred and thirty-one members, and three ministers. From the Susquehanna the Bridgewater was formed in 1826, and this in turn was the parent of the Wyoming in 1842.

Several of the Associations in this State had a very close connection with the churches of New York. For example, the Center Association (1831), owes its origin to the planting of a church in Milesburg in 1822 by the Rev. C. Phileo, then a missionary of the Hamilton Missionary Society.[1] The French Creek Association was formed in 1823

---

[1] Benedict, p. 614.

about equally of churches formerly connected with the Beaver and of others that had a membership in the Holland Purchase Association. The old Redstone proved, in the second quarter of the century, to be not without fruitfulness; her successive offspring were the Monongahela (1834), and the Pittsburg (1840). Besides those now mentioned, the Clarion was organized in 1838, thus completing the group of six western Associations and testifying to the growth of Baptists in this part of the State up to the year 1850.

The progress of the Baptist churches of Pennsylvania, outside of the Philadelphia district, was greatly due to the agency of the State Convention. The first annual report of this body (1828) says that a church had been constituted at Bethesda, Chester County; and this beginning was followed by large achievements of the kind. In the first ten years of its existence the Convention raised and expended fourteen thousand five hundred dollars, organized thirty-nine churches through its missionaries, and assisted in building fifteen meeting-houses, while between four thousand and five thousand conversions were reported as the direct result of its efforts. One of the most zealous and successful of the early missionaries of this body was the Rev. Eugenio Kincaid, but he soon felt called to the more needy missionary field of Burma. His brethren bore hearty and affectionate testimony to his faithfulness and parted from him with great regret, though recognizing his divine call to the larger work.

In the year 1838 the Convention was reorganized, and in the Minutes of that year we find the first statistical tables covering the whole State. According to these figures there were now fifteen Associations, two hundred and twenty-eight churches, and seventeen thousand two hundred and seventeen members. No immediate increase of interest seems to have followed the reorganization, the report for the following year showing an income of only fourteen hundred dollars; but there was steady growth of income and broadening of the work from this time forward. In 1843 the receipts rose to five thousand four hundred and fifty-nine dollars, which continued to be high-water mark for some years, being for the first time exceeded in 1851. This increase was not due to the benevolence of churches, but to gifts from individuals who became members for life by the payment of ten dollars each. There were reported in this year three hundred and seventy-six such life-members, with two hundred and sixty more who had signified their wish and intention speedily to do likewise.

In another decade the churches had increased to two hundred and thirty-two and the members to twenty-seven thousand five hundred and eleven, a gratifying growth in membership but a very small net increase of churches. In the Minutes of 1848 seven counties were mentioned, with a population of one hundred and fifty-six thousand five hundred and forty-five, in which there was not a single Baptist church. In seventeen counties, having a population of five hundred and twenty-nine thousand six hundred and thirty-eight, nearly one-third of the whole population of the State, there were but seven hundred and eight Baptists. These facts were made the basis of a stirring appeal to the churches to engage with more zeal and liberality in this work of State missions. The appeal was heeded and a great advance was made during the following ten years, for in 1858 there were three hundred and eighty-five churches in the State and thirty-seven thousand five hundred and twenty-seven members. The gain in members was about the same as in the previous decade, but in place of an increase of four churches in ten years there had been added during this decade one hundred and fifty-three churches.

In 1877 was held the semi-centennial of the Convention—the fiftieth anniversary of the first organization having been celebrated ten years before. Great cause for rejoicing was then found in the fact that during the last ten years of its history there had been a sudden and great increase in the liberality of the churches, the receipts being one hundred and twenty-two thousand six hundred and fifty-two dollars against sixty thousand three hundred and fifty-six dollars in the previous decade. But there was a still greater cause for joy in the fact, then officially announced and never disputed, that two hundred and thirty-three of the five hundred and sixty-one Baptist churches then existing in the State owed their organization to the labors of the Convention's missionaries and their continued life to its fostering care. In addition to this, seventeen thousand had been baptized into the fellowship of the Baptist churches by these missionaries. Certainly these facts constitute a record of efficient service and substantial progress that is creditable to any domestic missionary organization and probably has been surpassed by few.

The second great westward advance began with the close of what was known as King George's War, which was ended in 1748 by the treaty of Aix-la-Chapelle. In that year the Ohio Land Company was formed, and some adventurous settlers began to push their way into the Western wilderness. This movement was brought to an abrupt termination by the renewal of hostilities between the French and English, and the defeat of Braddock in 1755 seemed to give this region beyond the Alleghanies and north of the Ohio to the French. But the supreme struggle for the possession of this continent was yet to come; and the victory of Wolfe at Quebec in 1759 decided that North America was to belong to the Anglo-Saxon race. Then began that mighty movement of the American people westward that in a single century transformed the face of the continent as, in so short a time, no similar expanse of territory on the earth's surface was ever transformed. When we reflect that it required twelve centuries to bring the Britain of Cæsar's day to the semblance of general cultivation and Christian civilization we may well be dumb with astonishment before a development that reduces the Arabian tale of Aladdin and his lamp to the level of the prosaic and the commonplace.

It was about the year 1769 that the first serious advance westward occurred. Then the hardy pioneers of Virginia and North Carolina, men like Daniel Boone, began to make their way across the Alleghanies and into what are now the States of Kentucky and Tennessee. In 1794 the settlement of the famed Western Reserve was begun, and from Ohio the frontiers were rapidly pushed onward into Indiana and Illinois. By the year 1800 there were probably not fewer than half a million white people dwelling beyond the Alleghanies; it is known that the four Territories of Kentucky, Tennessee, Ohio, and Indiana contained three hundred and seventy-six thousand eight hundred and seven; and the regions beyond must have contained many thousands more.

In 1803 occurred an event that had momentous consequences upon the history of American Christianity, the so-called Louisiana purchase. Thomas Jefferson had been noted during Washington's administration as the opponent of Hamilton and the

Federalists, the champion of a strict construction of the Constitution. As president, patriotism proved stronger with him than party feeling, nor was he unduly devoted to that vice of feeble minds, consistency. With noble disregard of his past contentions, he bought of France for fifteen million dollars a strip of territory that more than doubled the area of this country. Before his administration the United States included eight hundred and twenty-seven thousand eight hundred and forty-four square miles; the Louisiana purchase added to the national domain one million one hundred and seventy-one thousand nine hundred and thirty-one square miles. It may help us to comprehend these figures by recalling that from this new domain were afterward formed the States of Louisiana, Arkansas, Missouri, Iowa, Kansas, Nebraska, Wyoming, the two Dakotas, and Montana, besides a large part of Minnesota and Colorado, and the Indian Territory, including Oklahoma.

Settlement of this new territory proceeded very slowly however during the next decade, for two reasons: the Indians were hostile and threatening on the north, and the possession of the southern part was menaced by the British. The energies of the country were too much absorbed by the war of 1812, the struggle to preserve the independence so hardly won in the Revolution, to have much surplus for colonization. The battle of Tippecanoe, in 1811, broke the power of the Indians, who were never formidable again east of the Mississippi; while the battle of New Orleans in 1815, assured the integrity of our possessions. Peace came soon to crown this victory, and then the great westward movement fairly began. The next fifty years saw a material growth without a parallel in history.

To the Baptist churches of that time belongs the praise of having been leaders in the work of evangelizing this new region. Devoted Baptist missionaries kept pace with the progress of the people westward. In many of the new States they were the first to preach the gospel. Baptist preachers from the older States first told the old, old story in Tennessee and Kentucky, in Illinois and Indiana and Missouri. Many of the Associations appointed missionaries for this purpose, and out of their poverty the churches made liberal contributions thus to carry the gospel to the regions beyond. Others of these pioneer preachers were men of faith who went forth not knowing where they should find a night's rest or food, but trusting that God would lead them and that the people to whom they ministered would supply their actual wants. Nor were they disappointed. The life of these settlers was rude, their food was coarse, their shelter was often inadequate, but the minister was heartily welcomed to his share of such as they had. And so churches were planted in all this new region, and denominational foundations were solidly laid on which we of to-day are building.

K

In this work the Baptists of the Middle States bore their full part. The churches of New York and Pennsylvania furnished a large quota of those Baptist families and Baptist preachers who went to build up the new West, to subdue the wilderness for Immanuel. It seems wonderful to us, as we look back, that so great a work of evangelization could have been carried forward with so little system and co-operation. Every Association, in many localities every church, in hosts of cases every individual, did what seemed good, without reference to what might be done by anybody else. And yet, by this method, unpromising as we should consider it in these days of organization for everything, this hap-hazard evangelization accomplished results of great and lasting value. There was hardly a hamlet of the new West into which the pioneer preacher did not penetrate and where he did not make converts.

We have already seen how the need for greater unity and co-operation in this home evangelization produced the State Conventions. The formation of these missionary bodies, however, was felt to supply only a part of the need; an organization was seen to be necessary that would represent the whole country in domestic missions as the General Convention represented the whole country in foreign missions. An attempt was indeed made for a time, as has been related, to have the Convention do both kinds of work, but this was abandoned after a brief trial as unsatisfactory, if not as impracticable, in itself. The

Massachusetts Missionary Society, at its meeting in 1831, strongly impressed by the account of the religious needs of the West brought back to that body by Dr. Jonathan Going, resolved that the Baptists of the United States ought to form a general society for the prosecution of missionary work, especially in the Mississippi Valley. Consultations were had with brethren representing the New York Convention, and a meeting was called in New York, beginning April 27, 1832. A constitution was adopted, officers were elected, and New York was selected as the headquarters of the new organization. The first president was Heman Lincoln; the first treasurer, William Colgate; and the first corresponding secretary, Jonathan Going—all men who remind us of the Scripture, "There were giants in those days."

And they have been succeeded by men of like stature: John P. Crozer, Martin B. Anderson, and James L. Howard, among the presidents; Jay S. Backus, Nathan Bishop, and Henry L. Morehouse, among the secretaries—these and others like them are men who have worthily carried forward the work so well begun. The history of the Home Mission Society belongs to the Baptists of the United States; or, if any section might claim a peculiar property in that organization, it is the West that owes so much to its beneficent labors. It is not practicable to pause here even for a sketch of its great and manifold activities, though it would be a grateful task to recount its pioneer work in missions throughout the great West; its evangelizing work among foreign populations in the East; its services to the freedmen of the South since 1869; the educational institutions established and maintained by its agency; its invaluable assistance to new churches in the West in the building of houses of worship; and the general and great denominational advance due to the energy and persistence and wisdom that have marked all these missionary labors. At the semi-centennial of the society, in 1882, it was reported that four million dollars had been raised and expended in this work. In the fifteen years that have followed, this sum has been more than doubled.

CHAPTER VI

EVANGELISM AND REVIVALS

AFTER the Great Awakening of 1740 and the years immediately following, there was a long period in the history of American Christianity in which special seasons of religious interest were almost unknown. Doubtless the troublesome period of the Revolution, with its military operations and social disorder, had much to do with producing this state of comparative religious lifelessness. The influence of English and French deism was also quite marked toward the close of the eighteenth century, and the cause of religion languished in all parts of the country and among all Christians. About the year 1800 revivals occurred almost simultaneously in various localities, and a marked increase of religious interest was manifested from this time forward. No one denomination experienced this influence in special measure, and no part of the country was entirely exempt from its power. The revivals were, however, most marked in their depth and fervor in the frontier regions. Among the new settlements the religious feeling was very strong, and beyond the Alleghanies revivals of extraordinary extent and power were frequent. It was in these regions and during these revivals that the camp-meeting originated, and from this time periodic religious gatherings were more frequently held.

The reflex influence of this revival interest was perhaps felt more strongly at first in Western Pennsylvania than it was in New York. The churches in the western counties were powerfully awakened, and the work continued with little abatement for several years. In 1802 there were numerous revivals in New Jersey, especially about the city of Newark. The church now known as Peddie Memorial Church, of that city, had been constituted the previous year and participated largely in the results of that revival. The general period from 1800 to 1830 was marked by continuous, or, at least, frequent revivals among Baptist churches. In those thirty years, the Baptists of the United States are said to have increased from one hundred thousand to three hundred and thirteen thousand one hundred and thirty-eight. In this increase the Baptists of the Middle States certainly had their full share. They cannot be estimated in the year 1800 at more than twenty thousand. In 1834 they numbered, according to "Allen's Register," over seventy-six thousand.

From 1830 a period of some twenty-five years elapsed in which there was no such general revival interest, either in the United States as a whole or among the Baptists of the Middle States, as have marked some other periods of their history. There were, however, numerous cases in the State of New York of very powerful revivals at this time. Most of these were connected with the labors of the Rev. Charles G. Finney, the celebrated evangelist and theologian.[1] Mr. Finney was a Presbyterian who had been bred as a lawyer, and who entered upon his work as an evangelist soon after his conversion, with very little special preparation. From the first he was remarkably successful. Many of his meetings were held in connection with Baptist churches, or in towns where these participated in the benefits of the general religious awakening. One of the most remarkable series of meetings that he conducted at this period were those held in Rochester in the year 1830. The great majority of the leading citizens of the place were converted, and a great change was made in the moral state and after history of the city. Twice subsequently, in 1842 and in 1855, Mr. Finney held meetings in Rochester with equally marked results. These three revivals left traces that have never been eradicated. They permanently changed the character of the city and gave to it a Christian tone that even the large influx of foreign population in recent years has not sufficed wholly to overcome. Revivals of similar power under Mr. Finney's preaching occurred at Utica, Auburn, Troy, New York, Philadelphia, and Buffalo.

It was in connection with these meetings that great opposition was developed to what were called

---

[1] "Memoirs of Rev. Charles G. Finney," New York, 1876.

Mr. Finney's "new measures." In one of his early meetings, when he had been preaching about three hours, Mr. Finney attempted to bring people to a decision in the matter of their salvation, by requesting them to rise if they desired to accept Christ; and a few years later, in 1825, on a single occasion he asked those who desired to be saved to come forward to the front seat while the rest of the congregation prayed for and with them. It was not until his first series of meetings at Rochester, that he made much use of either device, but from this time onward the practice of inviting inquirers forward became usual with him. This was known as "coming to the anxious seat," and Mr. Finney's use of this method was severely criticised.

The objection to it really rested on a theological ground. The old-school, extreme Calvinists were not willing to allow that the human will had any self-determining power. In their belief conversion *followed* regeneration, a mysterious process wrought immediately by the Holy Spirit on the hearts of the elect. They were accustomed merely to urge their hearers to use the means of grace and wait on the Lord until it was his good pleasure to renew them. Mr. Finney, on the other hand, assumed that the sinner had sufficient power of self-determination to accept the divine promise of salvation at any time, and that nothing but his own wicked perversity stood in the way of his immediate salvation. Consequently, in all his preaching he attempted above all things to sweep away every excuse that men had for their inaction, and strove by every means in his power to bring them to an immediate decision for Christ. The "anxious seat," the rising for prayers, and the attendance at inquiry meetings were simply devices to make one whose conscience was roused and who felt a desire for salvation commit himself by taking some public stand. He rightly judged that this was more than half the battle, and that when people were induced to take this step, if they were really sincere, they were not far from the kingdom of God.

Other new measures of Mr. Finney that were severely criticised were the prolonging of meetings to unseasonable hours, sometimes throughout the night. It was also objected that he was occasionally harsh and rude in the pulpit, saying unkind and censorious things; that he himself prayed for people by name in public assemblies, without their consent, and encouraged others to do the same; that he permitted, if he did not encourage, the practice of women speaking and praying in promiscuous assemblies. Some of these charges were not justified by facts. Others of them were true, however, and a difference of opinion regarding the advisability of such measures existed for years among the evangelical churches. It was generally thought, after due trial, that the methods in the main vindicated themselves. Nearly every evangelist has since adopted these or similar methods, and as the people have become wonted to them the criticisms have diminished and finally disappeared.

Two other contemporary evangelists are noteworthy for their labors among Baptists of the Middle States: Jacob Knapp and Jabez S. Swan. The former was especially active in New York, though his labors extended over the Northern States, as far west as California. Mr. Knapp had few educational advantages, and his language was often ungrammatical, especially in moments of excitement, but he had a mind as robust as his body (which was notably sturdy and muscular), and his knowledge of the English Scriptures was immense. Like Finney, his preaching was strongly doctrinal, and he appealed habitually to the conscience of his hearers rather than to emotion. His preaching would be considered severe, and even coarse, at the present day, but in his own time it was marvelously effective. Powerful revivals attended his labors, in the course of which he is said to have preached sixteen thousand sermons, baptized four thousand persons, and led two hundred young men to become preachers of the gospel. Probably one-fourth of these labors were performed in New York State.[1]

Mr. Swan was a man of rather more culture, having had a partial course of study at the Hamilton Literary and Theological Institution. In knowledge of the Scriptures, in directness and power as a revival preacher, he was a worthy peer of Jacob Knapp.

---

[1] "Autobiography of Elder Jacob Knapp," New York, 1868.

The greater part of his work was done in the State of Connecticut, of which he was a native, and where he spent the larger part of his life. He had, however, several periods of service in New York, both as pastor and as evangelist. The most marked of these was the decade between 1830 and 1840, when he was nominally pastor of the churches at Oxford and Preston, but was preaching far and near among the Baptist churches of the State, with marked results in the conversion of hearers of all sorts and conditions. It is said that over ten thousand conversions occurred during his ministry, but how large a part of these were in New York we can only guess.[1]

The influence of this period of revivalism on the life and growth of the churches was profound, and manifested itself in many ways. It had a great effect on the preaching. To a large extent it banished the written sermon from the pulpit, and made the preaching of all—even of those who continued to read their sermons—more personal and pungent. A certain type of doctrinal sermon disappeared by degrees. Mr. Finney's own preaching was strongly doctrinal, and evangelists in later years who have been most successful have been precisely those who have been most doctrinal in their preaching ; but there is doctrinal preaching and doctrinal preaching. Mr. Finney's aim in all his preaching

---

[1] "The Evangelist; or, Life and Labors of Rev. Jabez S. Swan," edited by Rev. F. Denison, Waterford, Conn., 1873.

of doctrine was to influence the will. He never taught theology *per se* in the pulpit, he never discussed philosophy for its own sake. His sermons were not essays on theological themes, but he used doctrines to give weight and point to his appeals to the conscience, to produce conviction, and to stimulate men to action.

The influence of evangelism during this period was also to simplify pulpit style. Preachers no longer indulged in florid rhetoric and stilted language, but talked to men in the language of ordinary life. It used to be objected to Mr. Finney that he brought his illustrations from the streets and men's workshops and other humble sources, but nowadays instead of being considered a blemish this is reckoned a merit in a preacher. The effect of revivalism on church life was also marked. Prayer meetings were increased in frequency and attendance. Participation in them was no longer confined to the ministers and deacons but became general among the members. The vital piety of the churches was confessedly greater. Religion became a more real thing to men, a thing affecting their every day life, and not something reserved for one sacred day of the week. This was especially manifest in the Middle States, where from the beginning a more active and robust type of piety prevailed than was found in New England. As the people of New York moved westward into the newer regions, which they have done by hundreds of thousands during this century, they naturally determined to a great degree the type of piety in the newer States. The Baptist churches of the Middle States have had a far greater effect upon the religious life of the West than have those of New England, partly because of their larger numbers, and partly because of their more active and demonstrative piety.

In 1857 there was a very marked wave of revival interest extending throughout the country. Its first manifestation was in the city of New York, one of its firstfruits being the establishment of the Fulton Street daily noon prayer meeting. Similar meetings were established in other large cities. It is said that three hundred thousand were added during this revival to the membership of the evangelical churches of the country. The Civil War which soon followed was a great interruption to the religious life and progress of the whole land, but with the return of peace new spiritual life was manifest in many parts of the country. After 1870 this interest was seen to be rapidly increasing, and from 1874 to 1877 the great Moody and Sankey meetings caused larger masses of people to attend religious meetings than had ever been brought together at one time. These revivals were not confined to any one denomination, but the Baptist churches of the Middle States fully shared in their blessing.

It will be an interesting study to note the effect of this evangelism upon the growth of the Baptist denomination in the Middle States. In New York the effect is distinctly traceable in the rise of new churches and Associations. In 1800 there were ninety-four churches; by 1810, eighty-three more had been organized; in the next decade ninety-six were formed; by 1830, one hundred and eleven, had been added to the number; and in the next two decades the number of new churches is one hundred and twenty-seven and one hundred and three respectively. When we look at the growth of Associations the facts are even more striking. Four were in existence in 1800; and the increase by successive decades was as follows: five by 1810; seven by 1820; ten by 1840; five by 1850; and since that date but six more in all have been constituted, and these by division or reunion of existing bodies. The conclusion from these data is irresistible: the period of most rapid growth among New York Baptists, in all their history, was between 1800 and 1840, in which time considerably more than one-third of all the existing churches, and almost two-thirds of the Associations of the State, came into existence. But this was precisely the period of evangelism and revival, in its most active manifestation. The coincidence cannot be accidental. Though there were other causes of growth, the most important cause of all must have been the prevalence of revivals and the prominence given among all the churches to the immediate work of soul-saving.[1]

---

[1] It may as well be noted here as elsewhere that directly after

Similar results, though perhaps less striking, are reached when we study the progress of Baptist churches in New Jersey. Twenty-two churches had been formed in that State by the year 1800. By the year 1825 there had been eighteen added to the number, and in the next twenty-five years the increase of churches was forty-three. The associational growth of New Jersey mainly belongs to this period also. Up to 1811 the Baptist churches of this State had been, with few exceptions, attached either to the Philadelphia or the New York Association. The first organization of churches within State lines was that known at first as the New Jersey Association—which has now for years borne the name of the West Jersey Association—which was formed in 1811 by delegates from fourteen churches. The Central Association was formed next, in 1828, and was followed by the North

---

the second evangelistic period (beginning about 1855) there was a marked and inexplicable decline in the number of Baptist churches in New York. In 1861 there were eight hundred and thirty-six churches, and from this time there was a steady decline for some years, the number falling as low as seven hundred and sixty in 1867—an average extinction of over twelve churches a year. A close examination of the Minutes shows that this mortality of churches was not confined to any one locality, but was general throughout the State. A small percentage of these disappearances may be accounted for by unions that were formed, which resulted in the apparent loss of a church, no record of this union appearing in the State Minutes; but this still leaves something like fifty extinct churches to be accounted for. The Civil War cannot be a sufficient cause, for the churches as a whole increased in numbers during these years, and none of the causes of disunion to be considered in Chapter VII. was then in operation. Who will solve this mystery?

(1833), the East (1841). The Sussex, which was organized in 1833, is now extinct, and the Camden and Trenton are of later origin. The inference is proper from these facts that if the influence of evangelism in New Jersey is less impressive than in New York during the corresponding period, it is still somewhat noteworthy.

Materials are not accessible for a similar study in detail of the growth among Pennsylvania Baptists. We may fairly assume that there were not in 1800 more than fifty churches in the State. By 1848 they had become two hundred and thirty-two, or little more than one-third of their present number. It is not possible to trace the details of this increase, as in the case of the other States, because the exact facts have not been ascertained and tabulated, either in State or associational Minutes; but it seems a warrantable inference, from such facts as have just been cited, that this wave of evangelism did not profoundly affect the Baptists of this State. Their most rapid growth did not begin before 1850, a year that marks almost the conclusion of the special evangelistic era in New York.

As we might suppose, this evangelistic era was marked by special activity in State missions. A New Jersey Baptist Mission Society was formed previous to 1811, and reports of its work were printed annually in the Minutes of the New Jersey Association. It was rather a feeble organization and never obtained the support of the churches of the entire State. Between 1812 and 1830 it collected and expended only one thousand eight hundred dollars in all. There came to be a general dissatisfaction with work on this scale, a desire to accomplish more, and to secure the co-operation of all the churches. A conference of brethren whose hearts were much moved in this matter was held at Nottingham Square, April 13, 1830, at which five churches in New Jersey and one in Pennsylvania were represented. The result of their deliberations was the issuing of a call, in which all the churches of the State were invited to send delegates to a meeting at the same place on July 27, for the purpose of forming a suitable State missionary society. At the appointed time and place ten churches were represented by delegates, who voted that "it is expedient to organize a State Convention for missionary purposes," and proceeded to adopt a suitable constitution and organize under it. Immediately steps were taken to secure the co-operation of the churches represented in the constituent body. A careful canvass of the State during the first year of the new Convention's work disclosed the following facts: There were in New Jersey at that time fifty-five Baptist churches, with four thousand one hundred and sixty-four members.[1] Five of these

---

[1] The fifteenth annual report of the Board gives the number of Baptists in the State at the organization of the Convention as 3,967, but the figures above given seem to be the more trustworthy. The first Convention statistics are found in the Minutes for 1834; then there were 63 churches and 5,954 members.

churches positively refused to co-operate with the Convention, and of the others twenty-four had merely a nominal existence. But twenty-six churches, therefore, could be depended on for any real co-operation, and of these but two had over two hundred members, and only ten a membership exceeding one hundred. These facts, while they must have been depressing, indicated clearly the need of just such an organization, and the work of the Convention was successful from the first. The growth of the churches was steady, at times even rapid; and when the Jubilee was celebrated at New Brunswick it was found that one hundred and eighteen thousand three hundred and seventy-six dollars has been raised for the work, and two hundred and sixty-six missionaries employed among the churches. These missionaries had baptized six thousand converts, while the total number of baptisms in the half-century had been more than fifty-four thousand.[1]

In New York, State missions also received a considerable impetus from evangelization. One special manifestation was seen in a work undertaken among the Indians. This began as early as 1819, when a committee of the Board visited the Oneidas, as a result of which the chiefs called a council and much interest in the gospel was manifested, so that a mis-

---

[1] Historical address of Rev. J. M. Carpenter, in "Minutes of the New Jersey State Convention" for 1879. For further details of growth, see table in Appendix B.

sionary was sent them the following year. A missionary church was constituted among this tribe in 1824, which for nearly a generation continued to be the only Baptist church among the Indians. The work continued, however, and in 1867 the annual report of the Board calls attention to some encouraging facts: Twenty-three years before there was only one Indian Baptist church, and it occupied a rude log house; now there are three other churches, all with respectable church edifices, supplied with regular pastors, having Sunday-schools, whose aggregate membership is nearly five hundred, while it is believed that three hundred more have been saved. Of late years this work among Indians has languished, and is now practically given up.

The general operations of the Convention were prosecuted during this period with varying degrees of success, and it seems plain on reviewing the facts that the periodic lack of spirit and fruitfulness was largely due to defective methods of organization. After the Convention became fairly established, by the absorption of the Hamilton Missionary Society in 1825, it was soon found necessary to adjust its relations with the American Baptist Home Mission Society. It was finally determined that the State Convention should become an auxiliary to the national society. It collected the funds, and a certain percentage was appropriated to State missions, at one time two-fifths of the whole amount collected for domestic missions, the rest going to the larger work. Pastors were as nervous then as they are now, and with as little reason, about increasing the number of collections; their theory being that the members of their churches are unwilling to make frequent offerings for purposes outside of their local work. This arrangement was therefore made to avoid the necessity of taking separate collections for State and Home missions.

But there are worse things than multiplying collections, as the pastors of New York soon found out, and this plan was so far from satisfactory that a readjustment was called for after a few years. It was then agreed that two collections constituted the less of two evils—a greater far being decline in the interest of the churches in both State and Home missions—and New York became thenceforth the common field for representatives of both societies until 1868. Then a plan of co-operation was adopted—it should rather have been called consolidation—and once more only one collection was to be taken for domestic missions, the whole of which was to go into the treasury of the Home Mission Society; but that body became responsible for the payment of the missionaries of the Convention. This plan did not work so badly so far as the finances were concerned, but it reduced the State organization to little more than a nominal existence, and caused great dissatisfaction in a short time.

In 1874 the Convention reorganized under a new constitution, which made it a distinctively State organization, devoted to missionary, education, and Sunday-school work. Since that time the Convention's work has shown steady progress, and the result on denominational growth has been marked. During the presidency of the late Rev. Edward Bright, D. D., from 1874 to 1885, the receipts of the Convention rose from six thousand and twenty-four dollars to fourteen thousand and fifty-nine dollars, and during the same period the Baptists of the State increased from one hundred and four thousand three hundred and thirty-nine to one hundred and sixteen thousand three hundred and forty. Of course, other things contributed to this denominational growth, of which the increased activity of the Convention is as much a symptom as a cause; but it was in part a cause, and must be allowed to be a very significant symptom. Since 1885, under the presidency of Rev. John B. Calvert, D. D., the Convention has more than made good this record, having quite doubled its contributions and correspondingly enlarged its operations, and each year sees it becoming a more important factor in denominational life and growth.

It is an equally interesting study to note the progress of Baptists in the chief cities during the period of evangelism. It would require a separate volume to do justice to the history of Baptist churches in New York, and a long chapter even to outline it. It is a history marked by great vicissitudes, and the investigator of it finds his path strewn with the wrecks of churches once flourishing—some wrecked by debt or other unwise financial management, others wrecked by dissensions and schisms, others left stranded and dying by inches through the movement of population. Before 1810, nine churches had been organized in the city, of which three were already extinct. Between 1810 and 1845, thirty-seven other churches were constituted, of which twelve had ceased to exist, and of the remainder only seven remain to the present day, though several others have been absorbed into existing churches. This was the period of the most rapid growth, though the gains made were not steadily held.[1]

Disunion has been mentioned as a cause retarding the growth of New York Baptists. There was not only lack of harmony in the churches at times, but lack of harmony between the churches most of the time. In 1843, when the first statistical tables of the State Convention were printed in the Minutes, we see this clearly. Part of the city churches are members of the old New York Association, but a still larger number—including the Tabernacle, Oliver Street, Stanton, Amity, and Norfolk Street—were members of the Hudson River Association.[2] This

[1] Greenleaf, "History of the Churches in the City of New York," New York, 1846, p. 274.

[2] The cause of this is not hard to conjecture. The Bible Society fight was on (see Chapter X.), and there was among the churches what we may call, from the names of the leaders, a Cone faction and a Williams faction. The churches of the former remained in the New York Association, while the latter sought more congenial companionship in the Hudson River.

state of things continued until 1871, when, the old feuds having become less intense and a desire for closer union being general, the Southern New York Association was organized with fifty-four churches and twelve thousand eight hundred and fifty-two members.[1] The divisions had borne their natural fruitage; between 1843 and 1865 the Baptists had lost ground, not only relatively to the growth of the city but absolutely, there being eight thousand five hundred and twenty-five fewer members in the latter year than in the former. The first report of the new body shows that the tide had begun to turn; and since that day Baptists have had, if not so rapid progress as might be wished, at least a solid and substantial growth. Twenty-seven of the sixty-eight churches at present constituting the Association have come into being since its organization, many of them under its direct fostering care. For, from the first this became a missionary body, and the Baptist City Mission—until recent years the agent of the Association, but now strictly a city organization—has been an effective means of church extension in the upper parts of the city. Work under its auspices in the down-town districts has been less conspicuously successful.

The vicissitudes of New York churches have been mentioned, but a stranger to things in that city can have no just idea of them. They are not to be matched by anything in the history of Baptist

---

[1] There were in 1895, 68 churches and 18,604 members.

churches in this country, or probably in the world. Take the old First Church as an example. It was founded as we have seen, in 1762, and its first house of worship was far down-town in Gold Street. In 1842 the church removed to Broome and Elizabeth Streets, then well up-town, but now in the heart of the business section. In 1871 it dedicated another house of worship at Park Avenue and East Thirty-ninth Street; and twenty years later, almost to a day, it laid the corner-stone of the house it now occupies, at the Boulevard and Seventy-ninth Street—a locality that even ten years previously would have been thought a preposterous site for any church edifice. The Calvary Church has had a much briefer history, but has been subject to nearly as many changes. Beginning in 1847 as Hope Chapel, on Broadway, in 1854 it established itself on Twenty-third Street, only to remove in 1883 to West Fifty-seventh Street. Few Baptist churches have remained in one church home in New York for more than a generation; those that have remained have remained to die.

But besides this movement of population up-town, the churches have had to contend with a movement of the population out of town. New York is a city of great contrasts, of extremes of fortune and social position—a city of paupers and of millionaires, of hovels and of palaces. People who belong to neither the highest nor the lowest stratum, who are neither poor nor rich, find it a hard city to live in, and are continually seeking homes in the suburbs. This is the class of which our Baptist churches are mostly composed; there are few paupers in them, and there are still fewer millionaires. In 1872 a careful study of the facts showed that within a generation fifty churches had sprung into existence within twenty miles of the City Hall, to which several thousand members had been dismissed by the Baptist churches of New York.[1] The same causes are still producing the same effects. In making comparative estimates of growth, when we find New York Baptists apparently falling behind others we must in fairness take these facts into consideration.

The Baptists of Philadelphia have had a less difficult problem to solve, and the several churches have been less subject to vicissitude, but there have been curious fluctuations in their history, for some of which it is difficult to conjecture any reasonable explanation. Between 1776 and 1781 the Philadelphia Association lost over half of its members —to be exact, they fell from three thousand and thirteen to one thousand four hundred and thirty-five; but this is easily accounted for by the war, the British occupation of the city, and the like. But a decline[2] between 1791 and 1802, similar though not so marked, is not so easily explained.

---

[1] Historical paper of Rev. James L. Hodge, in "Minutes of Southern New York Association" for 1872.

[2] From 3,253 members in 1791 to 2,695 in 1802. Then the tide turned, for in 1803 the number was 2,898, and during the rest of the decade there was rapid growth.

In 1784 the members were two thousand and seventy-seven and in 1788 they were three thousand one hundred and ninety-eight. In the decade between 1800 and 1810 there was a very rapid increase —from two thousand six hundred and twenty-six to four thousand three hundred and fifty-five ; and then ensued another inexplicable decline, the numbers falling as low in 1824 as two thousand six hundred and seventy-six. Between 1830 and 1840 the numbers more than doubled, and in view of this rapid increase it seems odd to read in the Minutes of 1841 a plaintive reference to the change in the style of preaching, which was conceded to be "well adapted to arouse, convict, and convert, but probably not so well adapted to edify and instruct." From 1840 to 1850 there was almost equally rapid progress—the thirty-eight churches becoming sixty-three and the six thousand six hundred and thirty-three members multiplying into ten thousand and twenty-nine. Now ensued another decline, for which also no explanation is forthcoming; in the next decade the number of churches decreased from sixty-three to fifty-eight, and the total increase of membership was only one thousand eight hundred and forty-two in the ten years. From 1860 to 1890 there was steady progress, especially in the organization of churches, which rose from fifty-eight to ninety-six, while the membership increased from eleven thousand eight hundred and seventy-one to twenty-eight thousand six hundred and ninety-four.

EVANGELISM AND REVIVALS 171

Disunion has been less a bar to progress among the Baptists of Philadelphia than in New York, but there was one controversy among the churches that must not be passed by. This was caused by a schism in the First Church. After its formal constitution, in 1746, this body enjoyed at least the average peace and prosperity that obtain among Baptist churches, until the pastorate of Rev. Henry Holcombe, D. D. This divine was a man of much ability, an eminent preacher, a man of warm heart and generous impulses, but somewhat rash and prone to violence of language when excited. A difference of opinion arose in the Philadelphia Association regarding the First African Church, which had fallen into dispute over a pastor. One of the factions into which the members became divided was recognized as the church by the Association at its meeting in 1816, there being only two negative votes. This gave great umbrage to Dr. Holcombe, and at his instigation the First Church issued a pamphlet protesting against the Association's act in language emphatic to the verge of abuse.

The Association could not very well let this pass, or so that body thought, and accordingly at the meeting of 1817 a minute was adopted recording regret at the "unchristian temper" and "very palpable misrepresentations" of the document, and adding: "They consider its tendency as mischievous, calculated to mislead the uninformed, and are of opinion that said church owe it to this body, to retrace their unwarrantable steps, or, in case of perseverance in their present unhappy course, that the Association owes it to her own honor and harmony, and to the cause of truth, to separate from her body a church with whom she cannot hold communion. The Association suspend any further proceedings, leaving the whole for the solemn consideration of said church until the next Association."

The amount of solemn consideration that an admonition of this kind, with a threat at the end of it, received under the circumstances was probably not large. At any rate, the Minutes of the following year contain this item:

Resolved, That this Association, conscious of the rectitude of her own acts in relation to the First Baptist Church of Philadelphia, and from the persevering conduct of said church, as manifested by her present delegation, are constrained to say, they cannot continue her any longer a member of this body.

Some years after this severance of relations, there arose a contention in the First Church itself. Many of its members were accused by other members of holding beliefs not in accordance with the Confession of Faith. It is beyond question that some had been infected with notions of the final restoration of the wicked and other kindred heresies, but the majority of the church always insisted that, as a body, they held no such errors and were loyal to the Confession. A strong and compact minority, however, still urged the accusations, and finally called a council in October, 1825, containing such men as William Parkinson, Horatio Gates Jones, Spencer H. Cone, and Joseph H. Kennard, who confirmed their view of the facts. Both factions finally applied for readmission to the Philadelphia Association in 1826, each claiming to be the First Baptist Church. The Association decided, sixteen churches favoring and but four opposing, that the minority were entitled to admission as representing the principles on which the church had been founded, and they were accordingly readmitted to the body as the First Baptist Church of Philadelphia, and soon after obtained an incorporation under the same title. The majority was afterward incorporated under the name of the "First Baptist Church of Philadelphia worshiping in Second street," but in 1835 purchased from the minority the legal right to the title of "First Baptist Church of Philadelphia," which the majority has ever since held. The minority, after thus selling the name to which it had a legal right—but not selling, as it was careful to specify, its history—changed its name to that of the "Spruce Street Baptist Church," which it still bears.

These are the facts, all of them that are essential to the case. Which, then, is the original First Baptist Church of Philadelphia? This is a problem like to that other famous in Baptist annals, Which is the oldest Baptist church in America? In an evil hour, with the confidence born of youth and inexperience, the author of this volume once expressed an opinion on this latter problem, for which he has been berated ever since. Grown wiser with added years, he now throws the responsibility of deciding between the two Philadelphia rivals on those who have read the unadorned facts.

CHAPTER VII

THE PERIOD OF CONTROVERSIES

THE first half of the nineteenth century will always be memorable in the religious annals of the United States, for in it originated three movements that were claimed by their leaders to be reformations of religion. The earliest, led by Alexander Campbell, resulted in the establishment of the Disciples of Christ as a separate religious body. The second was the rise of Mormonism, through the united labors of Joseph Smith and Sidney Rigdon. The third was the growth of Spiritualism, beginning with the "rappings" of the Fox sisters. The so-called Reformation of Alexander Campbell stands apart from the other two, in that it purported to rest on no new revelation, but professed to be nothing more nor less than a return to primitive Christianity. Study of the origin of the Disciples has, therefore, some special elements of interest at this time; and the propriety of such a study here is vindicated—if it needs vindication—by the fact that the beginnings of the Reformation were among the Baptists of Western Pennsylvania. On the other hand, Spiritualism and Mormonism did not originate among Baptists, had no appreciable connection with them, and therefore need not engage our attention.

The men to whom the Disciples owed their origin were Thomas and Alexander Campbell, and though the superior abilities and energy of the latter soon brought him into chief prominence, the share of the former was considerable. Thomas Campbell was a preacher of the Seceders, a Presbyterian sect of Scotland, the formation of which dates from 1733, when the General Assembly suspended the Rev. Ebenezer Erskine and others. From 1820 this body was called the United Secession Church, and since 1847, when a union was consummated with the Relief Church, it has been called the United Presbyterian Church. Mr. Campbell came to this country in 1807, a minister of the Seceders' church, in full fellowship.[1] For a time he labored in connection with the Presbytery of Chartiers, in Western Pennsylvania, but he soon became dissatisfied with what he believed to be its sectarian spirit, and in the early autumn of 1809 organized what he called "The Christian Association, of Washington, Pa." A "Declaration and address" issued at this time made known at length the purposes of this body. It was not a church; it disclaimed that character explicitly. Nor was it the intention of Campbell and his associates either to separate themselves from their existing denominational relations or to found a new denomination. The fun-

---

[1] "Memoirs of Alexander Campbell," by Robert Richardson, Vol. I., pp. 81, 85.

damental principle of the Association was the securing of Christian union on the basis of the Bible alone. All articles of faith, as terms of communion, were opposed, and the principle was laid down "That with respect to the commands and ordinances of our Lord Jesus Christ, where the Scriptures are silent as to the express time or manner of performance, if any such there be, no human authority has power to interfere in order to supply the supposed deficiency by making laws for the church."[1] At the organization of the society[2] Thomas Campbell had announced this principle with brevity and point in these words: "Where the Scriptures speak, we speak; where the Scriptures are silent, we are silent."

Before this declaration was printed, Alexander Campbell had arrived at his father's house; and, on reading the document in proof, gave it his hearty approval. Up to the time of his leaving Scotland, he too had been in full outward fellowship with the Seceders, though in his heart he had renounced their doctrines and practice, and had refused to partake of the communion at their last semi-annual communion season.[3] He did not scruple, however, to apply for and receive the usual certificate of good standing

---
[1] Tyler's "History of the Disciples," American Church History Series, Vol. XII., pp. 49–54.
[2] Richardson, Vol. I., pp. 236, 237.
[3] *Ibid.*, pp. 189, 190. There seems to be no authority for the statement by his biographer in the "Schaff-Herzog Encyclopædia," that he "came to America as a licentiate of the Seceder Church."

M

before setting out for America. He had spent some time, while a student at the University of Glasgow, in the society of Greville Ewing, one of the leaders of the Sandemanian sect, and had been strongly influenced by the peculiar notions of this able and eccentric divine.[1] Many of these notions were afterward worked out in the Reformation, especially the Sandemanian doctrine of faith—that it is mere intellectual assent to the teaching of Scripture, a simple belief in the historic Christ. His obligations to Ewing, and to the writings of Glas and Sandeman, Campbell never denied or concealed. He did not profess that his teachings were original. He only claimed that they were true. "I am," said he, "greatly indebted to all the reformers, from Martin Luther down to John Wesley. I could not enumerate or particularize the individuals, living and dead, who have assisted in forming my mind. If all the Hebrew, Greek, Roman, Persian, French, English, Irish, Scotch, and American teachers and authors were to demand their own from me, I do not know that I would have two mites to buy incense to offer upon the altar to my genius of originality for the honors vouchsafed me."[2]

Alexander Campbell became a member of the Christian Association, and before it he preached his first sermon, on July 15, 1810. In October, 1810, the Association applied through Thomas Campbell

---

[1] Richardson, Vol. I., Chapter IX., *passim*.
[2] "Millennial Harbinger," 1835, p. 304.

to the Synod of Pittsburg for membership, and the application was refused on these grounds, as stated in the official record:

It was not for any immorality in practice, but, in addition to the reasons before assigned, for expressing his belief that there are some opinions taught in our Confession of Faith which are not founded in the Bible, and avoiding to designate them ; for declaring that the administration of baptism to infants is not authorized by scriptural precept or example, and is a matter of indifference, yet administering that ordinance while holding such an opinion ; for encouraging or countenancing his son to preach the gospel without any regular authority ; for opposing creeds and confessions as injurious to the interests of religion ; and, also, because it is not consistent with the regulations of the Presbyterian Church that Synod should form a connection with any ministers, churches, or associations.

Finding that, by persisting in a denial that the Christian Association they had formed was of the nature of a church, fellowship with any religious body would probably be impossible, on May 4, 1811, this body organized itself into a church. No further attempt, however, seems to have been made to secure admission to the Presbyterian Synod. This was due to an impending change of conviction and practice in the church regarding the subjects and act of baptism. Some weeks before the Brush Run Declaration was issued, in 1809, this question seems first to have seriously presented itself. At that time it was pointed out that the principle, "Where the

Scriptures speak, we speak; where the Scriptures are silent, we are silent," would require the abandonment of infant baptism, because no explicit command to baptize infants is found in the Scriptures; and accordingly this matter was from the beginning left optional in the Brush Run Church.[1] This fact was, as we have seen, a reason why the Synod of Pittsburg refused to receive the Brush Run body into its fellowship. We find also, that on at least one occasion during the next year or two, Alexander Campbell took part in a warm private debate with a Baptist preacher on the question of baptism.[2] By the third of January, 1810, though his mind was still unsettled, he was led to say of baptism, in a sermon on the Great Commission: "As I am sure it is unscriptural to make this matter a term of communion, I let it slip. I wish to think and let think on these matters."[3]

About this time Mr. Campbell was convinced that he must decide the subject one way or the other: "Abandoning then all uninspired authorities he applied himself to the Scriptures, and searching out critically the signification of the words rendered baptism and baptized in the original Greek, he soon became satisfied that they could mean only immersion and immerse. From his further investigations

---

[1] Richardson, Vol. I., pp. 238, 250. Compare the objections of the Synod of Pittsburg already quoted. See also Alexander Campbell's reply to the Synod's objections in Richardson, Vol. I., p. 344.
[2] *Ibid.*, p. 362. [3] *Ibid.*, p. 392.

he was led finally to the conviction that believers, and believers only, were the proper subjects of the ordinance. He now fully perceived that the rite of sprinkling to which he had been subjected in infancy was wholly unauthorized, and that he was consequently, in point of fact, an unbaptized person, and hence could not consistently preach a baptism to others of which he had never been a subject himself. As these points were for some time matters of anxious inquiry, he frequently conversed upon them with his wife, who also became much interested in them, and finally came to the same conclusions with himself." [1]

Having reached this point, he determined to make known his convictions to his father, and accordingly went to see Thomas Campbell:

> Soon after arriving, his sister Dorothea took him aside and told him that she had been in great trouble for some time about her baptism. She could find, she said, no authority whatever for infant baptism, and could not resist the conviction that she never had been scripturally baptized. She wished him therefore to represent the case on her behalf to her father. At this unexpected announcement Alexander Campbell smiled, and told her that he was now upon his way to request the services of Mr. Luce, as he had himself determined to be immersed, and would lay the whole case before their father.

Accordingly, on the 12th day of June, 1812, Alexander Campbell and his wife were baptized by

---

[1] Richardson, Vol. I., p. 395.

the Rev. Matthias Luce, a Baptist minister. At the same time his father and mother, his sister, and two other persons were baptized; but not until after they set out for the place where the ceremony was to be performed did Alexander Campbell know that his father and mother had decided also to be baptized, so little concert of action was there in this entire matter. The members of the Campbell family arrived at their convictions with entire independence, and were mutually surprised when they discovered each other's views. These circumstances, as related by Mr. Richardson, cannot be questioned. He was the chosen biographer of Mr. Campbell, and at his disposal all the manuscripts in the family were placed. He was familiar with much of Mr. Campbell's life personally, and derived other facts from conversation with him and with members of his family. We have our choice between two alternatives: Either Professor Richardson has deliberately fabricated this whole story, or the Campbells were influenced solely by such a change of conviction, due to the study of the Scriptures, as led men like Alexander Carson and Adoniram Judson to forsake former relations and obey Christ in baptism.

At the next meeting of the Brush Run Church thirteen other members requested baptism, which was administered by Thomas Campbell, and in a short time the great majority of the church consisted of baptized believers, and the rest soon after withdrew.[1] At the time they were baptized the Campbells "had no idea of uniting with the Baptists more than with the Moravians or the mere Independents.[2] The Baptist churches of that region had mostly adopted the Philadelphia Confession as a bond of union, and the Brush Run Church was violently opposed to all such creeds. Moreover, the Baptist ministers of the time were mostly uneducated, and the Campbells believed them to be narrow and illiberal. Nevertheless, when the news spread, as it did very rapidly, of the action of the Brush Run Church, they were naturally regarded as Baptists in all but the name, and the suggestion was often made that the church unite with the Redstone Association. The matter was formally laid before the church in the fall of 1813, and after much discussion it was determined to apply to the Association for admission, with a full statement of their views. This statement filled eight or ten large pages, and made known fully the objections of the Brush Run Church to all human creeds as bonds of union or communion, but expressed a willingness to co-operate with the Association, provided they should be allowed to teach and preach whatever they learned from the Scriptures. A considerable majority favored their reception on these terms, and accordingly the Campbells and their church became members of

---

[1] Richardson, Vol. I., p. 403.
[2] Alexander Campbell's own words in 1848, "Millennial Harbinger," Series 3, Vol. V., p. 344.

the Baptist denomination.[1] Thomas Campbell approved this step much more warmly than his son.

From the first, however, there was a party in the Association opposed to the Campbells and the Brush Run Church. Undoubtedly there were differences between them and the Baptist churches of that day and region. From all accounts it appears certain that the Baptists of this region were strongly tinged with hyper-Calvinism, and the preaching of their ministers was more doctrinal than practical. The Campbells were as evidently what was in those days called Arminian; they believed in a universal atonement, and in their appeals to the unconverted gave the free will of man a greater importance in conversion than was welcome to the Calvinists. It was not long before charges of heresy were made, especially against Alexander Campbell, who was by this time the acknowledged head of the new movement, to which the name of a Reformation already began to be given. Much fuel was added to this fire by Mr. Campbell's preaching of his famous "Sermon on the Law," at the meeting of the Redstone Association in 1816. At this day it is difficult in the extreme to understand why this discourse should have aroused such a furore.[2] It seems orthodox to the point of truism and dullness now in its affirmations of the relation of the law to the

---

[1] "Millennial Harbinger," Series 3, Vol. V., pp. 346, 347.
[2] The complete text may be found in the "Millennial Harbinger," for 1846, p. 493.

gospel. The most unwelcome thing in it at the time was probably the preacher's insistence that there is no necessity for preaching the law in order to prepare men for receiving the gospel. How anybody could read the New Testament with his eyes open and dispute this is a marvel indeed; but it must have been wormwood to his fellow Baptist preachers, for they attempted to secure a protest against its heresy on the spot, but were discouraged by one of their number, shrewder than the others, who said: "That would create too much excitement, and would injure us more than Mr. Campbell. It is better to let it pass, and let the people judge for themselves." [1]

Moved by this constant opposition and accusation of heresy, Alexander Campbell and about thirty others obtained letters of dismission from the Brush Run Church in August, 1823, and constituted a church in Wellsburg; and in September, 1824, the Wellsburg Church was received into the Mahoning Association, of Ohio.[2] The churches composing this body had been members of the Beaver Association, of Pennsylvania, until 1819, when they withdrew and formed a separate organization. Of this Association Mr. Campbell remained a member in good standing until it formally disbanded in 1827, the majority having come to hold that there is no war-

---

[1] Richardson, Vol. I., p. 472.
[2] Mr. Campbell presented a very brief statement of doctrine on this occasion. Richardson, Vol. II., p. 100.

rant in Scripture for such organizations. This action was contrary to the wishes and views of Alexander Campbell, who held that a specific "Thus saith the Lord" is not required in such a case, and that some organization of Christian churches is needed.[1]

In the meantime, however, divergences from Baptist doctrine and sentiment more marked than anything in the "Sermon on Law" had been manifested by Alexander Campbell. In June, 1820 he had a public debate with Rev. John Walker, a Presbyterian minister of the region, on baptism, in the course of which he for the first time mentioned publicly what was to be thenceforth one of his peculiar teachings. "Baptism," said he, "is connected with the promise of the remission of sins and the gift of the Holy Spirit."[2] This is, however, only a passing glance, but interesting as showing the tendency of his thinking. In August, 1823, he began the publication of the "Christian Baptist," a newspaper whose sole object was avowed to be "the eviction of truth and the exposing of error in doctrine and practice." Before this he had complained of the persecutions he had received from the clergy; he now carried the war into Africa on a large scale. No polemic literature in this country has surpassed, if it has equaled, the issues of the "Christian Baptist" in sarcasm, bitterness, and unrelenting severity of attack upon the chief existing religious institutions and methods. Campbell included in

---
[1] Tyler, p. 71.   [2] Richardson, Vol. II., 20.

one sweeping condemnation the building of costly churches, the use of organs, the selling or renting of pews, "missionary wheels" and other forms of church gambling, Sunday-schools, missionary societies, education societies, Bible societies. The violence of his language is so absurd that one is at a loss how so sane-minded a man could have used it, or why it was not received as the ravings of a madman. That both he and his hearers treated the whole matter with tremendous seriousness shows how utterly destitute of a sense of humor they all must have been.

At the same time, Campbell had not broken with Baptists, and was still in some sort regarded as not only one of them, but a champion of their peculiar tenets. In October, 1823, he engaged in another debate with the Rev. W. L. McCalla, a Presbyterian minister of Kentucky, and a man of much higher standing in his denomination than Mr. Walker. The whole question of the subjects, "mode," and design of baptism, was thoroughly gone over by these doughty champions; and it appeared that Campbell's views regarding the design of baptism had been decidedly developed. He now said: "Now, we confess that the blood of Jesus Christ alone cleanses us who believe from all sins. Even this, however, is a metaphorical expression. The efficacy of his blood springs from his own dignity and from the appointment of his Father. The blood of Christ, then, really cleanses us who believe from all sin. Behold the goodness of God in giving us a formal token of it, by ordaining a baptism expressly 'for the remission of sins.' The water of baptism, then, formally washes away our sins. The blood of Christ really washes away our sins. Paul's sins were really pardoned when he believed, yet he had no solemn pledge of the fact, no formal acquittal, no formal purgation of his sins until he washed them away in the water of baptism. To every believer, therefore, baptism is a *formal* and *personal remission*, or purgation of sins. The believer never has his sins formally washed away or remitted until he is baptized."[1] There is nothing in this that is really beyond the limits of Baptist orthodoxy; if we believe that "baptism unto remission of sins" means anything in the New Testament, we can hardly attribute less than this to it. There is here not the slightest trace of baptismal regeneration; on the contrary, baptism is made to show forth in form what has already been accomplished in reality, which is and always has been Baptist doctrine regarding the ordinance. Nevertheless, it requires but a single step forward to land one who thus teaches in baptismal regeneration.

It was not Alexander Campbell, however, who first took the step in the new Reformation that really separated it from the Baptists. This was

---

[1] "Debate with McCalla," quoted by Richardson, Vol. II., p. 82. Italics Campbell's own.

done by the Rev. Walter Scott. He had been a teacher in Pittsburg, and at the time Campbell made his acquaintance was delivering weekly lectures to a little church in that town composed of baptized believers, but not in union with the First Baptist Church of Pittsburg, of which the Rev. Sidney Rigdon was then the pastor. Mr. Scott was not an ordained minister, but he soon became a preacher of the new Reformation and he carried Mr. Campbell's teaching regarding the design of baptism into practical effect. During the course of some meetings that he was holding with churches of the Mahoning Association in November, 1827, in one of his discourses he taught that in the beginning of Christianity believers were immediately baptized into the name and into the death of Christ, receiving in this symbolic act the remission of sins and the promised Holy Ghost. His hearers, we are told, were charmed with such a novel view of the simplicity and completeness of the gospel, but most of them doubted whether the teaching could be true. When he closed his sermon with an exhortation inviting any present to come forward and be baptized for the remission of sins, a stranger who had entered toward the close of the discourse accepted the invitation. Mr. Scott was nonplussed for the moment, but, on questioning the man found him intelligent and seeing no reason for delay, baptized him in the presence of a large concourse for the remission of sins. This was the eighteenth of November, 1823. The matter caused a great excitement and discussion. Mr. Campbell himself was inclined to fear that Mr. Scott had been precipitant and indiscreet and might be the means of injuring the cause. Thomas Campbell accordingly went to examine the progress of affairs, and upon hearing Mr. Scott's preaching and witnessing his method of receiving and baptizing converts, he saw at once that what he and his son Alexander had plainly taught was now reduced to practice and that the simple primitive method of administering the gospel (as they conceived it) was really restored.[1]

From this time onward the Reformation took a new turn. The new doctrine and practice regarding baptism was discussed by the Baptists of the region and discussed only to be rejected. It seemed to Baptists then, as it seems to them still, that to reduce faith to the mere assent of the intellect to the teachings of the gospel regarding Christ is to nullify the gospel; that to baptize people, even on their personal confession of faith, without any evidence whatever of regeneration, is to introduce unregenerate persons into the church, to protest against which is the one thing for which Baptists have existed from the first. Or, taking the other horn of the dilemma, if regeneration is supposed to be accomplished in the act of baptism, the regenerate character of the church is saved only at the ex-

[1] Richardson, Vol. II., pp. 209-220.

pense of asserting a doctrine regarding sacramental grace which is the essence of Romanism. Accordingly, strong opposition was manifested among Baptists from the first to these teachings and practices. The Mahoning Association was indeed deeply permeated by the teaching of the new Reformation, and practically followed Messrs. Campbell and Scott in a body. The Redstone Association in 1827 withdrew fellowship from the followers of Alexander Campbell, and in 1829 the Beaver Association issued a circular in which they denounced the Mahoning Association and Mr. Campbell as " disbelieving and denying many of the doctrines of the Holy Scripture," giving a list of the alleged heresies. This document, which is usually known in Disciple literature as " The Beaver Anathema," was diligently circulated and roused many other Associations to take similar action.

In the autumn of 1832 the Dover Association, of Virginia, after careful deliberation, advised the churches constituting it "to separate from their communion all such persons as are promoting controversy and discord under the specious name of ' Reformers ' ! " They did so on the avowed ground that the doctrines taught were " not according to godliness, but subversive of the true spirit of the Gospel of Jesus Christ; disorganizing and demoralizing in their tendency, and therefore ought to be disavowed and resisted by all the lovers of truth and sound piety." Twenty years after, the Rev.

Jeremiah B. Jeter, one of the committee that presented this report to the Dover Association, and largely instrumental in procuring its adoption, frankly admitted that it contained " some unguarded and unnecessarily harsh expressions," and he particularly acknowledged that this representation of the doctrines of Campbell as "demoralizing in their tendency" was unjust.

From this time on the new Reformation assumed all the characteristics of a sect or denomination, adding one more instructive instance to the large number existing, of men who have set out to secure a union of all Christian sects and have ended by adding another to the number. The further history of the Disciples of Christ, as the followers of Alexander Campbell came generally to be called, does not belong to the subject of this volume.

Although the new body originated in Western Pennsylvania it failed to obtain a strong foothold there, and has never shown much ability to extend its influence and numbers eastward. Its principal success has been in the West and Southwest, where the Baptist churches of the time held to hyper-Calvinistic, almost Antinomian theology, and the preachers seemed to think that they were called to the ministry for no other purpose than to proclaim and vindicate a few abstruse and barren points of the Calvinistic creed. Naturally such preaching was not acceptable to the people at large, and they were ready to listen to any minister whose preaching was more juicy and practical. Moreover, in these regions, since the Great Awakening and the emotional disturbances that had attended its progress through the central South, undue importance was attached to the emotional elements in religion, and to the relation of a Christian experience approaching the miraculous before a candidate was accepted for baptism. The Baptist churches had lost sight of the fact that the only thing to be required as a prerequisite to baptism and reception into the church, according to the New Testament standard, is evidence of regeneration, not the experience of certain emotions. The only value attaching to the emotions is that, in some cases, they are presumptive evidence of that change known as the new birth. The Disciple movement was a reaction from these abuses. Its Calvinism was of the mildest type, if indeed it were not more properly Arminian in its theology; and by utterly rejecting the narration of marvelous experience as a prerequisite to baptism, and substituting for this a mere confession of faith in Christ, the Disciples made the way easy for many to enter the church who had remained out of it through disgust with the exaggerated requirements common among the Baptist churches of that day. In the Eastern communities, where a more evangelical type of doctrine prevailed, and where the practice conformed more closely to the New Testament order, the new Reformation made little or no progress. Almost no impression was made upon the churches of New York and Pennsylvania, except in a few isolated cases, but in the South it is not too much to say that the denomination was rent in twain and its growth retarded for a generation.

Another controversy that had more disastrous results upon the churches of the Middle States affords a fruitful study to those who are interested in the rise and progress of an enthusiasm. The history of the Anti-Masonry excitement is a fine instance of the power of mental contagion. In 1826, one William Morgan, a bricklayer by trade, who lived at Batavia, N. Y., wrote a book purporting to expose the secrets of Free Masonry. The Masons of his neighborhood discovered what he had done and attempted to secure the manuscript. They failed, for the book was actually published, and pamphlet copies of it may be bought now. Morgan was arrested on a frivolous charge, and when released was seized by masked men, placed in a carriage and taken to Fort Niagara, from which time no certain trace of him was ever found. A few days later a body was discovered floating in the river, which many positively identified as the body of Morgan, but the identification was disputed and very likely was wrong. Great excitement followed this event, as Morgan was believed to have been foully murdered by members of this secret order. The real facts were never disclosed. They soon became so entangled and intermixed with political and religious passion that no court could have sifted them and discovered the truth. Some of the officials were lax and indifferent in the discharge of their duty to discover and punish the perpetrators of this outrage, hence many inferred that a Mason was not a fit man to be entrusted with public duties.

The politicians attempted to suppress the agitation, but they underestimated its power. It gradually took the form of a crusade against all secret and oath-bound societies. When the politicians found that they could not crush the movement, they attempted to turn it to their advantage and to a considerable extent succeeded. At first the Masonic question became an issue in a few local contests, many citizens having resolved that they would not vote for any candidate for a public office who was a Mason. From this, an organization of Anti-Masons was quickly developed and conventions were held and candidates formally nominated. It is astonishing to find how many able men were drawn into this movement. Such men as William Wirt, John Quincy Adams, William H. Seward, Joseph Story, became leaders in the movement, which reached its culmination when, in the Jackson–Clay campaign of 1831, Mr. Adams could seriously write as he did in his diary: "The dissolution of the Masonic institution in the United States I believe to be really more important to us and our posterity than the question whether Mr. Clay or General Jackson shall be chosen president at the next election."

As the Anti-Mason movement began in New York, that continued to be its stronghold, but it also spread through Pennsylvania and had a large following in Ohio, Connecticut, Massachusetts, and Vermont. In the States named it nominated candidates for governor; in 1831 it nominated William Wirt for President, and he actually recived the electoral vote of the State of Vermont. In the next presidential election the Anti-Masons did not nominate a candidate, but, as the event showed, their strength was enough in the State of New York to secure the election of Van Buren. From this time on the political power of the organization died out as rapidly as it had grown.

If the political excitement or agitation caused by the Anti-Masonic crusade had been all, there would have been no occasion for mentioning the matter here; but there was unfortunately an accompanying agitation in social and religious circles. The excitement among the people could not be allayed by simply carrying the question into politics. It was discussed everywhere, including all gatherings of religious people.[1] It became with many the article of a standing or falling church. The Baptist churches were no exception to the rule. Sentiment among the Baptists was by no means uniform on the question. While probably a majority of them were more or less opposed to all secret societies, there were many who were by no means in favor of mak-

---

[1] For an amusing instance, see Appendix D.

ing this a question of church membership. Others who saw in Free Masonry deadly sin against God and the rights of man, would be content with nothing less than having it declared unchristian and wicked, and with refusing the hand of fellowship to such as persisted in continuing in alliance with an institution so unholy. The result was that, between the years 1830 and 1845, the Baptist churches in the Middle States, especially in some parts of New York, were greatly harassed and troubled by the continual discussion of this question. Some churches refused to continue in fellowship, not merely with actual Free Masons, but with any who would not vehemently denounce Masonry as an anti-scriptural institution. Many churches were divided by the question, and the growth of the denomination was seriously interfered with. The lesson of the agitation should be plain to all Baptists.

In the year 1831 considerable interest was aroused among the Baptists in the State of New York by a series of lectures delivered by William Miller. He was born in Pittsfield, Massachusetts, in 1782. He was the son of a Revolutionary soldier and was himself in the American army during the war of 1812, where he rose to the rank of captain. Afterward he was sheriff and justice of the peace. These facts warrant the conclusion that he was a man of some force of character and capacity for leadership among his fellows, but, so far as is known, his educational opportunities were only those afforded by the common school. In early life he was a deist, but somewhere about the year 1818 he was converted and became a member of the Baptist church at Low Hampton, Washington County, N. Y. Immediately after his conversion he became a close student of the Scriptures, but without any knowledge of exegesis or theology, his sole rule of interpretation being the comparison of scripture with scripture. In this comparison he utterly neglected the principles of interpretation now made familiar to us by the science of biblical theology, though little practised then even by scholars. To him the Bible, consisting as it does of sixty-six books, written at varying intervals during a period of more than a thousand years, was one book, originally composed in the English language. God was the author and therefore a word used in a certain sense by the prophet Daniel, for example, must necessarily mean the same thing when used by the Apostle John in the Apocalypse. To interpret the Bible according to his system, all that one needed was a concordance and industry. Mr. Miller possessed both, and therefore believed himself to be a competent exegete. His attention was concentrated upon the prophetic portions of Scripture, especially those relating to the second coming of Christ. His first conclusions he set forth in a series of articles contributed to the "Vermont Telegraph" in 1831, and the following year he gathered these into a pamphlet. In 1838 a more elaborate exposition of his views was published in Troy, N. Y., with the title: "Evidence from Scripture and History of the Second Coming of Christ about the year 1843, exhibited in a course of lectures by William Miller." The eighteen lectures in this book are composed in a better literary form than we might reasonably expect of a man with Miller's antecedents. Perhaps we may attribute their comparative accuracy to the assistance of some more scholarly friend, or to the labors of a faithful proof-reader, but the substance of the book is thoroughly characteristic of the author.

Mr. Miller, as has been intimated, by no means confined his labors to propagating his views through the press. He lectured far and wide through New York and the adjacent New England States, and obtained a large following. His interpretation of prophecy had that shallow plausibility very captivating to untrained minds. He found his starting point in the prophecy of Daniel, from the ninth chapter to the end of the book, and taking as his point of departure the time of the going forth of the decree to build the walls of Jerusalem in troublous times—which according to the received chronology of his time was in B. C. 457—and assuming that the twenty-three hundred days of Daniel meant a similar number of years, by a very simple calculation the end of the world should occur in the year 1843. By a little juggling with Scripture and arithmetic it was easy to find numerous confirmations of this date in the Old Testament and in the New, and with every confirmation of this kind his faith in the accuracy of his prediction was strengthened. Without doubt, Mr. Miller was wholly sincere in believing that he had made a great discovery in the interpretation of Scripture, and that the time of our Lord's second advent was at hand. It is impossible to read his book, with its fervent appeals to the unbelieving and unconverted, without giving him credit for the best of motives ; but no student of Scripture ever furnished a better justification of the poet's familiar lines :

> A little learning is a dangerous thing !
> Drink deep, or taste not the Pierian Spring.

His little learning was dangerous, not merely to Miller himself, but to his converts, who soon became very numerous. In 1838 the Rev. Josiah Litch, a minister of the Methodist Episcopal Church in Lowell, Mass., became a convert to Mr. Miller's views and likewise began to lecture and publish pamphlets. At Exeter, N. H., Mr. Miller, on one of his lecture tours, met the Rev. J. V. Hines, of the Christian Connection, pastor of a church of that order in Boston. He not only became a convert but invited Miller to preach in his pulpit. A revised edition of the lectures was issued about the close of 1839, and it is said that five thousand copies were sold in a few weeks. Other ministers and laymen of greater or less prominence accepted the new doctrine, and the believers in Christ's second advent began to exhibit the first signs of organizing themselves into a separate sect. In October, 1840, a conference of them was held in Boston and other conferences followed. In the spring of 1842 Mr. Miller and Mr. Hines, who had now become his chief coadjutor, began meetings for the propagation of their belief in Apollo Hall, New York. By this time the excitement had become intense; camp meetings were held in various localities; powerful revivals of religion occurred among the churches. In many of the rural communities the ferment became so violent that the reason of not a few was unbalanced and some became insane.

As the expected consummation of this world drew near the believers in Miller's doctrines showed strong evidences of enthusiasm and fanaticism. Many neglected their business—why should they labor for things that were soon to perish in the great final conflagration? Some sold their property and spent all that they possessed in the propagation of their beliefs. The eyes of all were turned toward the day (April 23, 1843) fixed for the end of the present order. It was even currently reported that many of the saints prepared ascension robes, and on the fatal day donned these and, ascending to the housetops, confidently awaited their translation to the kingdom of Christ. But when the day passed without any convulsion of nature, though their faith had received a considerable shock, the Millerites evolved a theory that would account for their disappointment, namely, that the second coming of Christ would occur at the end of the Jewish year, not at its beginning. Accordingly they fixed a second time for the advent (March 22, 1844), but when the day came it was as calm and bright a spring day as ever shone upon the earth. This time the disappointment was bitter. The leaders of the movement, indeed, kept fixing days from time to time, but faith in their predictions rapidly dwindled, and after a few years the excitement died away in the natural course.

It must not be supposed that the sober-minded Christians of the Middle and New England States were either silent or idle during this time, but to those upon whom this madness had descended they prophesied in vain. Very numerous and very able tracts, sermons, and books were published by orthodox ministers during this period, but they made comparatively little impression. The delusion was like an epidemic, and had to run its course, and finally die out because there was nothing more for it to feed upon. Its effects upon Baptist churches, among which it originally started, were disastrous. Some were completely destroyed by the fanaticism, and scores of others were seriously weakened. Those who did not withdraw from their churches in order to join the new sect were greatly disturbed; and in numerous cases, after the final disappointment, those who had been converts to Millerism lost all faith in the Scriptures and in every form of religion, and lapsed into blank infidelity. For years the spiritual condition of some parts of the State of New York was not unlike that of a prairie after it has been swept by fire. All was blackness and desolation and death.

This period of storm and stress cannot be dismissed without a brief sketch of another controversy, though it affected the Middle States less than other parts of the country—the conflict that led to the final separation between the " Primitive " or " Old School " Baptists and their more progressive brethren. There had always been two parties among the American Baptists, one of which inclined to an extreme form of Calvinism. We have already seen that this difference in theology led to divisions, in Virginia and elsewhere, some of which had been apparently healed. But the two were not agreed and therefore could not walk together. As the greater part of the Baptist churches lengthened their cords and strengthened their stakes, engaging in missionary operations both domestic and foreign, establishing Sunday-schools, founding educational institutions, assisting in the organization of Bible societies, and the like, a small but stubborn minority protested with great vigor against these things. The ground of their objection was their conviction that this policy of the majority involved the substitution of human instrumentalities for the Spirit of God as the agency for the conversion of men.

Many of the oldest churches and some of the oldest Associations in the Middle States were carried away by this opposition to what they called " the works of man," and the crisis was reached in September, 1835, when the Chemung Association, then composed of eight churches in both Pennsylvania and New York,[1] passed the following:

WHEREAS, A number of the Associations with whom we have held correspondence, have departed from the simplicity of the doctrine and practice of the Gospel of Christ, and have followed cunningly devised fables (the inventions of men), uniting themselves with the world, in what are falsely called benevolent societies founded upon a moneyed base, with a profession to spread the Gospel, which is another Gospel differing for [*sic*, but evidently a misprint for "from"] the Gospel of Christ.

Resolved, Therefore, that we discontinue our correspondence with the Phila., Abingdon, Bridgwater, Franklin, Madison, Steuben, and all other associations, which are supporting the popular institutions of the day; and most affectionately invite all those Churches, or members of Churches among them, who cannot fellowship them, to come out from among them and leave them.

In May of the following year the Baltimore Association passed a similar resolution; from this time, therefore, the separation between the two par-

---

[1] Twenty-four of the churches that formerly composed this body had withdrawn and formed the Canisteo River Association in New York and the Bradford in Pennsylvania. This was the action of a "rump" only.

ties became rapid and was soon complete. The Old School churches were not long content with issuing affectionate invitations; they adopted rules, and embodied them in some cases in the constitutions of their Associations, that if any of their members should unite with any society for the spread of the gospel or the promotion of reform, such members should *ipso facto* be expelled from their membership and communion. These prohibitions not infrequently extended to the making of any contribution to such societies—an interference with the private rights of members that one would have supposed any Baptist would be prompt to resent as intolerable. That any were willing to take such a yoke on their necks is the best witness to the strength of the party spirit underlying this action of the Old School churches.[1]

It has been common to represent the Old School Baptists as having rapidly declined since that date. As regards the Middle States, this appears to be markedly true. Few of their churches have become wholly extinct, but most of them have sadly decreased in numbers and influence. Even where there has been little actual decrease in members, there has been relative loss, by reason of the failure

---

[1] A circular issued by the Warwick Association in 1840 is a good example of the violence of language indulged in during this controversy. It alleges that God carries on his own work "without the least instrumentality whatever," and that "all the preaching from John the Baptist until now, if made to bear on one unregenerate sinner, could no more quicken his poor dead soul than so much chattering of a crane or of a swallow."

of the church to keep pace with the growth of the community and adjoining churches. As regards the United States it may be questioned whether the Old School Baptists have not increased. The "Baptist Almanac" of 1844 assigned them sixty-one thousand one hundred and sixty-two members. Doubtless these figures were incomplete, but they must have been approximately correct; and in 1890 they had, according to the official figures of the census, one hundred and twenty-one thousand three hundred and forty-seven members.[1] In any case, however, their growth has been relatively slow, and they are an insignificant body compared with those from whom they separated a half-century ago.[2]

---

[1] In the Middle States, according to the last census, the strength of the Old School Baptists is as follows: New York, 31 churches, 1,019 members; New Jersey, 4 churches, 258 members; Pennsylvania, 15 churches, 314 members; Delaware, 6 churches, 183 members; total, 56 churches, 1,774 members.

[2] There are now five Old School Associations in the Middle States: the Warwick and Lexington (formed in 1825) in New York; the Chemung and Delaware River in Pennsylvania (the latter also embracing churches in New Jersey), and the Delaware. Every one of these Associations, without exception, was for some years a hearty supporter of Sunday-schools, missions, and the other enterprises against which they afterward inveighed so loudly. There were probably among them from the first those who opposed these things as "innovations," but their opposition was not prominent for a decade or two. It gradually gained strength and finally carried all before it. (See Hassell, "History of the Church of God," especially of the Kehukee Association, Chap. XXI. Middletown, N. Y., 1886.)

CHAPTER VIII

BAPTISTS AND EDUCATION

THE Baptists of the Middle States were the pioneers of the denomination in the cause of education. They were not a unit in this, however, for not a few among them doubted both the scripturalness and the expediency of educating the ministry; and it was to train the rising ministry that educational institutions of a higher grade than the district school were established by Baptists. Opposition to higher education was mainly confined to the older and less intelligent men; there was a thirst for learning among the young men who felt themselves called to preach the gospel. Morgan Edwards met such frequently, and specially commends in New Jersey "one of those lay ministers who think they may be wiser than they are already, or than ordination, and *reverend Sirs*, have made them." "Were I twenty years younger," he adds, "I would make another tour into Europe to try at raising a fund for the sake of giving learning to such."[1]

It was doubtless a knowledge of this desire that

---

[1] "Materials," Vol. I., p. 19.

led the Rev. Isaac Eaton to establish the first school "for the education of youth for the ministry" at Hopewell, N. J., where he was then pastor. This school, which was of what we should now call academic grade, began its sessions in a modest wooden structure in that town in the year 1756, and continued its work for eleven years. Though it was intended primarily for the education of ministers, and among its first graduates were such men as James Manning and Hezekiah Smith, others were by no means shut out.[1] A large part of the pupils engaged in secular callings, but almost without exception they were men of exemplary piety, and many of them were most useful as teachers or became Baptist pioneers in other States. The Philadelphia Association early gave countenance and support to this school, raising toward its support a fund of four hundred pounds, which was mostly lost through the fluctuations of the Continental money. Mr. Eaton's natural endowments and scholarly attainments well fitted him for this work, which might have been far more successful had the financial support of the academy been equal to the excellence of its training. The work that he was unable to continue was taken up and carried on by his gifted pupil, James Manning, whose conversion

---

[1] John Gano, a native of Hopewell, and a member of the Baptist church there, on yielding to a long-resisted call to the ministry received some instruction from Mr. Eaton, his pastor, but he was not a student of the academy, for the very good reason that Mr. Eaton had not yet established it.

occurred at the school and is largely ascribed to the influence of his teacher.

While the school continued, the worth of its work so generally commended itself as to raise the question whether it were not expedient for Baptists to establish a school of still higher grade, in short a college. Manning, Smith, and others received a collegiate education at the College of New Jersey (Princeton), but this was practicable only in a few cases, and, besides, this was an institution strongly tinctured with Presbyterian principles. It is said that the friends of the Hopewell Academy were the prime movers in the matter; certain it is that Dr. Samuel Jones, an early graduate, was one of the chief advocates of the new college. At its meeting in 1762, the Philadelphia Association took the first step forward in this enterprise, by far the greatest and the most far-reaching in its consequences that American Baptists had yet undertaken. There were serious if not insuperable difficulties in obtaining a charter for a Baptist institution from any of the Middle States, but the Association had now "obtained such an acquaintance with the affairs of Rhode Island as to bring themselves to an apprehension that it was practicable and expedient to erect a college in the colony of Rhode Island, under the chief direction of the Baptists, in which education might be promoted and superior learning obtained, free from any sectarian tests."[1] To Morgan Ed-

---
[1] Backus, Vol. II., p. 137.

wards and Samuel Jones the practical conduct of the preliminary business was committed. Both were active and useful, Edwards pre-eminently so.

From 1764 onward we find frequent entries in the Minutes of the Association that testify to the warmth and constancy of its interest in this project. In that year it was voted to ask liberal contributions from the churches for the establishment of the college; in 1767 the churches were requested to forward their subscriptions. In 1774 the Association approved the plan already adopted by the Charlestown and Warren Associations, of requesting every Baptist to pay sixpence annually for three successive years, to their elder or some suitable person, the money to be paid to the treasurer of the college. This plan was to encourage systematic giving for education on the part of the poorer people, in addition to larger sums that might be subscribed by those well to do.

The Rev. James Manning drew up a plan for a college, and presented it to a company of New England Baptists at Newport, in July, 1763. It was approved, and a committee was appointed to prepare a charter for legislative enactment, corresponding to Manning's plan and giving that legal effect. In the drafting of the charter, aid was asked of the Rev. Ezra Stiles, afterward president of Yale College, the committee pleading unskillfulness in an affair of this kind. The charter when presented to the legislature was found to contain provisions that practically vested the control in the Fellows rather than in the trustees; and though nineteen of the thirty-five trustees were to be Baptists (a bare majority), eight of the twelve Fellows were to be Congregationalists, and the other four might be, for all that was said in the charter as drawn.[1]

Fortunately, this was discovered in time, and the charter as finally passed, in February, 1764, made the number of trustees thirty-six, of whom twenty-two were always to be Baptists, five Quakers, four Congregationalists, and five Episcopalians. Eight of the twelve Fellows were to be Baptists, and the other four "indifferently of any or all denominations." It was also provided that the president should always be a Baptist, but that all other positions in the faculty should be open for all denominations of Protestants. It was distinctly specified that no religious tests should ever be introduced; that the youth of all religious denominations should be fully and equally admitted to all advantages, emoluments, and honors; and that sectarian differences, though they might be studied and explained, should make no part of the public instruction.

This charter secured absolute control of the institution to Baptists, but also made it absolutely unsectarian from the outset. No instance of similar liberality can be named among the early educational institutions of America, and to this day the college

---

[1] For the full history of this discreditable episode, see Guild's "Manning and Brown University," Chap. I.

thus founded is unsurpassed in true catholicity and genuine liberality. In all this the Baptists of America were a unit, and they of the Philadelphia Association were chiefly instrumental in the founding of the first Baptist college in the world. From this time onward the history of Rhode Island College—after 1804 called Brown University in honor of its generous benefactor, Nicholas Brown—belongs, of course, to New England rather than to the Middle States, though the Philadelphia Association for many years was most active in the efforts for its endowment, and has never ceased to take a peculiar interest in its welfare. The War of the Revolution and the long occupation of Philadelphia by the British, necessarily interrupted this practical co-operation with the Rhode Island institution, and it seems never to have been fully resumed after peace was proclaimed. By that time the college had struck its roots into the soil of New England, and influential friends were springing up about it.

For a half-century the Baptists of the Middle States took no further step forward in the cause of education. A number of private academies, similar to the Hopewell institution, were indeed established[1] and rendered service by no means to be despised, but this was all. In the early part of the present century, however, there was a general revi-

[1] Benedict mentions that of Dr. Jones, at Lower Dublin, 1766-1794, Dr. Stanford's, in New York City, Dr. Burgess Allison's, in Bordentown, N. J., and Rev. Stephen S. Nelson's, at Mount Pleasant, N. Y.

val of interest in higher education throughout the United States, and particularly in theological education. Within a single decade seven institutions [1] for the education of ministers were founded; of the seven three were Baptist and two of the three owed their origin to the Baptists of the Middle States.

The first manifestation among Baptists of this renewed interest in education was the formation of education societies. In this the Baptists of the Middle States, and especially of the Philadelphia district, were in the van. In 1812 was organized The Baptist Education Society of the Middle States, the second article of whose constitution said: "Its avowed and explicit object is, with a divine blessing, the assisting of pious men in obtaining such literary and theological aid as shall enable them, with greater ease to themselves and usefulness to the churches, to fulfill the public duties of the Christian ministry." A similar society, called the Massachusetts Baptist Education Society, was formed in Boston in 1814; in 1816 an Education Society was formed in the Warren Association; in 1817 the New York Baptist Education Society was

---

[1] The seven institutions were: Andover Theological Seminary, 1808; the Seminary of the Reformed Church, New Brunswick, N. J., 1810; the Princeton Theological Seminary, 1812; the Theological Seminary (Congregational) at Bangor, Me., 1814; the Maine Literary and Theological Institution, 1813; the Columbian University (which really dates from 1807, but was not chartered until 1821); and the Hamilton Literary and Theological Institution, whose history begins with 1817, though it was not formally opened till 1820.

formed at Hamilton and in the same year was organized the Baptist Society in South Carolina and Georgia, for the Education of Pious Young Men Designed for the Ministry, and in 1819 the Baptists of Maine established an Education Society. Thus it will be seen that while the Baptists of the Middle States were the leaders in this new phase of denominational activity, their priority was of no long standing; the movement was general and almost simultaneous.

The establishment of a new institution did not invariably follow the organization of an education society, though such was the result in the majority of instances. Both the Middle State societies found that to be the logical result of their attempt to educate their students for the ministry. As early as 1807 Dr. Wm. Staughton had begun to receive such students into his household. He was a native of England (born in 1770), was baptized at the age of seventeen, and was graduated from Bristol College about 1792. Feeling strongly drawn to America, he soon after left England and became pastor of a Baptist church in Georgetown, S. C. Coming North, he labored in various places, until in 1805 he became pastor of the First Church, Philadelphia, from which in 1811 he led forth the colony that became the Sansom Street Church. He had some experience as a teacher before coming to Philadelphia, particularly at Bordentown, N. J., and felt himself called to this work. His fitness for it was recognized by his brethren, and when the time came to choose the head of an educational institution their minds turned naturally toward him. After the formation of the Baptist Education Society of the Middle States, Dr. Staughton was formally appointed tutor, and a small class of theological students was begun in his house.[1] This was felt to be an inadequate provision, but the society was poor and nothing better seemed possible at the time. It seems evident, however, that from the first the men who were active in this society had in mind the establishment of a permanent theological school, on a scale commensurate with the importance of the work. Baptists of New York City cordially coöperated in this society, among its first trustees being the Rev. Messrs. John Williams, Archibald Maclay, and John Stanford—the latter of whom had a private school in New York at which not a few students for the ministry then and afterward were trained. Two of the first students in the Philadelphia school were nominated by the Baptists of New York, who in the first year of its work raised upward of seven hundred dollars for it.[1] One of these students was Charles G. Sommers, afterward a useful and honored pastor in New York for many years. A regular course of studies, including classical, biblical, and theological branches,

---

[1] Lynd, "Memoir of the Rev. William Staughton, D. D.," Boston, 1834, p. 160, seq.

[1] "Minutes" of the society, Philadelphia, 1813, p. 9.

was planned for the school, and so far as appears, was faithfully carried out.[1]

The real work of establishing another institution of higher grade was done by the Baptist General Convention. During his tours about the country, both prior and subsequent to the Convention's organization, the Rev. Luther Rice had his attention painfully called to the need of higher culture in the Baptist ministry, and the cause of advanced literary and theological training assumed in his mind and heart a place side by side with that of foreign missions. His view was evidently shared by the men who shaped the Convention's policy, for its first form of constitution, while it said nothing specifically about education, contained this very plain hint of a future policy, when among the duties imposed on the Board were to "employ missionaries, and, if necessary, to take measures for the improvement of their qualifications." The first address to the churches of the new Convention also laid great stress on the education of pious youth called to the ministry, and the need of "a general theological seminary, where some, at least, might obtain all the benefit of learning and mature studies." Though it was this very sense of need that led to the founding of Brown University, theological instruction had been carefully excluded by the charter from the

---

[1] Thinking this curriculum of the first Baptist theological school may be of some interest to present-day Baptists, I have placed it in Appendix A.

curriculum of that institution. Baptist youth could now obtain a college training under Baptist auspices, but there was no provision for distinctively theological training, whether for college graduates or for others.

At the second meeting, in 1817, the Convention authorized the Board, "when funds of a sufficient amount should have been contributed for this purpose, to institute a classical and theological seminary." The Baptist Education Society of the Middle States having once and again offered its co-operation, the Board in the following year elected Dr. Staughton principal of the proposed institution, and the Rev. Irah Chase professor of languages and biblical literature. A house was now hired in Philadelphia, and from the autumn of 1818 instruction was given on a larger scale. During the next three years the work was continued in this way, at the end of which time eleven students had completed creditably a course of instruction and were dismissed as having been graduated. In the meantime, Mr. Rice and some others had obtained a plot of land in Washington, which they offered to the Convention as the site of the institution. The offer was accepted, and a charter was obtained from Congress in February, 1821, incorporating "the Columbian College in the District of Columbia," with full powers to establish faculties in ordinary classical instruction, law, divinity, and medicine—a university charter in fact, though not in name. Dr. Staughton was elected president, and in consequence, the Philadelphia school was removed the following September to Washington, as the theological department of Columbian College, Professor Chase and eight students constituting the new "department."[1]

No long experience was required, however, to demonstrate that the new school was a failure, so far as the education of the ministry was concerned. The efforts of the friends of the college were concentrated on the other departments, and the theological department languished. Accordingly, when the Newton Theological Institution was established in 1825 by the Massachusetts Baptists, the theological department of Columbian College, with its professor, students, and good-will, was transferred to Newton, Dr. Chase becoming the first president of that institution. Columbian College (now University), however it may have disappointed the expectations of its founders, will remain to all time a monument of the zeal of the Baptists of the Philadelphia Association in the cause of higher education.

The New York Baptist Education Society owed its life mainly to Deacon Samuel Payne, of Hamilton. The farm of Deacon Payne is now the campus of Colgate University, he having thus fulfilled a vow that he made in his earlier days : he felled the first tree in the virgin forest, on that part of the hill where the Colgate Library building now stands, and kneeling down consecrated himself and all that

---

[1] Lynd, "Memoir of Staughton," Chapter IX.

he had to the service of God, particularly promising that this land should be given to his cause. As early as 1816 Daniel Hascall suggested the idea of an institution of higher learning to Nathaniel Kendrick, who visited Hamilton that year, this idea having been suggested to him by an address written by Dr. Jeremiah Chaplin.[1] Seven brethren of kindred thought and purpose came together in Deacon Payne's house, in May, 1817, to converse on this subject, and this led to another meeting, September 24, in Deacon Olmstead's house, where "The Baptist Education Society of the State of New York" was formed.[2] As in the case of the Philadelphia organization, the object of this movement was to provide the churches with a better trained ministry, and the characteristic feature of the constitution was this article: "The object of this Society shall be to afford means of instruction to such persons of the Baptist denomination as shall furnish evidence to the churches of which they are members, and to the Executive Committee hereafter named, of their personal piety and call to the ministry." Members of the Board were required to be members in good standing of some Baptist church.

---

[1] This address was also a chief agency in the founding of Waterville College (Colby University) and the Newton Theological Institution. Rarely has a single address been so fruitful of good as this. "Missionary Jubilee," p. 334.

[2] Thirteen came to this meeting: Daniel Hascall, Nathaniel Kendrick, P. P. Root, John Bostwick, Joel W. Clark, Robert Powell, Jonathan Olmstead, Samuel Payne, Samuel Osgood, Thomas Cox, Elisha Payne, Charles W. Hull, Amos Kingsley.

The new Society began its career with thirteen dollars in the treasury, each of the constituent members paying one dollar, and the expenses during the first year amounted to forty-one dollars and twelve cents, of which twenty-seven dollars and twelve cents was paid to Jonathan Wade, the first beneficiary of the Society.[1] It is said that then there were in the State twenty-eight thousand Baptists, with three hundred churches and two hundred and thirty ministers.[2] That it was the intention of the Society from the first to establish a school of the higher learning may reasonably be inferred, not only from their subsequent action, but from the earliest records. The first annual report of the Executive Committee contains these significant words: "On the twelfth of February, 1818, they convened for the examination of Bro. Jonathan Wade, who exhibited a letter of his membership and liberty to preach from the Baptist church in Hartford, Washington County, N. Y. After examination he was received to the privileges of the institution. Since this time he has been studying under the instruction of Elder Hascall." A literary and theological institution at Hamilton was already begun in fact, if not in name, with one instructor and one student.

At the second annual meeting of the Education

---

[1] And the second student was like unto him, Eugenio Kincaid.
[2] Dr. Eaton's Historical Discourse, in "First Half Century of Madison University," p. 25.

Society, Hamilton was selected from several competitors as the site of the proposed institution, on condition of the payment of six thousand dollars in a specified time and way, which condition was fulfilled. "This gift," said Dr. Eaton in 1869, "was fully equal to sixty thousand dollars now." The Hamilton Literary and Theological Institution was formally opened May 1, 1820, in the third story of a building, of which the first was occupied by the district school, and the second by the Hamilton Academy. Soon the number of students so increased as to make necessary a large separate building, which was completed in 1823; and another still larger building was dedicated in 1827.

Until 1839, the institution was strictly confined to its original purpose of educating students for the ministry; but by that time its friends were convinced that this was too narrow a basis for the conduct of the institution. The resolution passed by the Board in that year allowed the faculty "for the time being, to receive into the collegiate department of the institution a limited number of young men who have not the ministry in view." In spite of this very cautiously worded resolution, it was opposed by Nathaniel Kendrick as an entering wedge to a change in the object and character of the institution. In this it certainly justified his prevision, but Baptists of the present day would be slow to admit that the change has altered for the worse the character of the institution. The education of the laity is quite as important in the thought of Baptists now as the training of the ministry. For a time the graduates of the collegiate department were admitted to the usual degrees by the Columbian College, but this was not a satisfactory arrangement. A regular charter was desired, but this the State was unwilling to grant to a body composed, like the Education Society, of delegates chosen from year to year by churches scattered over the State.[1] The collegiate department was finally chartered as Madison University, in 1846, a majority of the members of the new corporation being taken from the Board of the Education Society. It was thought best to keep the two corporations legally distinct, in order that purely theological education might not be in any wise subjected to the supervision of the State, or be controlled by a secular corporation. Nevertheless, by a special compact between the two Boards, a close connection and sympathetic co-operation was secured. The university bound itself to sustain a course of secular education adapted to the proper training of the Baptist ministry, and to leave theological education exclusively to the Education Society; and upon violation of this agreement the university was subject to a notice to quit within two years.

---

[1] A similar difficulty had previously been experienced in the establishment of the Columbian College, Congress being unwilling to give the General Convention an act of incorporation, because it was a strictly denominational body with a constantly changing membership.

Hardly had these wedded institutions—the Madison University and the Hamilton Theological Seminary—begun their new life when their very existence was threatened by one of the fiercest contests that ever divided the Baptists of the Middle States. To write of this controversy is somewhat like an excursion to the crater of a half-extinct volcano—underneath the apparent quiet are hidden fires, and the molten lava is covered by a very thin crust. The conscientious historian must not be frightened away by these dangers, however, and possibly he may avoid all danger by close adherence to fact. This is the easier for him to do, as looking back on the controversy, he finds it possible to credit both parties to it with equal honesty, sincerity, and disinterestedness. No doubt, in the heat of the conflict, unworthy motives were suspected and imputed on both sides, without adequate reason, but this generation need not repeat that mistake of the fathers.

Not long after the charter was granted to Madison University the question of its removal was agitated. The site of Hamilton had been selected in the early history of the State, when Western New York was a wilderness, and nothing larger than a village was to be found west of the Hudson. At that time it was impossible to foresee the future centers of population. The completion of the Erie Canal in 1825, and the construction shortly afterward of what is now the New York Central Railway System parallel with the Hudson and the Erie Canal, determined the points where the centers of population would be located. The direction thus given to the growth of the State made it reasonably certain that Hamilton would remain for generations a small village in a secluded district of the interior, away from the main lines of travel and therefore difficult of access. Then as now, some Baptists thought a rural community the ideal site for educational institutions, a place where young men may be withdrawn from the rush and distraction and temptations of a city, and give themselves uninterruptedly to their studies. Now as then, some Baptists think a city the better place for the location of a college or university, where the student may study not only books, but men; where he may learn none the less of ancient civilizations, while he is brought into actual contact with a thriving and busy community, and is graduated a scholar indeed, but also to some extent a man of affairs.

Those who held this latter view, about the year 1847, began to agitate the question of the removal of the institutions from Hamilton to a site, as they thought, more favorable for development. At about the same time, the Baptists of Western New York began to consider the propriety of establishing an institution of learning in that part of the State. Rochester speedily became the center of that feeling, and the removal question soon ceased to be a vague sentiment of preference for some more central location and became a definite project for the removal of the two Hamilton institutions to Rochester. A considerable portion of the faculties and Boards of both were enlisted in favor of the new movement, which was expected to place both the college and the seminary in a flourishing city on a great main thoroughfare of the nation and provide them with an ample endowment. The legislature passed an Act in April, 1848, authorizing the trustees to make the transfer, if in their judgment it seemed wise so to do, with a condition, however, that if fifty thousand dollars should be raised by the friends of Hamilton before the following August the removal should not be made.[1] At the anniversary of 1848 a majority of both Boards voted in favor of removal; but it was afterward alleged that the votes were obtained by "extraordinary appliances" that deprived them of all moral force. The legality of subsequent proceedings was disputed and the case was finally carried into the courts.

While the case was pending in the courts an educational convention was held in Albany on October 9, 1849. At this meeting another "compromise" was adopted in these terms: "That the university

[1] This was the result of a compromise between the two parties. The time originally named was June, and the advocates of removal were pledged not to hinder the raising of the money. They held themselves absolved from the pledge by the extension of the time from June to August, and appealed to the Baptists of the State not to tie the hands of the Board by subscribing the required amount. Charges of bad faith were bandied to and fro over this, greatly embittering the contest.

be surrendered to Rochester by the friends of Hamilton, and that the project for a theological department be abandoned by the friends of Rochester." In case the friends of Hamilton declined to accept these terms, it was advised that a college with a theological department be established at Rochester.[1] Whether this advice—for the action of this convention was nothing more—would have been accepted under different circumstances it is useless to speculate; it was completely nullified by the absolute victory in the courts of the opponents of removal. In April, 1850, the Supreme Court perpetually confirmed the preliminary injunction obtained by this party, and so established forever at Hamilton both institutions. Three weeks after this decree (May 10) the Board of Trustees of Madison University met at Rochester, ten being present; and the reorganization of the Board was completed by the resignation of seven "removalists" one after the other, and the election, also one at a time, of seven stanch friends of Hamilton. In the fall, the vacancies made in the faculties by the withdrawal of professors to Rochester, were filled and the term opened with thirty-three students in attendance; before the end of the year they had increased to eighty-four; and at the end of three years the number was two hundred and sixteen, more than at the

---

[1] "The Baptist Register," in its report of the convention, said that this alternative was "so entirely unsupposable" that it hardly attracted a moment's attention. But, of course, the friends of Hamilton at once construed it as a threat.

beginning of the removal agitation. Before the end of the first year sixty thousand dollars was added to the endowment. Those who had opposed removal felt morally bound to demonstrate to the Baptists of the State that nothing had been lost by keeping the institutions at Hamilton, and they made a convincing demonstration indeed.

With the outbreak of the civil war the university in particular experienced a marked decrease of good fortune. At the close of that struggle its property is said to have been worth only sixty-two thousand dollars. This had grown in 1870 to two hundred and twenty-five thousand dollars, and in 1880 to four hundred and thirty thousand dollars. In 1891 Mr. James B. Colgate added to his previous large benefactions a gift of one million dollars, and in grateful recognition of the generosity of this giver and the family of noble Baptists bearing that name, the institution has been named Colgate University. Before this gift his liberality had made possible one of the notable steps forward in the institution's life when, in 1873, the preparatory school, until then maintained in an inefficient way, was firmly established in a handsome building and with sufficient funds, as Colgate Academy.

Perhaps the greatest change of recent years in this institution was that effected in 1893 by a radical reconstruction of the compact between the Boards of university and seminary. By the new compact the actual direction of the affairs of the seminary was made over to the university, so that the administration, instead of being shared by two bodies, is now controlled by one body. The Education Society, however, retains a right of visitation and has an influential part in the election of theological instructors, while it still continues its original work of aiding young men in their preparation for the ministry.

Madison University has been fortunate in its presidents. The first of these was Nathaniel Kendrick, teacher of theology in the institution from its formal opening in 1820, virtually president for many years before his formal election in 1836. He had only an academic education himself and such theological training as he could pick up in the studies of several Baptist ministers, including Drs. Stillman and Baldwin, of Boston. But nature had endowed him with a mind of uncommon capacity, and much thinking and reading had made him the intellectual peer of the best trained men of his time. He towered above his contemporaries in mental power as much as his six feet four inches of physical stature surpassed the average height. His was the guiding mind of those who wished to retain the institutions in their original home; but he died too soon (September 11, 1848), to see the triumph of what he firmly believed to be the righteous cause. The next president, Stephen W. Taylor, elected in 1851, was a graduate of Hamilton College, devoted his life to the profession of teaching, and was connected with different departments of the university for eighteen years. He was an excellent organizer and executive, and when he died in 1856 had left an ineffaceable mark on the institution. In the same year George W. Eaton was chosen as his successor and filled the office until 1868. He was a graduate of Union College, and from 1803 to the time of his death (August 3, 1872), he was connected with the Hamilton institutions. To him and to Drs. Hascall and P. B. Spear was mainly due the retention of the institutions at Hamilton and the subsequent endowment and growth of the university.

Of Ebenezer Dodge, president from 1868 to 1890, it is difficult to speak in fitting words. His life and work are too near us to be seen in their true proportions and significance. He was a graduate of Brown University (1840) and the Newton Theological Institution (1845), and after a pastorate of several years at New London, N. H., became professor of biblical criticism in the seminary at Hamilton. From this time until his death he was an instructor both in the seminary and the university, filling the chairs of evidences of Christianity and metaphysics in the latter, and from 1861 that of Christian theology in the former. From 1871 he was also president of the seminary, and for nineteen years was the head of both institutions, thus continuing and strengthening the traditions of unity in the administration of the two that prevailed from the first and have done so much to make both strong and prosperous. Dr. Dodge wrote comparatively little, and like many of our greatest educators, has left behind no books that will seem to future generations to justify his reputation as a thinker and preacher. His real "works" are the men who came under him, and who owed so much of their mental and moral character to his teaching and personal influence.

The Hamilton institutions were also fortunate in the noble laymen who supported them from the first, devoting "their lives, their fortunes, and their sacred honor" to the upbuilding of both. Deacon Payne has already been mentioned; worthy companion spirits were Deacons Jonathan Olmstead and Seneca B. Burchard. But it is no disparagement of the deeds of others to say that chief among the names of the early benefactors of the institution stands that of William Colgate. From 1823 he was one of the firm friends of Hamilton, equally ready with counsel and purse, and which was of the greater value to the struggling institution it would not be easy to decide. He was one of the sturdy opponents of removal, and an equally sturdy opponent of the permanent endowment of the institutions. He gave liberally from year to year, but believed that the institutions should be kept in close touch with the Baptist churches, and that an endowment, by making them independent of control, would eventually lead to heretical teaching and perhaps to the loss of the institutions to the denomination. Mr. Colgate's greatest gift to Hamilton was his two sons, Samuel and James B. Colgate, who have more than repaired this error of their father, if error it was. The noble library building will ever remain a monument to the wise liberality of the former, and the great collection of historical documents already deposited in it, and constantly increased by the founder's generosity, will be better appreciated by coming generations of Baptists than it seems to be at present.

The story of the founding of the Rochester institutions has already been told in part. There was, prior to 1850, no college in Western New York, in a district as large as the State of Massachusetts, with a population of over half a million, evidently destined to be one of the richest as well as most populous parts of the Empire State. The desire of this section for an educational institution of the first rank was natural, and certain before long to be gratified. The Baptists of Western New York saw their opportunity, and it seemed to them that the most easy and natural solution of the problem was the removal of the institutions at Hamilton to Rochester. Accordingly a "meeting of the friends of Madison University" in that region was held at the First Baptist Church of Rochester, September 12, 1847, and it was decided to be "the sense of this meeting that Madison University be removed to

Rochester." On October 28 following a meeting of citizens of Rochester, without regard to denomination was held; the project was heartily approved, and money was pledged in considerable sums for the endowment of the university. Then ensued the removal controversy, already related with sufficient fullness. After the legal question was decided, and removal was negatived by the courts, those who had favored the removal applied for a charter of a new institution, and the Regents of the University of New York granted a provisional charter to the University of Rochester on January 31, 1850; and on February 14, 1851, the Regents granted a permanent charter, investing the corporation "with all the privileges and powers conceded to any college in this State." Proof had been submitted to the Regents that suitable buildings had been provided for the use of the institution and that one hundred thousand dollars had been raised in valid subscriptions. The charter provided that within five years one hundred thousand dollars must be permanently invested for the benefit of the university to make the charter perpetual.

This charter did not vest the control of the university in the Baptist denomination; it created a "close corporation" of twenty-four members, of whom twenty were Baptists. In the Board, in the faculty, in the recitation rooms, various denominations of Christians have been represented from the first. The distinction between a sectarian and a denominational college was clearly understood by the founders of the institution, and has been faithfully maintained throughout its history. Rochester has been and is a denominational college, under the control of Baptists, who comprise a majority of its trustees and faculty, and thus assure the higher education of youth of Baptist parentage under influences that shall not be hostile to their fathers' faith. In such a college no attempt is made to inculcate directly the distinctive beliefs and practices of the denomination; but all students, of whatever faith, or of no faith, are freely admitted to its privileges on an equal footing with Baptists. This may or may not be the highest ideal of a college—that is a matter where honest difference of opinion may be expected —but it is the ideal of the University of Rochester, as tacitly recognized in its charter, and exemplified in all its history.

At a meeting held September 16, 1850, the trustees organized and appointed the following faculty for the college: Asahel C. Kendrick, Greek language and literature; John F. Richardson, Latin language and literature; John H. Raymond, history and belles lettres; Chester Dewey, natural sciences; Samuel S. Greene, mathematics and natural philosophy. Instruction was begun the following November, and a class of ten was graduated in July, 1851.

A part of the Rochester project from the beginning had been to establish a theological institution as well as a college. In fact, the interest of the Baptists of Western New York was mainly in this part of the plan, though they fully approved the other part. Like their brethren elsewhere, their chief anxiety was for the training of the Baptist ministry, and they desired a college largely if not chiefly that it might be a feeder to and auxiliary of the theological school that they meant to found. In carrying out their plan Rochester Baptists duplicated the organizations at Hamilton. The university obtained a separate charter, as we have just seen. The New York Baptist Union for Ministerial Education was organized, and its Board established the Rochester Theological Seminary, instruction being begun simultaneously with the college, in the same building, and to some extent by the same professors. Thus Dr. John Maginnis was professor of theology in the seminary, and acting professor of intellectual philosophy in the college; and Dr. Thomas J. Conant, professor of Hebrew in the seminary, gave elementary instruction in that language in the college, which at first made this a part of its curriculum. The business affairs of the two institutions were, however, entirely distinct.

They were indeed too entirely distinct. At one point the Rochester founders failed to duplicate the Hamilton plan, and that they failed to do so has had unfortunate consequences ever since. There was a compact between the Board of Madison University and the Education Society that ensured the harmonious co-operation of the two institutions. The necessity of such an arrangement at Rochester seems not to have occurred to the founders; at any rate nothing of the kind was provided for. The result was that differences soon developed; the Boards and faculties of the two institutions could not work comfortably together; instead of harmony and co-operation there has been ever since more or less of friction, distrust, and opposition, some of the time confined to one or two individuals in either institution, at other times threatening to divide the Baptists of Rochester and the friends of both institutions into two hostile camps—a condition of affairs not merely embarrassing but distressing to the large number of men who are alumni of both institutions.

In 1853 presidents were found for both institutions, Martin B. Anderson being chosen as head of the university, and Ezekiel G. Robinson as head of the seminary. Both choices were admirable. Under the leadership of Dr. Anderson the university advanced with a rapidity truly remarkable. He was a great teacher, not so much excelling as a drill-master as in the capacity to rouse and direct students, impelling each man to think, investigate, and judge for himself. He was greatest, however, in the power of giving his students a lasting moral impulsion, a healthful and uplifting direction to their aspirations and ambitions. He regarded it as a great achievement to awaken a sluggish intellect, to spur a lazy will; but he valued still higher the awakening of conscience and the laying of solid foundations of character. The influence of an active mind, a firm will, and a strong character, like his, upon young men at the critical stage in the formation of their characters, was wonderful. It was not merely marked, but lasting. He was almost equally successful as an administrator. A large part of the money raised for buildings and endowment during Dr. Anderson's presidency was raised through his personal efforts and the rest was gained largely through his personal influence. To the public at large he was the university, its living embodiment. His was a personality that would have been marked anywhere. He never failed to impress profoundly even those strangers with whom he came into casual contact, and the better he was known the more impressive his personality became.

The only appropriation ever received by the university from the State was a sum of twenty-five thousand dollars in 1857, conditioned upon the raising of an equal sum by its friends. Gen. John E. Rathbone, of Albany, promptly met this condition by giving twenty-five thousand dollars for a library fund. In 1865 one hundred thousand dollars was added to the endowment. In 1880 two hundred and fifty thousand dollars was added in like manner. The total value of the assets of the university in 1895 was one million two hundred and three thousand and seventy-eight dollars, of which sum five hundred and ninety-seven thousand nine hundred and thirty dollars was in interest-bearing securities. The campus and buildings are estimated to be worth over four hundred thousand dollars. The grounds consist of more than twenty acres in one of the best parts of the city of Rochester, and the buildings are as follows: Anderson Hall, completed in 1861 at a cost of thirty-nine thousand dollars; Sibley Hall, completed in 1877 at a cost of one hundred thousand dollars, borne entirely by the Hon. Hiram Sibley, the sole condition of his gift being that the library of the university should be housed in it and be open to the citizens of Rochester as a free reading library; the president's house, purchased with funds subscribed by the citizens of Rochester in 1868, and valued at forty-eight thousand dollars. The Reynolds Memorial Laboratory was built by Mortimer F. Reynolds, Esq., at a cost of fifty thousand dollars.

A year before his death Dr. Anderson retired from the presidency, and at his nomination David J. Hill was elected president.[1] Under his administration the university made marked advances. A scientific department was established, enlarged, and improved. The old catalogues used to contain a statement to the effect that when their studies coincided the scientific students recited with the classical; while the boys had a witticism to the effect that "when the studies do not coin-

---

[1] Dr. Hill resigned in 1896, and as this volume goes to press the university has no president.

cide the scientific students do not recite." This fairly expressed the state of the case. The scientific course was then a title; it is now a reality. The chemical laboratory is not exceeded for convenience and completeness of appointment by any in the country, and an excellent biological laboratory has been established in recent years in which practical training in the methods of modern biological resorts is given by a competent instructor. The Ward cabinets that early became the property of the university by the generosity of the citizens of Rochester, are unexcelled for their purpose by any collection of the kind in the country. The specimens are excellently adapted for practical demonstration in the geological course, and while their value was largely theoretical in years past, it has in these later years come to be actual. The whole number of students graduated from the University of Rochester up to and including the commencement of 1894 is one thousand one hundred and twenty-two. Of these students a very large proportion are men distinguished for their high character and the attainments they have made in their callings. Few even of the more famous institutions can show in their roll of alumni so large a proportion of men who have made their mark in the world as can the University of Rochester.

Dr. Robinson was equally successful as a teacher and administrator in the theological seminary. His personality was not less striking than Dr. Anderson's. Tall and lithe, with a face almost Grecian in the delicacy of its outlines and quite Roman in its strength, he was a man whom one could not pass in the crowd without looking back at him. His power as a stimulating teacher has probably never been excelled. He hated shams, hated slipshod thinking and pernicious sciolism, and was merciless in their castigation; but a man who came under him with any capacity for honest work, strenuous thinking, and clear expression, was sure to have that capacity developed. The men he trained have always been noted for a certain independence and fearlessness, a love of truth, and faithfulness to duty that belong to the highest type of ministerial character. Large additions for the times were made to the endowment during his presidency, just at the close of which Trevor Hall was erected, at a cost of forty-two thousand dollars, by John B. Trevor, Esq., of Yonkers.

The largest advances in the material prosperity of the seminary belong to the administration of his successor, Augustus H. Strong, who was chosen president in 1872. The gymnasium building, adjoining Trevor Hall, together with its ground, cost twelve thousand dollars, and were given to the seminary by Mr. Trevor in 1874. In 1879, Rockefeller Hall, costing thirty-eight thousand dollars, was built by John D. Rockefeller, Esq. Great additions have been made to the library during Dr. Strong's administration, through the

Bruce fund of twenty-five thousand dollars and a special subscription of the same amount by William Rockefeller in 1879. When the institution began it had no endowment. It required the first ten years of its existence to secure the sum of seventy-five thousand dollars, and in 1868 its productive fund had reached only one hundred thousand dollars. At an early period of his service Dr. Strong made special efforts to increase the endowment, and in 1874 the funds and subscriptions amounted to two hundred and eighty-one thousand dollars. In 1881 they had risen to five hundred and twelve thousand dollars, and in 1896 to six hundred and eight thousand seven hundred and forty-three dollars. The real estate is valued at one hundred and five thousand dollars, and including other items the total assets of the institution are about seven hundred and eighty-seven thousand dollars.

During the forty-four years of the seminary's existence, to and including the commencement for 1894, one thousand one hundred and seventeen students had been connected with it, of whom eight hundred and eleven were in the English department. Five hundred and seventy of these had completed the full three years' course, including the study of Hebrew and Greek Scriptures, and an average of twenty-two students had been sent out each year. Fifty-one of these students have filled places in the faculties of our theological seminaries or colleges, forty-three have become foreign missionaries, thirty-one have been home missionaries in the West, twenty-two have been secretaries or agents of our benevolent societies, and six have become editors of religious journals. It cannot be said that the Rochester Theological Seminary has not contributed its full quota of men to every department of our denominational life and work.

In 1854 the increasing number of German Baptists in the United States suggested the propriety, not to say the necessity, of providing a theological training for their rising ministry, and a German department of the seminary was organized. In 1858 Rev. Augustus Rauschenbusch was secured to take charge of this work, and a course of studies was laid out for the German department occupying six years. Inasmuch as most of the young men have had little preparatory training, their instruction is necessarily literary as well as theological. Two hundred and thirty-six young men have been trained in this department, which now has a separate German Students' Home, purchased in 1874 at a cost of twenty thousand dollars, and rebuilt in 1890 at a cost of thirty-seven thousand dollars.

The other theological school of the Baptists of the Middle States has an entirely different history. It owes its existence not to a great denominational effort, but to the wise liberality of the family whose name it bears. Its virtual, though not its actual, founder was John Price Crozer, who was born in

Delaware County, Pa., in 1793, and was baptized in early life into the fellowship of the First Baptist Church of Philadelphia, by Dr. William Staughton. He accumulated a large fortune in the manufacture of cotton goods and other business enterprises, and unlike many men who thus acquire wealth, did not forget that he was a steward for his Lord. He was always a warm friend and generous benefactor of established educational institutions, such as the college at Lewisburg, but he wished to found a new institution. In 1855 he erected a large building on the crest of a hill near Upland, at a cost of forty-five thousand dollars. But even while the walls were rising he had not fully settled in his own mind the nature of this institution, though he was strongly inclined to a school of a more popular character than a university—something of the nature of a high school, with a normal department for both sexes. One thing he especially desired, that in it young people of slender means should be able to gain a thorough training for practical life.

The school was finally begun on these lines, but it was a disappointment to its founder from the first. Contagious diseases twice broke out and interrupted the work; it was difficult to procure the right sort of teachers; and it failed to help appreciably the class for which it was designed—most of the pupils being the children of people who could well afford to give them an education in schools previously existing. The enterprise having thus practically failed, the school was closed, and during the war the building was placed at the disposal of the government and used as a military hospital. It was afterward temporarily let for the purpose of a private military school, and so the question of the ultimate disposition of the property dragged on until Mr. Crozer's death, in 1866. Shortly after, one of his children suggested that it be devoted to ministerial education, a work in which their father had for many years been deeply interested. The location was favorable for a Baptist theological seminary, almost on the border line between North and South, and the building could hardly have been better adapted to the purpose if it had been especially constructed for it.

But there were difficulties in the way, problems to be solved, before this proposition could be adopted. Was such a theological seminary needed? Would the denomination sustain it? How could it be adjusted to the work of the University at Lewisburg? There had been for some years a theological department at the Lewisburg institution, maintained by the Baptist churches of the State. Mr. John P. Crozer had long been a friend and liberal supporter of this department, and though they believed it inadequate to the needs of the State, his children were disposed to do nothing that could possibly injure the university. The project was submitted to the Philadelphia Conference of Baptist Ministers in September, 1866, and after due consideration they adopted the following resolutions with perfect unanimity and great enthusiasm:

Resolved, That we approve, and heartily recommend the appropriation of the building for this purpose.

Resolved, That we have a high appreciation of the University at Lewisburg, and desire that it may continue permanently in its present location, enlarging its means of usefulness year by year. Yet in our judgment the time has come when its real prosperity will be promoted by transferring the work of theological instruction to a distinct and well-endowed institution near to this city, leaving it with all its present endowment and apparatus to prosecute its literary work.

Resolved, That a committee of five be appointed to convey to the Messrs. Crozer, and the Boards and faculty of the University at Lewisburg, our action on this subject, and to take such measures as may be necessary for the securing of the important object which we contemplate.[1]

The president and faculty of the university had also been consulted, and shortly after this friends of the institution held a meeting in Philadelphia and adopted the following:

Resolved, That we express to the brethren Crozer our high gratification at learning of the purpose which they are contemplating, to establish a theological school at Upland on the most munificent basis, our hope that this plan may be carried out, and our gratitude to God that he has suggested to them so grand an enterprise, promising incalculable good to the church of Christ.[2]

---

[1] Smith, "Life of John P. Crozer," Philadelphia, 1868, p. 257.
[2] *Ibid.*, p. 259.

The way seemed now to be fully open, and on the second of November, 1866, the family[1] of Mr. Crozer jointly agreed to establish and endow "The Crozer Theological Seminary." The property dedicated to this purpose was valued at two hundred and seventy-five thousand dollars, of which one hundred and forty thousand dollars was in cash endowment, the rest being the estimated value of the building and grounds (eighty-thousand dollars), and money to be devoted to the erection of other buildings. This was a princely sum to be given at one time for theological education, and constituted an endowment then equal to or larger than that of any similar Baptist institution. This property was duly conveyed to a Board of Trustees, incorporated by the legislature of Pennsylvania, April 4, 1867. The trustees met for organization June 12, and resolved to establish four departments of instruction: (1) Interpretation of the Bible; (2) Christian Theology; (3) Church History; (4) Preaching and Pastoral Duties. The theological department at Lewisburg was discontinued, and Crozer has been to this day the only denominational school of the prophets in Pennsylvania.

The next thing was to obtain a faculty. A fortunate choice was made of a president when

---

[1] The family consisted at this time of Mrs. Sallie Knowles Crozer; her four sons, Samuel, Lewis, George, and Robert; her three daughters, Mrs. Bucknell, Mrs. Griffith, and Emma; and her sons-in-law, William Bucknell and Benjamin Griffith.

Rev. Henry G. Weston, then pastor of the Madison Avenue Church, New York, was called to this position. A native of Massachusetts and a graduate of Brown University (1840), and the Newton Theological Institution (1843), he had had a varied experience in the ministry. First a missionary in Illinois at his own charges, then pastor of the church at Peoria, Illinois, and after that in New York, he had been brought into contact with all sorts and conditions of men, and had learned human nature thoroughly. His administration has been particularly wise and tactful, and he early secured and has ever held the respect and esteem of trustees, professors, and students—a feeling that has deepened, as the years have passed, into affection and veneration. Rev. Drs. G. D. B. Pepper and Howard Osgood were secured as professors, and the institution was opened for instruction in the fall of 1868, and graduated its first class in 1870. Its career has been one of uninterrupted prosperity, and of late years its accommodations have been all too small for the students who have flocked to its walls. While recommending that all students for the ministry shall procure the most thorough education possible, it has never turned from its doors any worthy applicant who was able to profit by even a part of its advantages. During its history not fewer than seven hundred students have been in attendance, of whom about three hundred and sixty have received a graduate's diploma; and those still living are filling honorable places in nearly every State of the Union. The faculty has been increased to seven, and the course of study is thorough and varied. Crozer was the first of our Baptist institutions to establish a chair of biblical theology—a fact that is an index of the character of its instruction, which is pre-eminently biblical.

Prosperity has also attended its business management. From time to time houses have been built for the professors, until there are now six on the campus; and Pearl Hall, a fireproof library building, was erected in 1871 at a cost of twenty-five thousand dollars, by the liberality of the late William Bucknell, Esq., who also gave nearly thirty thousand dollars outright for the purchase of books, and endowed the library with a permanent fund of ten thousand dollars. A commencement hall was built in 1881, and a lectureship fund of ten thousand dollars has been given by Mr. Samuel A. Crozer, the income of which provides instruction for the students from men of eminent qualifications outside of the seminary faculty. The total value of the property was estimated in 1895 at five hundred and fifty thousand dollars, of which four hundred thousand dollars is productive endowment.

The institutions at Lewisburg owe their origin to the desire on the part of some Baptists of the Northumberland Association for a school in which their sons and daughters might be educated under

Baptist influences. Nothing more was at first projected than the establishment of an academy of the first grade. Such a school was begun in the fall of 1846 in the basement of the Baptist church at Lewisburg, that town being chosen because of its central location and healthfulness. The principal was Stephen W. Taylor, who had formerly been a professor at Hamilton, N. Y., and his assistants were his own son, Alfred Taylor, and I. N. Loomis. Very soon there was an enlargement in the ideas of its founders, and a charter was obtained from the legislature incorporating "The University at Lewisburg," on condition that one hundred thousand dollars should be raised, one-fourth to be permanently invested in a productive form. The sum was subscribed by July, 1849, through the efforts of Eugenio Kincaid and William Shadrach, the chief givers being David Jayne, M. D., John P. Crozer, and William Bucknell. About the same time an academy building was completed on beautiful grounds that had been secured near Lewisburg. In 1851 the college building was partly finished and the first session of this department began, with Rev. Howard Malcom, D. D., as president. His chief coadjutors were George W. Anderson, professor of Latin, and George R. Bliss, professor of Greek. Dr. Bliss continued to be a chief educational factor in the college until 1874, when he was called to Crozer, where he did an equally valuable work until his death in 1893.

When the academic and collegiate departments were separated, the former was placed in charge of Isaac N. Loomis. It was not until 1888 that the academy had a distinct faculty of its own, and its work has since shown a great increase of efficiency. In 1888, Mr. William Bucknell erected an additional building for its use, the Bucknell Cottage for Young Men. In 1894 Principal William E. Martin, A. M., after twenty-four years of service in the academy, was promoted to a professorship in the college. Thomas A. Edwards, A. M., who was elected to succeed him, has fully maintained the character of the school.

In 1852 the "University Female Institute" was added. Five years later a campus of six acres was secured and a building capable of accommodating ninety boarders was erected. In 1869 the south wing, containing rooms for students and a commodious gymnasium, was added, and Mr. William Bucknell in 1889 erected the Bucknell Cottage for Ladies. The institute offers three courses of five years each, and there are now eleven teachers. The theological department, to which allusion has already been made, was established in 1855, but discontinued in 1868.

Dr. Malcom continued to serve as president until 1857, when Rev. Justin R. Loomis, LL. D., was elected president, and on his resignation in 1879, David J. Hill, a graduate of the college a few years before and then professor of rhetoric, was chosen as his successor. After his call to Rochester, already related, John H. Harris was elected president in 1889.

By successive gifts the endowment of the university has been increased until it now amounts to four hundred thousand dollars. Besides the one hundred thousand dollars raised to validate the charter in 1849, a second one hundred thousand dollars was raised in 1865; a third one hundred thousand dollars was raised in 1881, and a fourth in 1892. Other sums have been given for buildings, library, apparatus, and scholarships, aggregating a large amount. The main college building was begun in 1852 and completed in 1858, at a cost of nearly one hundred thousand dollars. The building has a front of three hundred and twenty feet, and consists of a central structure eighty feet square, with wings each one hundred and twenty feet in length. The chapel was erected in 1886; the observatory in 1887; the gymnasium in 1890; the chemical laboratory in 1890. The real estate of the university is valued at two hundred and fifty thousand dollars. The founders of the institution raised and expended a large amount of money upon the library and apparatus, and additions have been made constantly. At present the library numbers over sixteen thousand bound volumes and many thousand pamphlets. The astronomical apparatus, including a Clark equatorial telescope, the chemical, the physical, the electrical, the biological, and other apparatus have received gifts and appropriations aggregating many thousand dollars. The museum contains over eleven thousand specimens, besides duplicates. There have been four hundred and ninety-seven students graduated from the collegiate department, and since 1891 there has been a steady and rapid increase of students. In 1886, in recognition of the liberality of the late William Bucknell, Esq. (who had given the institution considerably over two hundred thousand dollars), the name of the institution was changed to Bucknell University.

In the providence of God, the Baptists of the Middle States were to be leaders in the higher education of women, not, however, in virtue of any general denominational movement, but through the liberality of a single man. A generation ago there were in the United States several schools of considerable repute for young women, at least one of which was nominally of collegiate grade; but there was not one that was generally recognized as a college of the first rank, with a curriculum as severe and instruction as thorough as could be found in any college for young men. It was reserved for Matthew Vassar to found such an institution. He was a resident of Poughkeepsie, N. Y., a Baptist in sentiment, and a warm friend and benefactor of the Baptist church there, who had accumulated a large fortune, no inconsiderable part of which he determined to devote to the higher education of women. He found a coadjutor and executive in John H. Raymond, who became the first president of the college, which began its career in September, 1865, with property valued at seven hundred thousand dollars, fully five hundred thousand dollars being in productive funds.[1] No American college up to that time had begun its work with resources so large; nevertheless they speedily proved to be quite inadequate to the work.

In a few years Vassar had not only a main building—a structure five hundred feet long, with chapel, lecture rooms, and dormitories—but a library building and an astronomical observatory. To these it has since added Strong Hall, a residence building accommodating one hundred students; the alumnæ gymnasium, one of the best gymnasia in the country; a laboratory of physics and chemistry, due to the generosity of the Vassar Brothers, and amply equipped with the best apparatus; biological, mineralogical, and geological laboratories; a museum of natural history; an art gallery; a conservatory and various residences for professors.

The successor of Dr. Raymond in the presidency of the college was Samuel Lunt Caldwell, and after his resignation in 1886, James M. Taylor was chosen president. A preparatory department was maintained in connection with the college during

---

[1] Lossing, "Vassar College and its Founder," New York, 1867, pp. 87-109.

its early history, but this was long ago discontinued. In 1895 the value of the grounds and buildings was estimated at seven hundred and ninety-five thousand dollars, and its productive endowment had reached nearly a million dollars. Vassar has enjoyed from the beginning constant growth and increasing fame. The number of graduates up to the commencement of 1895 was one thousand one hundred and eighty-two. No college in the United States has before it a brighter prospect. Its growth, both in wealth and usefulness, is as certain as anything earthly can be.

While the Baptists of the Middle States are thus amply supplied—some might say supplied beyond all needs—with educational institutions of the higher grades, they have from the first lacked good academies, and that want is still only partially supplied. Besides the academic schools maintained in connection with Colgate and Bucknell Universities, there are seven schools of this grade under the control of the denomination. Of these, three are in Pennsylvania (Hall Institute, at Sharon; Keystone Academy, at Factoryville; and the Western Pennsylvania Classical Institute, at Mt. Pleasant). Two are in New York (Cook Academy, Havana; Marion Collegiate Institute, at Marion); and two are in New Jersey (Peddie Institute, Hightstown; South Jersey Institute, Bridgeton). These academies are all fairly provided with suitable buildings, but they are very inadequately endowed. One of them has no endowment whatever; only two have permanent funds exceeding fifty thousand dollars; but one has a productive fund exceeding one hundred thousand dollars; and the combined endowments of all fall considerably short of the fund of our worst endowed higher institution. The mere statement of these facts is convincing proof that Baptists have made a serious error in their denominational policy regarding the establishment and maintenance of educational institutions—an error that they cannot too speedily recognize and repair. The earliest schools established by Baptists, as we have seen, were academies; it is surely anomalous and indefensible that these should be the schools systematically neglected and underrated, from the early days until nearly the present time. The absorption of the fathers in the question of ministerial education, while it was the cause of their establishing what have grown to be our chief seats of learning, had also the harmful consequence of withdrawing their attention almost wholly from the maintenance of academies. But it is the academy, not the college or the theological seminary, that is the corner-stone of an educational system.

CHAPTER IX

WORK FOR THE YOUNG—THE PUBLICATION SOCIETY

BAPTIST writers have sometimes asserted that their denomination gave birth to the modern movement for the religious education of children. Robert Raikes, "the founder of the Sunday-school," has often been claimed as a Baptist—a claim that must be relegated to the large, if not respectable, limbo of Baptist myths. It would be more correct to say that Robert Raikes founded Sunday-schools, but the Sunday-school as it exists to-day is an evolution.[1] No man, no denomination, can claim its exclusive parentage. As we have seen, the Dunkers of Ephrata established and maintained a Sunday-school more like that institution as it exists to-day than anything that Raikes ever did or saw; but it had no traceable influence on other American

---

[1] Sporadic cases of the establishment of Sunday-schools before Robert Raikes began his work were not infrequent. Such schools were known in Bath, England, in 1665; in Norwich, Conn., 1676; in Plymouth, Mass., in 1680; in Newton, L. I., in 1683; in Berks and Montgomery counties, Pa., by the Schwenkfelders, in 1734, and in many other places. (See Trumbull's "Yale Lectures on the Sunday School," p. 112, note.) Why was the work of Raikes not sporadic also? Dr. Trumbull is doubtless correct in ascribing its greater permanence to the influence of the Wesleyan revival.

Christians. Sunday-schools first began to be permanently and generally established in America about the year 1791, when schools were organized almost simultaneously in Philadelphia, at Providence, R. I., and Passaic Falls, N. J. The instruction given by these schools was largely secular, and the teachers were paid just as were teachers in weekday schools. It is believed that the first Sunday-school for exclusively religious instruction was organized by the Second Baptist Church of Baltimore, in 1804. In September, 1815, a Presbyterian school was established in Philadelphia, and a week later three women of the First Baptist Church organized another. Baptists may therefore very properly claim to have been among the foremost in recognizing the importance of this work, and to have had no inconsiderable share in giving to it the form that it finally assumed.

By 1825 the movement had extended to most of the large cities, and was beginning to invade the small towns; that may therefore be taken as the date when the new institution had become so firmly established as to secure its permanence. Since then the growth of Sunday-schools has been simply amazing. It did not merely keep pace with the growth of the churches, but led the way. Even in the Middle States, probably more than half of the churches organized since 1850 trace their first beginnings to a Sunday-school established as a " mission " in a new field by members of some older church. In the West this has been still more the case; there the first religious interest in a new town is generally a little Sunday-school, which in process of time grows into a church. Any survey of denominational growth that should neglect to take this institution into account would be fatally defective. Baptists everywhere, and especially in the Middle States, took up the work with enthusiasm and success. The Sunday-school supplied a need especially felt by them, for Baptists, as a rule, never much practised catechetical instruction of their children, and the religious training of their children at home was only too prone to be spasmodic and unsatisfactory. While the Sunday-school is in no proper sense a substitute for parental instruction of children who have Christian homes, it is an admirable supplement to home training, and supplies much needed instruction for thousands of children who would otherwise receive little or no religious teaching.

Not only did Baptists early recognize the importance of the Sunday-school work, but they were quick to see the need of a distinctively Sunday-school literature. This feeling had much to do with the progress of an enterprise which, though it did not originate among the Baptists of the Middle States, nor appeal alone to them for support, soon found its home among them, and has had their peculiar interest and especial aid. In 1823, or earlier, Rev. Noah Davis, of Maryland, became im-

R

pressed with the idea that a Tract Society should be organized among Baptists, and proposed the matter to various others. In consequence a call appeared in the "Columbian Star," of Washington, of February 21, 1824, for all persons disposed to assist in forming such a society to meet at the house of Mr. George Wood. Washington was chosen as the headquarters of such a society because, owing to the recent establishment of the Columbian College there the interests of Baptists of that part of the country centered in the capital city. The meeting was held on the 25th of February, twenty-five Baptists being present. Dr. William Staughton, president of the college, was chairman of the meeting. The society defined its sole object in the first article of the constitution adopted, to be "to disseminate evangelical truth and to inculcate sound morals by distribution of tracts." A depository was established April 2d of the same year, in the office of the "Columbian Star," and auxiliary societies were established in various places.

The unsuitableness of Washington as the headquarters of this organization was felt almost from the outset. The first tracts were printed from type, and when the editions were exhausted, as they speedily were, it was found advisable to stereotype all future publications. There were no facilities for doing this in Washington, so that all the printing had to be done in Philadelphia, whence the tracts were shipped to the Washington Depository, to be sent thence all over the country. The advantage of having the headquarters located where the work was done was obvious. The removal would have been accomplished almost immediately had it not been for the opposition of Luther Rice, who was treasurer of the Society, as he was of the Columbian College. The force of his opposition was, however, broken by the charges of mismanagement (well founded), and of peculation (without foundation), that were made against him. Mr. Rice had had no training as a business man, did not understand the science of bookkeeping, and no man could have been found less fitted to be the financial agent of two struggling institutions like the Columbian College and the Tract Society. His honesty was never questioned by those who knew him, but his fitness for the financial management of these concerns was very seriously doubted. Late in the fall of 1826 the Society was removed to Philadelphia, where it has ever since remained.

At the first annual meeting in 1825 the Society reported that it had printed eighty-five thousand five hundred copies of nineteen different tracts, established ten central depositories and thirty-eight auxiliary societies; had expended five hundred and eighty-two dollars and forty cents, and including its stock on hand had a balance of one hundred dollars in its favor. This creditable report showed that the Society met an actual need among Baptists, and had fair prospects of usefulness and of growth.

In 1827 the Society received a proposition to become an auxiliary to the American Tract Society. The Board of Directors considered the proposition, but however tempting it may have been, they properly decided that they had no power under their constitution to become an auxiliary to any other body. In this year the publication of the "Tract Magazine" was begun, and such a publication served as a means of communication among the friends of the work, and largely promoted the circulation of tracts. The Minutes of the annual meetings from this time forth gave evidence of a rapid extension of the work. Not only were tracts circulated in our own country, but Dr. Judson was assisted in the publication and circulation of tracts in the Burmese language on his missionary field, and Oncken, the beginner of the modern Baptist movement in Germany, was generously furnished with supplies of evangelical and denominational tracts in German.

In spite of its general prosperity, however, the Society was badly hampered by lack of funds. It had begun its work in Philadelphia in a single room on Front Street, below Market. From time to time it was moved into more convenient quarters, but the necessity was felt for a building in which its property might be safely preserved and its business carried on with more regularity, economy, and system, particularly in the printing and bookbinding departments. A subscription was opened for this purpose, but very little was ever received for it. In the year 1840 sixteen years of the Society's work had been completed, and the following results were reported : The receipts were eighty-six thousand and forty-eight dollars, three million three hundred and forty-one thousand nine hundred and six tracts had been printed, twenty-eight branch depositories were in existence, four hundred and thirty auxiliary societies, and the Society owned three thousand six hundred and fifteen stereotyped plates.

As early as 1830 the Society began to take special note of the growing interest among Baptists in Sunday-schools, and a suggestion in the annual report of that year was to the following effect: "The time may come when the number of schools in our denomination will be so great as to require the Tract Society to publish a series of Sabbath-school books suited to their wants." In 1835 the proposition was made at the meeting of the General Convention at Richmond to enlarge the scope of the Society's work, but struggling as it was under financial difficulties and lack of co-operation, so as to be threatened with speedy dissolution, how could larger plans be undertaken? The Hudson River Association, at its session in 1839, called the attention of Baptists to the necessity of a Baptist Sunday-school Union, to furnish literature for our Sunday-schools in accord with our convictions of Scripture truth. The Board of the Tract Society took advantage of this circumstance to issue through the denominational press a plan for reorganization and enlargement. This was actually accomplished in 1840, when the annual meeting of the Tract Society was held in the Tabernacle Church, of New York. The constitution was so amended as to make the name of the Society the American Baptist Publication and Sunday-School Society, and to define its object as being " to publish such books as are needed by the Baptist denomination, and to promote Sunday-schools by such measures as experience may prove expedient." [1]

The first difficulty experienced by the new Society was, of course, the want of working capital. Appeals were made from year to year for special subscriptions to supply this lack. The churches were requested to raise a permanent fund by means of an average contribution of ten cents per member, but the plan proved to be a total failure, for instead of realizing as was expected, sixty or seventy thousand dollars, the Society only received about fifteen hundred dollars. An enlarged and more convenient building was also an absolute necessity if the

---

[1] After sixteen years of progress under the new organization it became a matter of interest to compare the progress made by the new Society, with that made by its predecessor in the same period. It was found that a gain of $60,000 had been made in the assets of the Society during these years in stock, funds, and cash. Of this $39,300 was working capital. Since 1840 the Society had issued books and tracts to the number of about 146,000,000 pages. In the first five years of this time the work had been distinguished by the introduction of colportage, and the steady increase of this force had been followed by an enormous extension of the circulation of tracts.

additional work was to be undertaken. It was not, however, until October 15, 1853, that a fund of twenty-five thousand dollars was raised for this purpose. So much being accomplished, a special attempt was made to raise a fund of one hundred thousand dollars as capital on which the business might be conducted. This attempt also proved a failure, but brighter days were in store for the Society. After it had successfully weathered the financial storms of 1857, a new era of prosperity dawned. The Rev. Benjamin Griffith was chosen general secretary, and under his administration there was a great and continuous advance. This was somewhat interrupted during the first years of the Civil War, but subsequently the growth was continued and rapid. There has never been a year since then that has failed to show an increase of receipts over those of the previous year. Not only was the management wise, but during these years many friends were raised up for the help of the Society.

The building on Arch Street occupied after 1850, seemed palatial quarters in comparison with what had been known before, but the increasing work of the Society soon rendered even this entirely inadequate. Accordingly the construction of a larger and better building was begun about 1870, and in March, 1876, the headquarters at 1420 Chestnut Street were completed and occupied. The cost of this building was two hundred and fifty-eight thousand dollars, all of which was provided for by the liberality of its friends, and the proceeds of the sale of its building on Arch Street.

This building was found at first to be all that was anticipated, but the business of the Society so increased beyond all forecasts as to make it quite inadequate for the manufacturing department after ten years' occupancy. A fund was gradually accumulated from the profits of the business, through the wise foresight of Dr. Griffith, and applied in due time to the erection of a fireproof building for the manufacture of the Society's books and periodicals. This building was completed and occupied in 1896. Its arrangement, machinery, and appointments are of the best, and no publishing house in the United States has better facilities for doing work of the highest grade. The cost of the building was one hundred and twenty-five thousand dollars.

Before this addition to its facilities could be made the Society suffered the greatest calamity in its history, the total destruction by fire of the Chestnut Street building, on Sunday, February 2, 1896. The building and stock were kept insured to nearly or quite their full value, but the loss of books and periodicals in process of publication, of valuable manuscripts, of engravings, and many things whose value was not computable in money or not replaceable at any price, was great. Still more disastrous, perhaps, was the interruption of business, and the necessity of immediate republication of much of the destroyed matter. All difficulties were, however, overcome; the next day business was resumed, all available presses in the city were set at work, and almost without break the business went forward—as splendid a proof of perfect system as any mercantile concern could give to the world.

Preparations were immediately made to rebuild on the same site, and on November 15, 1897, the Society occupied its new quarters in a new fireproof building of twelve stories, costing about five hundred thousand dollars. The beauty of its front, the excellence of its construction, the completeness of its appointments within make this one of the finest business buildings in Philadelphia. The Society occupies the first floor and also a part of the second and fourth floors. On the first floor it has the largest and most handsomely appointed bookstore in the United States, and none of our denominational societies is in all respects so well housed. There are about one hundred and fifty offices in the building, from which a large income will be derived, the profits from which will be devoted to missionary purposes. The location of the new building is unsurpassed in the city for an edifice of this kind.

In the early years of the Society's work there was no clear distinction between the strictly business and the benevolent work of the Society. From the year 1859, however, the two departments have been distinct; since 1862 they have had separate accounts, and for some years they had different counting rooms. The Society was first in the field with a body of colporters, leading even the American Tract Society in this work. In the plan for the reorganization of the Tract Society special stress was laid upon the appointment of traveling agents supplied with denominational tracts and books. This was embodied in the new constitution in that clause authorizing the Publication Society to promote Sunday-schools by such measures as experience may prove expedient. Experience soon showed that it was expedient to supplement colporters with Sunday-school missionaries whose work should be not so much the supplying of people with books and tracts, as the founding of new Sunday-schools, and strengthening and improvement of those already founded, and to assist in the organization of Sunday-school unions or societies that would promote the efficiency of the work in the newer States. The Society began to employ colporters about 1840. It was not until 1867 that Sunday-school missionaries were appointed, but in a few years twenty or more such missionaries were constantly laboring in the southern and western parts of the United States. No labor undertaken by the Publication Society has proved more fruitful of good than this. The chapel car work, that has grown to such proportions of late years and been so remarkably successful, is only colportage on wheels, and with the aid of steam.

But time and space alike would fail to tell adequately of the Society's work, nor would a complete history of it be germane to the purpose of this book. Through this agency Baptists have been among the foremost in providing a literature for Sunday-schools of high and steadily improving quality. The Society has devoted an ever-increasing part of its attention and business resources to the preparation and publication of such literature. In establishing the International Lessons Baptists also took a leading part, and in the more recent introduction of the inductive method Baptist scholars, teachers, and schools have taken a place second to none. To-day in the Middle States the number of Baptist Sunday-schools equals or exceeds the number of Baptist churches, and the pupils enrolled do not fall much below the number of church-members.[1]

Though the Society began its work as a publisher of tracts and Sunday-school literature, it did not long continue in a sphere so restricted. Poverty, if nothing else, compelled modest attempts in the earlier years, but ideals and purposes of a broader character were cherished from the first. As early as the year 1844 there was a beginning of their realization. An edition of Andrew Fuller's writings

---

[1] The exact figures, as reported in the "Baptist Year-Book" for 1897, are: New York: churches, 926; members, 147,907; Sunday-schools, 920; pupils, 124,757. New Jersey: churches, 255; members, 45,534; schools, 298; pupils, 41,350. Pennsylvania: churches, 718; members, 103,981; schools, 714; pupils, 83,972. Delaware: churches, 15; members, 2,209; schools, 22; pupils, 2,508.

issued in that year was the precursor of a long and rapidly increasing list of standard works in general religious literature. This is coming to be, if it has not already become, the most important part of the Society's work of publication. Already the number of such works far exceeds the number of Sunday-school publications,[1] and the excellence of these books has kept pace with their numbers. One risks little, therefore, in so far attempting the *rôle* of prophet as to declare that, while the Society will go on with the publication of tracts and Sunday-school literature, its greatest development during the next generation will be in its general publishing work.

There are reasons why there should have been delay in the development of this work, as there are reasons for now expecting its rapid advance. Poverty, as already intimated, was one controlling reason. Lack of means for pushing the sale of its publications, lack of qualified writers, lack of facilities for manufacturing, all contributed to the delay. None of these hindrances now exist; the Society has ample capital, through its branches and the denominational press it can market its books, while "the trade" no longer considers the imprint of the Society or its secretary fatal to a book designed for general circulation; and its facilities for making

---

[1] At the close of the year 1895-6, there were 206 works in the Society's Catalogue of general religious literature, as against 168 Sunday-school publications.

books, in all externals equal to the best, are unsurpassed.[1] Baptist writers are awaking to the fact that the Society is the natural medium of communication between themselves and the denomination. This broader view of the Society's opportunities has led to an enlargement of its policy, and recent years have seen a remarkable advance in the number of its religious publications, in the excellence of their contents, and the mechanical perfection of their form.

The Baptists of the Middle States were not only among the earliest supporters of the Sunday-school work, but among the first to recognize the importance of what is now known as "the young people's movement." Nothing in the history of modern Christianity is more clearly providential in origin and in guidance than this movement. The way had been prepared for it in several evangelical denominations by sporadic attempts toward the organization and development of the younger members of the churches. Young people's societies, of various names and types of organization, began to be common in the Middle States soon after 1860.[2]

---

[1] One of the best selling books of the year 1893, "Beautiful Joe," bore the Society's imprint. Within the year 20,000 copies were sold, and early in the present year (1897) the total sale had reached 250,000 copies. And yet some have an idea that books by Baptist writers do not sell!

[2] The Young People's Society, Tabernacle Church, Philadelphia, organized May 7, 1860, and the "Covenant Band," of the First Church, Troy, N. Y., organized by Dr. George C. Baldwin,

They were found alike in Baptist, Methodist, and Congregational churches—in a very few instances in Presbyterian churches also. Considerable opposition was manifested by the more conservative, both ministers and laymen, to the organization of such societies; and in cases not a few there were good reasons for anxiety regarding the probable influence of a young people's society. If it were what its name implied, and only young people constituted it, a patent objection was that it would tend to make an unwise and unscriptural line of division in the church. This was not wholly a theoretical objection; for there were societies in the "sixties" that actually accomplished such a division. The result of such an age-line, in a church of average human nature, would be an increasing feeling of independence on the part of the young people, and increasing perplexity and irritation on the part of the pastor and older members. Friction, if not conflict, was inevitable. Moreover these societies of young people were too frequently organized for social reasons mainly. Their chief ostensible purpose was the

---

April 30, 1863, are typical cases. There are, however, similar societies considerably older than these. There has been an organization of young people in the First Church, Rochester, N. Y., since 1848. The church records contain the following entry, under date of August 29 of that year: "Bro. A. G. Mudge, in behalf of the young members of the church, requested the church to recognize their Monday evening meeting as a stated meeting of the church." In other States similar societies were formed. Rev. D. E. Halteman, while pastor of the church at Marengo, Ill., in 1858, gathered his young people into a society known as "Pastor's Helpers."

maintenance of a young people's prayer meeting, and generally they did manage to keep such a meeting just alive, but often at what a poor, dying rate! The real purpose of many societies was to furnish their members "a good time." The sociable flourished when the prayer meeting languished; so-called "literary entertainments," with oysters and ice cream, would bring together crowds, while only a few could be drawn to the place of prayer; the gastric nerve was cultivated at the expense of piety, and "the cooking-stove apostasy" found some of its brightest exemplars in these societies.

While these organizations were thus distrusted by many, with only too much reason, they accomplished no little good where the pastor was possessed of tact and discretion. They were the only means then at hand for developing the prayer-meeting gifts of the younger members. Many of the best Christian workers of to-day gave their first testimony in one of these young people's meetings, and were in time graduated from them into the larger activities of the churches. But the conviction deepened among thoughtful pastors that a better means of training young Christians was needed, and that the work itself was second in importance to none committed to a minister of Christ. This conviction produced the young people's movement, by a series of events that fools call accidental, that Christians call providential.

One who had been pondering this problem as it

affected the young people in his own flock was the pastor of the Williston Street Congregational Church, of Portland, Maine, Rev. Francis E. Clark. His work had for a series of years been especially fruitful among the young, and in the winter of 1880-81 a revival brought into the church an unusually large number of young converts. More than ever he felt the need of an organization in his church for the training and development of these converts, in purpose and spirit quite differing from anything of the sort he had known. On the evening of February 2, 1881, a few trusty helpers met in the pastor's study, and there the first Society of Christian Endeavor was formed. The constitution then adopted was essentially the same as the model now suggested for all societies of the name. The distinctive features of this first society were two, and were recognized in its motto, "For Christ and the Church." Neither the motto nor the principles could be called new, but a quite original application of them was made to the young people's society. Christian Endeavor chose the right foundation by emphasizing the personal relation of the young Christian to his Saviour. The society was founded on a spiritual, not a social, basis. Next to this radical principle, the new society laid emphasis on the young Christian's relation to his church. No Christian Endeavor society can be independent of the authority and control of pastor and church; so soon as it becomes an independent organization it loses all right to its name. It is to regard itself, and seek to be regarded, as an integral part of the church, a department of its work, subject to its control, and deserving its sympathy and support.

Such were the principles of the new society, and they constituted it a novel feature of church work, a new departure in the training of young Christians. Its methods were equally novel in their application to this work, though neither of them was new. The first was the taking of a pledge that imposed on each member a high ideal of Christian living, and especially committed him to taking some part, aside from singing, in every prayer meeting of the society. The second novel method was the holding of a monthly consecration meeting by the members of the society—a feature that may have been suggested to Dr. Clark by the Methodist class meeting, with which it has an obvious affinity. Those two methods constitute the distinctive feature of the Christian Endeavor Society in practical work, and naturally they have provoked the most vigorous and prolonged criticism. Nevertheless, that these are precisely the features that have made Christian Endeavor such a power, those who have practical experience in the work are almost unanimous in testifying.

The success of this new organization was so immediate and so marked as to attract the attention of other pastors. Mr. Clark described the society's principles and methods in newspaper articles, which stimulated the formation of other societies on the same model. The founder of this first society discovered, like so many other leaders, that he had builded better than he knew; but even he could have no prevision of the magnitude that the work so simply and modestly begun would attain. The second society was formed in October, 1881, at Newburyport, Mass., and before the end of the year four societies had been organized in New England churches. The first Christian Endeavor Convention was held at Mr. Clark's church, June 2, 1882, at which time six societies were recorded. By the next year there were fifty-three, five of which were in New York, and seven in the West. From this time on the growth was rapid. In 1885 the United Society of Christian Endeavor was formed and incorporated, to give advice and help in the progress of the movement. The following year saw still another advance in the establishment of the "Golden Rule" as the organ of the movement, and the election of Dr. Clark as president of the United Society. Not by leaps and jumps, but by steady progress, bringing to naught all gloomy predictions of decline, this growth continued until at the great convention at San Francisco, in July, 1897, there were over three millions of young Christians affiliated with the United Society in America, and the Endeavor societies had been organized literally in every country in the world where evangelical Christian churches are found.

Such a great work did not progress without opposition, much of it, some of it bitter. The real nature of the movement was mistaken. Because the Christian Endeavor organization was adapted to any and every church, it found ready adoption in many denominations. The United Society was undenominational or interdenominational in character, and the conventions of the societies necessarily partook of the same character from the first. In these facts some minds saw the promise of an immediate blotting out of denominational lines; the sanguine radical hoped for such a result, the timid conservative feared it. The indiscreet friends of the movement, who saw in it the beginning of a long-hoped-for organic unity of the Christians, did the cause great harm by prejudicing against it many otherwise well disposed to be its friends. Men extreme in their denominational views looked upon the movement with alarm, and began a counter movement in their own denominations, with the intention of organizing their young people within denominational lines, and under a strictly denominational name. Such attempts were made in several cases. In the Methodist Episcopal Church, with its centralized government, the attempt was measurably successful. A conference of representatives of several forms of societies met in Cleveland, O., May 14 and 15, 1889, and effected a new organization for the entire church, under the title of the Epworth League. The bishops and the denominational press gave the new society a most enthusiastic welcome, showed especial honor to its representatives, and held forth every inducement to Methodist young people to separate themselves from Christian Endeavor. To a large extent this policy has proved successful, but not all the pressure that can be brought to bear through official and unofficial channels has sufficed to separate many Methodist societies from the organization of their choice. What cannot be done with complete success in a church organized on the principle of almost despotic episcopal powers was certainly foredoomed to failure in a denomination like the Baptist, in which the independence of each local church makes impossible the control of the local organization of young people by any outside power whatsoever.

The beginning of separate denominational organization among Baptist young people antedates Christian Endeavor. In October, 1877, the various Baptist young people's organizations of Brooklyn, N. Y., met and formed "The Young People's Baptist Union of Brooklyn"—a society that has had a history of uninterrupted growth and prosperity until the present time. The formation of this society was probably suggested to the young Baptists of that city by the existence of the Brooklyn Baptist Social Union of their elders; yet the new society was not mainly social in its purpose, but religious, missionary, evangelistic. Two years later a similar Union was formed in New York, but after a brief and feeble existence it died; and for a decade or more the Brooklyn Union continued to be the only organization of the kind among young Baptists in the country, and there seemed to be no prospect of further advance along this line of development in the East.

It was from the West that the first impulse proceeded toward the further organization of Baptist young people. The mind of a Kansas pastor, the Rev. O. W. Van Osdel, began to be greatly exercised about this matter, and on opening his heart to other pastors he found them similarly affected. He prepared and sent out a circular in the year 1887, in which he thus defined the object of those who had taken up this work with him: "The aim of the movement is to organize the young people as a department for work and special training in the interest of the church and denomination, and contemplates more efficiency in the work of the church and Sunday-school, and Baptist training and reading, rather than that which is undenominational." This circular suggested the name of "Loyalists" for societies of Baptist young people, and proposed the motto that has since become so widely known, "Loyalty to Christ, in all things, at all times."

From the beginning much was made of the training of the young people in distinctive denominational principles. In 1888 a course of lessons was prepared and printed on "The Apostles' Doctrine," and pastors were exhorted to use these in the instruction of their young people. Circulars of the

Loyalists issued during the following year said, among other things: "Baptists are making no systematic provision whatever for the doctrinal instruction or denominational interest of their young people, who are being sent into associations where it is unlawful for them to speak of their distinctive principles, and thus the tendency is to make them feel that Baptist principles are objectionable, and an element of division." In a similar spirit Mr. Van Osdel had written in 1888:

> It is not enough to say that the church has a popular and flourishing young people's society. They are organized and zealous, and magnified by members, to be sure; but what is the training and influence in which they are placed to produce twenty years hence? We labor for something more than the good cheer and smiling prosperity of the young of all denominations of to-day. To the hands of Baptists have been entrusted the oracles of God. The truth of the New Testament, uncorrupted and unchanged, is the ground of Christian union. Does the training of the young members of our churches tend to make them the firm defenders of those vital truths which have been committed to us through so much blood and treasure? Will the present form of organization lead our young members to contend earnestly for a regenerated church membership, to be loyal to the church of the New Testament, and to insist that the unevangelized regions shall have the pure word of God? These questions cannot be passed lightly by.[1]

Though Christian Endeavor was not explicitly named, such references were too plain to be mis-

---
[1] "Baptist Quarterly Review," Vol. X., p. 240.

understood. That organization had many warm friends among the Baptists, and they were provoked into an attitude first of suspicion and then of opposition by the aggressive and exclusive denominationalism of many Loyalists. This feeling of mutual repulsion increased as the months passed on, and at one time threatened results of the gravest character. Happily the first organization in the West was formed on broader lines. At the meeting of the Nebraska State Convention in October, 1889, "The Nebraska Convention of Baptist Young People" was organized, on the platform of inviting all Baptist young people's societies, of whatever name or method, to affiliate with it and come together under denominational auspices and for a common end. It was generally felt that this was the true basis for a general movement among Baptists—in fact, the logic of the Baptist polity made any other basis impossible. However strongly individuals might prefer this or that organization or method of work, it was obviously impossible to force the form preferred on those who preferred something else. The local church is the court of last resort for the decision of all such questions, in reality as well as in theory, and its choice of an organization for its young people is a fact against which all outside influence and authority strive in vain. Any general organization among Baptists must therefore be founded on the principle not of exclusion, but of inclusion—not of reorganization, but of affiliation. Some Baptists, however, were slow to see this, and therefore the movement at one stage seriously threatened the peace and unity of the denomination.

A further step was taken when the friends of the new movement held a conference in connection with the anniversaries in Chicago, in May, 1890. It was not thought best to attempt a general organization at that time, but in March of the following year another conference held in Chicago issued a call for a convention of all friends of the movement, to be held July 7 and 8, for the purpose of effecting a general organization.

In the meantime the originators of the Loyalist movement had begun the publication of a newspaper caller "The Loyalist," in Chicago. There was little capital at their command; and the basis on which they conducted their work was too narrow to command wide sympathy and support. The managers of the American Baptist Publication Society had watched the movement and had become convinced of two things: first, that the movement had come to stay, and second, that it needed broadening to give it the largest success. The society therefore purchased the paper, and began its publication in November, 1890, under the name of "The Young People at Work." The change of ownership and name marked a change of policy. The right of the local church was clearly recognized to determine what form of organization its young people should adopt, or whether they should be organized at all.

The principle was advocated that the associational, State, and national organizations, when formed, should be formed on a basis broad enough to admit to equal rights all Baptist young people. For a time the conflict seemed only to be intensified, and the lines appeared to be drawn more sharply than ever between the denominational movement on the one side and Christian Endeavor on the other. The call for a general convention only increased the feeling of apprehension and anxiety.

At this juncture the society took a course that proved to be the wisest possible, and in a few weeks the matter was removed from the field of controversy and conflict, and amicably settled on a basis satisfactory to all concerned. At least, if there were any who still had doubts and were rebellious, they had tact enough to hold their peace. The society called a conference of representative men of the denomination to consider all the questions involved, as Christian brethren. It included men known as among the foremost in support of Christian Endeavor, and men who had been most active and outspoken in the Loyalist movement, as well as others who had not been conspicuously identified with either, but were known to have at heart the interests of the Baptist young people. These men met in Philadelphia, April 22, 1891, and the whole question of organization for Baptist young people was thoroughly and dispassionately considered. Guided by the Spirit of God, the conference reached a conclusion that few had regarded as possible or had ventured to hope for, a conclusion that was embodied in a general address to the denomination. This is a document of hardly less significance in the denominational history than the resolutions of the Saratoga Bible Convention, and equally deserves a place in these pages with that memorable decision :

GENERAL BASIS OF ORGANIZATION.

The undersigned, cognizant of the fact that there is a widespread desire for a more thorough organization of the young people of the Baptist churches for indoctrination in distinctive Baptist principles and instruction in Baptist history ; for more effective service in the local churches ; for a better acquaintanceship among our young people ; for the better pushing of all mission work —domestic, home, and foreign—suggest the following basis for organization :

(1) That the Baptist national organization, when formed in July next, be on a basis broad enough to receive all Baptist young people's societies of whatever name or constitution ; (2) That no Baptist young people's society now organized be required to organize under any other name or constitution in order to obtain fellowship and representation in such body, either State or National ; (3) That such national organization adopt the "Young People at Work" as the organ of the young people's societies, with the understanding that the paper is to be impartially hospitable to all such societies, and that the paper shall especially devote itself to the indoctrination of the Baptist young people in the distinguishing tenets of Baptist churches ; (4) That all young people's societies in Baptist churches, of whatever name or constitution, be earnestly requested to heartily co-operate

in Associational, State, and National Baptist organization ; (5) That each young people's society shall be left to determine to what extent it will participate in interdenominational societies ; (6) That all societies of young people in Baptist churches be strenuously urged to subscribe for the "Young People at Work," and also to circulate other Baptist literature ; (7) That while the national organization may recommend some model constitution for local societies, the constitution shall be entirely optional with all societies in affiliation with the body.

(Signed) Wayland Hoyt, Albert G. Lawson, P. S. Henson, F. L. Wilkins, Benjamin Griffith, John H. Chapman, A. J. Rowland, C. R. Blackall, Alexander Blackburn, Joseph K. Dixon, Philip L. Jones, O. W. Spratt, O. W. Van Osdel, John T. Beckley, C. C. Bitting, A. W. Lamar, Chas. H. Banes, Frank M. Ellis, William R. Harper, O. P. Eaches, R. S. MacArthur.

On this basis a national convention was held at Chicago, Ill., and there, July 8, 1891, was organized the "Baptist Young People's Union of America." The object of this organization, and of all State and other organizations affiliated with it, was declared to be " the unification of Baptist young people; their increased spirituality ; their stimulation in Christian service ; their edification in Scripture knowledge ; their instruction in Baptist doctrine and history ; and their enlistment in all missionary activity through existing denominational organizations." As to membership, the constitution was in strict accordance with the foregoing agreement : " The membership of this Union shall consist of accredited delegates from young people's societies in Baptist churches, and from Baptist churches having no young people's organization." The Union thus avowed, and has steadily adhered to, the policy not of reorganization but of federation. Its growth was immediate and remarkable. At the convention held in Detroit, in 1892, four thousand one hundred and seventeen delegates and visitors were enrolled; at Toronto, in 1894, the number was five thousand seven hundred and fourteen; at Baltimore, in 1895, the registration was six thousand five hundred and fifty-nine; and at Milwaukee, in 1896, the number rose to ten thousand four hundred and two,—making these last three the largest conventions of Baptists ever held in America, if not in the world. Mere statistics, however, would give a very inadequate impression of the Union's real strength, which has not consisted in the attendance at its conventions, but in the solid work done through the year by the young people in their local societies.

The distinctive feature of this work has been its educational character, and this is the real *raison d'être* of the organization. The United Society of Christian Endeavor, from the very nature of the organization, could not undertake the guidance of young Christians in the work of studying their denominational principles and history. They must leave this to denominational agencies. Hence there was felt to be not only room, but a demand, for denominational societies that exist for the purpose of complementing the work of Christian Endeavor, not of antagonizing it. Early in the history of the Union there was planned a comprehensive scheme of instruction in the Bible, in missions, and in denominational doctrine and history. These Christian Culture Courses extend over a period of four years, and are the best system of denominational training that has yet been devised—the only one that is in practical and successful operation among any body of Christians. By the Union's purchase of the "Young People at Work," in November, 1891 (then "Young Peoples Union") and its publication later as the "Baptist Union," an effective means was provided of communication with local societies and of pushing the work. At the first annual examination of students in the Christian Culture Courses (popularly known as the "Three Cs"), held in June, 1893, three hundred and forty-nine persons enrolled themselves as candidates. One year later, owing to the systematic work done, the number of examinees had risen to three thousand one hundred and ninety-five, a surprising rate of increase; and in 1897 the number of papers sent in was thirteen thousand four hundred and seven. This work is still in its infancy, and it would require a gift of prophecy to tell whereunto it may speedily grow.

CHAPTER X

BAPTISTS AND BIBLE WORK

AMONG the foremost in the organization of the great societies for translating and distributing the Bible were Baptists. The British and Foreign Bible Society, the first organization of the kind, was formed in London in 1804, the meeting having been called by the Rev. Joseph Hughes, a Baptist, who was chosen one of the first secretaries. Not only so, but the aroused and enlightened Christian sentiment that made possible such a federation is plainly traceable to the missionary labors of Carey, Marshman, and Ward. The immediate success of this society in uniting, in the work of circulating the word of God, Christians who had never before had a single common interest, naturally led to the formation of Bible societies in America. At first the organizations were local. A Bible society was organized in Philadelphia in 1808, and others followed so rapidly that in eight years there were one hundred and twenty-eight such bodies. The continued usefulness of the English society suggested almost irresistibly the idea of one great organization for the whole country; and, accordingly, in 1816 the American Bible Society was formed.

Seven denominations of Christians were represented among the sixty delegates from twenty-eight local Bible bodies that organized this new league.[1] In the "address" issued to the public, explaining the constitution and work of the new society, its object was said to be "the dissemination of the Scriptures in the received versions, where they exist, and in the most faithful where they are required." From this it appeared that the society was constituted on a most catholic basis, and for years there was no sign of sectarian differences in its administration. Baptists were among its most active supporters, and in proportion to their wealth, not so great as that of some other denominations, were liberal givers.[2] Honored Baptists were from time to time chosen to fill vacancies on the Board of Managers,[3] and the Rev. Spencer H. Cone, D. D., was one of the secretaries, from 1833 to 1835.

When Adoniram Judson began his mission to the Burmese, he felt that his greatest service would be

---

[1] The local societies did not cease to exist when the American Bible Society was formed; on the contrary, they flourished more than ever as its auxiliaries, and there are now in the United States over 2,000 such local organizations for the circulation of the Bible.

[2] Up to the year 1836 the total of their gifts was calculated to be $170,000. Of this sum $18,500 had been appropriated for the circulation of versions in which Baptists were especially interested—a sum equal to little more than one-third of the bequest of a single Baptist, John F. Marsh.

[3] Among them may be named Drs. Archibald Maclay and Charles G. Somers, and such laymen as Garret N. Bleecker, William Colgate, and Timothy R. Green.

the translation of the Bible into their vernacular. Many years he labored, and in 1832 his version of the New Testament was printed at Moulmein, and the Old Testament followed in 1834. In the intervening year the Foreign Mission Board of the Baptist General Convention adopted a resolution requiring all its missionaries "to endeavor by earnest prayer and diligent study to ascertain the precise meaning of the original text, to express that meaning as exactly as the nature of the languages into which they translate the Bible will permit, and to transfer no words which are capable of being literally translated." This resolution was printed in the "Baptist Missionary Magazine" for May, 1833, and Dr. Cone personally presented copies of it to the Board of Managers of the American Bible Society, and to individual members. There could be no question, therefore, of lack of knowledge on the part of the Society; and with this knowledge they voted for the printing and circulation of Dr. Judson's version —five thousand dollars in 1833; in 1834, seven thousand five hundred dollars; and in 1835, six thousand dollars. During the same period appropriations were granted for the circulation of versions made by others than Baptists, and made on the same principle of translating every Greek and Hebrew word into the vernacular, if a suitable equivalent could be found.

At its anniversary in 1834 the society adopted a resolution "to distribute the Bible among all the accessible population of the globe, within the shortest practicable period." The secretaries, by order of the Board of Managers, prepared and sent to missionaries a circular announcing this policy and inviting their co-operation. In part as a result of this circular, an application was made, August 6, 1835, for aid in printing a version of the Scriptures in Bengali, made by the Rev. Messrs. W. H. Pearce and William Yates, on the same principle as the Burmese version already circulated by the society. There was also another reason for the application: aid in printing and circulating this very version had been lately refused by the British and Foreign Bible Society, in utter subversion of its previous policy, and in defiance of the rights of Baptists.[1] It remained to be tested whether sectarian prejudice would produce similar results in the American Bible Society.

After months of discussion in committee and Board, the managers finally decided (February 17, 1836) against the application by a vote of thirty to fourteen. They adopted the following, which became thenceforth a by-law of the society:

---

[1] Dr. Yates asserted, and was never challenged, that up to 1832 all the Pedobaptist missionaries, as well as the Baptist, uniformly translated βαπτίζω and its cognates, including the Persian and Hindustani versions of Henry Martyn, the Arabic of Mr. Thomason, the Hindu of Mr. Bowley, and all the versions made by Dr. Carey. For twenty-six years the British and Foreign Society had been assisting in the printing and distribution of versions like these, not only without a word of protest, but with frequent entries in its journals of praise for their excellence and the scholarship of the translators!

Resolved, That in appropriating money for translating, printing, or distributing the sacred Scriptures in foreign languages, the managers feel at liberty to encourage only such versions as conform in the principle of their translation to the common English version; at least so far that all the religious denominations represented in this society can consistently use and circulate said versions in their several schools and communities.

On April 7 the Baptist members of the Board presented a strong and dignified protest,[1] which the Board refused to receive or even hear read. That decision, adding discourtesy to unfairness, was followed by the action of the society at its annual meeting, on May 12, approving the course of the Board of Managers. This vote Baptists were compelled to accept as a final decision of the question. The American Bible Society had, after mature deliberation, concluded to transform itself from a catholic to a sectarian institution; it had repudiated its original platform, of circulating the most faithful versions where there were no received versions, and adopted the new rule that, in order to deserve its patronage, a new version must not be faithful. Two courses were open to Baptists—they might endure the wrong with Christian meekness, co-operate with

---

[1] One of its unanswerable points was the exposure of the American Bible Society's inconsistency in continuing to circulate Roman Catholic versions, which were neither conformed to the common English version in principle of translation, nor could be consistently used by all the denominations represented in the Society, while the translations of pious, faithful, and learned Baptist ministers were rejected.

the American Bible Society as before in the circulation of received versions, and provide in other ways for the circulation of their missionary versions; or they might secede in a body from the American Bible Society, establish a society of their own, and carry on their Bible work independently at home and abroad. Each course had its advantages, each had its advocates; perhaps either might have been successful. Unfortunately, Baptists chose both. The denomination was never a unit in regard to methods of Bible work, and the inevitable result followed—division, strife, failure.

For a time, to be sure, it seemed that the project of a separate society would carry all before it. Dr. Cone was at the height of his fame as preacher and platform orator, in the prime of life, influential in the denominational counsels,[1] and a man of great resolution and untiring industry. He had been in the thick of the controversy, the champion of his denomination in the Board, the one on whom the blows of opposing champions had fallen thick and hard. Ever an uncompromising Baptist, though generally a man of catholic spirit, his denominational pride was now at white heat. He felt that Baptists must, for their own honor and for the work committed to them, establish a society of their own. On the very day after the final action of the American Bible Society was taken, a meeting was held in

---

[1] From 1832 to 1841, when he declined re-election, he was president of the General Convention.

the Oliver Street Church, New York, where Dr. Cone was then pastor, and a provisional organization was formed. Before this the Foreign Mission Board of the General Convention, at a meeting held in Hartford, April 27, anticipating an adverse decision in the Pearce-Yates application, voted that in such case it would be "expedient to call a convention of delegates from churches and Associations, and other religious bodies, to meet in Philadelphia in the month of April, 1837, to adopt such measures as circumstances, in the providence of God may require."

Such a convention was called, and met on April 26, being composed of three hundred and ninety delegates from twenty-three States, and was pronounced by one whose competence to judge no one will dispute (Rev. James D. Knowles) "the largest and most intelligent assemblage of Baptist ministers and laymen which has ever been held." The American and Foreign Bible Society was formally organized, and it was voted during the ensuing year to confine its efforts to the circulation of the word of God in foreign tongues, the denomination being requested to express at the next annual meeting "their views as to the duty of the society to engage in the work of home distribution." Of this society Dr. Cone was, as a matter of course, elected president. He was virtually its founder, without question its leading spirit.

Great enthusiasm seemed to attend the organization of the new society. Even during its year of provisional existence it had raised and sent (July, 1836) five thousand dollars to print the rejected Bengali version of Messrs. Pearce and Yates. The annual meeting in 1838 was held in the Oliver Street Church, New York, and it appeared that thirty-eight thousand seven hundred and fourteen dollars and fourteen cents had been subscribed. In Dr. Charles G. Somers, the corresponding secretary, and William Colgate, the treasurer, Dr. Cone had helpers who were men after his own heart, stanch in their Baptist principles and as untiring in labors as himself. The "little rift within the lute," however, was that undecided question about the work of the society in home distribution. At no time was it possible to unite Baptists on this question. With regard to the missionary translations, on the contrary, there was substantial unanimity, and had foreign work been the only thing in question, Baptists would never have been divided in Bible work. But as to the home work there were three views, each of which had its strenuous advocates: (1) That Baptists should co-operate with the American Bible Society in circulating received versions. (2) That Baptists should do their home work through their denominational society, but circulate only received versions. (3) That Baptists should apply their rule of translation to all languages, especially to the English, and proceed to make a new version in English for circulation.

The last view was the really troublesome one. The question was one about which Baptists of equal piety and loyalty to principle might and did differ. The discussion went on until, in 1849, the managers of the American and Foreign Bible Society unanimously declared that the Scriptures ought to be faithfully and accurately translated into every language, but, regarding an English version, it was prudent to await the instructions of the society. At the annual meeting, May 25, 1850, after a discussion that extended through three sessions, it was decided that the society should circulate only the Received version in English, without note or comment. That decision, without doubt, represented the wish of the great majority of the Baptist denomination at the time, nor was there any considerable change of sentiment at any time thereafter. Both then and afterward, however, there was a minority, small in numbers, but worthy of all respect for the scholarship, piety, and zeal of those composing it, who were much aggrieved by this decision. They could not be convinced that it was not the duty of Baptists, by themselves if need be, to make a new version of the Scriptures in English; nor could they be convinced that even Baptists themselves would refuse to accept such a version, whatever scholars might say as to its merits, in place of the old King James version. In short, these brethren, deeply conscious of the defects of the Received version, were not sufficiently appreciative of its merits, and above all, they did not in the least understand the strength of the religious sentiment, in which the Common version was entrenched. Baptists of the present day understand it better, after seeing a Revision fall flat that had been produced by the labors during ten years of fourscore scholars, the ablest on both sides of the Atlantic—a version in which nine denominations bore a part, and for that reason had no sectarian prejudices to overcome.

But in 1850 this was by no means so clear, and five days after the above action was taken a meeting of twenty-four Baptists was called at the house of William Colgate, at which it was resolved to invite the co-operation of all who believed it to be the duty of Baptists to form a Bible society whose object should be to procure and circulate the most faithful versions of the Scriptures in all languages. On June 10 the American Bible Union was formed on this basis at the Baptist Tabernacle, in Mulberry Street, New York. It was ordered, as the fundamental principle on which all versions were to be made by this union, that "the exact meaning of the inspired text, as that text expressed it to those who understood the original Scriptures at the time they were first written, must be translated by corresponding words and phrases, so far as they can be found in the vernacular tongue of those for whom the version is designed, with the least possible obscurity or indefiniteness." This work was at once begun and prosecuted with energy.

The American Bible Union was not avowedly a Baptist society. It obtained co-operation from representatives of nine different denominations. It published revised versions of the Scriptures in Spanish and Italian, published the New Testament complete in the Chinese written character, in the Ningpo colloquial, in Siamese, and in Sgau Karen. Nevertheless, in common fame, its English version was alone recognized, and that was stigmatized as "a Baptist Bible," because it rendered $\beta\alpha\pi\tau i\zeta\omega$ and its cognates by "immerse" and its cognates. Great pains were taken with this English version. That of the Old Testament was never completed; that of the New Testament has passed through four careful revisions, and in its present form is recognized by competent scholars as the most faithful, accurate, and idiomatic version of the New Testament in the English tongue, alike valuable to the learned and the unlearned. More than half a million copies of this version were issued prior to 1880, and it had much to do with the undertaking of the Anglo-American revision, while its influence on the Revised New Testament of 1881 may be traced on every page of that book. Nevertheless, as a popular version it was a distinct and unmistakable failure. The Received version was too closely associated with the most sacred things in the experience of all Christians to be displaced by another that seemed strange and uncouth; and no matter how much the scholarly might insist on the superior merits of the new, the people shook their heads and clung to the old.

Many and fierce were the denominational combats while this work was going on. The great men among Baptists were ranged on opposite sides; the press was divided; hard blows were given and taken; old friends became alienated, or even became the bitterest mutual opponents. At every denominational gathering the strife was renewed. Rival agents scoured the country and alternately besieged pastors and churches. After a generation of this sort of thing the denomination tired of it, and all were ready to say right heartily, "a plague o' both your houses." The people showed their sentiments unmistakably by drawing their purse strings tight. The receipts of both societies, except from occasional legacies, dwindled to an amount barely sufficient to pay their expenses of administration. The denomination had lost faith in both, yet it was by no means ready to cease doing its proportion of circulating the Scriptures in all languages, both in the home and in the foreign fields.

From time to time various efforts were made at union between the two Bible societies, either with each other or with some other denominational agency. The first of these attempts seemed at one time to have been crowned with success—a union between the American and Foreign Bible Society and the American Baptist Publication Society. A "basis of union" was agreed upon by the respective Boards of Managers, and almost unanimously adopted at the annual session of both societies held in Tremont Temple, Boston, in May, 1869. By this agreement the Philadelphia society was to change its name to "The Bible and Publication Society," alter its constitution to correspond with the new title, recognize the privileges of life-members and directors of the other society, and carry on the Bible work to the extent of the means furnished for that purpose. On these terms the Bible Society was to wind up its affairs and turn over all its property to the Bible and Publication Society. Enabling acts were procured from the legislatures of New York and Pennsylvania, but that procured in New York was deemed defective in that it made the "basis of union" statute law, so that the constituency of the united society could make no change of policy except by permission of the New York Legislature. This Act was repealed, but another was practically vetoed by the governor, and the American and Foreign Bible Society was left without legal authority to effect a union. Injunctions and other legal proceedings were threatened by a minority of the Board of this society, who had all along been opposed to the union, and the project therefore came to naught. In May, 1873, the Philadelphia society resumed its name, The American Baptist Publication Society, and the restoration was formally legalized June 6, 1874.

Thus foiled of its purpose, the American and

Foreign Bible Society made overtures in May, 1874, for consolidation with the American Bible Union, under the title of "The American and Foreign Bible Union." The same motions were again gone through, but all efforts to secure from the legislature the requisite enabling act were vain; and, though the project was once formally abandoned, it was several times renewed, as late as 1880 being proposed as cheerfully as if it had never before been mentioned. Hope springs eternal in the Baptist breast, surely.

In the meantime it had seemed that the Baptists might again be brought into co-operation with the American Bible Society, at least in the distribution of the English Scriptures. There were many Baptists who had never ceased to take a warm interest in this society, and to engage actively in its work. Among these was Nathan Bishop, LL. D., who was a member of the Board of Managers from the year 1861 until his death. In the year 1879 the by-laws of the society were amended so as to remove the offensive restriction that had caused the division in 1836. The new by-law was as follows :

> The committee on versions shall have charge of all translations of the Bible published or distributed by the society; they shall recommend measures for securing new versions or revisions of old versions in foreign languages; shall examine new versions presented for the consideration and adoption of the society, especially in regard to their catholicity and the fidelity of their trans-

lation; and shall recommend such as they approve for the use of the society.

It seemed to Dr. Bishop that this opened the way for a union between Baptists and other denominations in the work. At his own expense he called a conference of twelve of the most eminent ministers and laymen of the denomination, which met in New York in March, 1879. They were in session for nine hours, in connection with one of the secretaries of the society; and every act of the Board of Managers from the year 1829 to that time, that could possibly concern the interests of Baptists, was read to them and carefully considered. After this thorough examination of the facts, and a full discussion of them, there was a unanimous conviction that no obstacle remained in the way of the co-operation of Baptists with the American Bible Society. A statement to that effect, signed by these twelve Baptists, was issued to the denomination under date of March 4, 1879, and was published in the denominational papers on March 20.[1]

At this time Prof. Howard Osgood, D. D., of the Rochester Theological Seminary, was the Baptist member of the committee on versions. He was requested by the committee to state what would satisfy

---

[1] This statement was signed by M. B. Anderson, Edward Bright, John A. Broadus, Wm. A. Cauldwell, S. S. Cutting, Alvah Hovey, Jas. M. Hoyt, Edward Lathrop, J. N. Murdock, Henry G. Weston, J. L. M. Curry, and G. W. Northrup. The last two, though invited to the conference, could not be present, but concurred in the statement.

the Baptist denomination and harmonize the differences between Baptists and the Bible Society. He told them that "Baptists, having been wrongfully excluded from common rights in the Bible Society, had no requests to make; that the only condition on which Baptists could be induced to return were those of the earlier years of the society, when scholarly Baptist versions with $\beta\alpha\pi\tau\iota\zeta\omega$ translated by words signifying *dip* or *immerse* were treated with the same favor as other versions." The committee expressed an earnest desire to put away all grounds of discord, and in May, 1880, the following substitute for the old law was adopted by the committee and the Board of Managers.

In the matter of Scriptures in foreign languages, the Board will favor versions in any language which, in point of fidelity and catholicity, shall be conformed to the principles upon which the American Bible Society was originally founded.

This new by-law was published and an official copy was sent to the Executive Committee of the American Baptist Missionary Union in June, 1880. In the following October the committee made an application to the Bible Society for a grant to aid in the circulation of Dr. Judson's Burmese version of the Scriptures and the revised Karen versions.

When the application was presented the objection was at once raised that the word $\beta\alpha\pi\tau\iota\zeta\omega$ was translated by words signifying *dip* or *immerse*. Action on the application was delayed for fifteen months. At the meeting of the Board of Managers in March, 1882, this decision was reached:

> The Committee on Versions reported their conclusion, based upon careful inquiry and correspondence, that the Burmese and Karen versions, for publishing which an appropriation had been asked by the American Baptist Missionary Union, are deficient in the quality of *catholicity*, as that term is used in the by-laws of the American Bible Society and the regulations of the Committee on Versions.

It would be putting it mildly to say that Baptists were surprised and chagrined at so lame and impotent a conclusion of this matter. The "Independent" said, with as much point as candor:

> The officials of the Bible Society are guilty of real sectarianism. It is vain to deny that the only objection they had to Judson's translation is that it may have a certain effect in certain controversies. But what has the Bible Society to do with sectarian controversies? If a certain translation is incorrect, let them condemn it. But what have they to do with the question how it will effect this or that dispute? If a certain translation seems to be scholarly, they should publish it, no matter what effect it may have on ecclesiastical conflicts. The officials of the society abandoned the majestic neutrality of scholarship and love of truth which asks merely whether a given version is correct. They stoop to inquire how it will affect the interests of contending sects.[1]

There were many who did not hesitate to pro-

---
[1] "Independent," February 23, 1882.

nounce the course of the society disingenuous and tricky. In this they were hasty and unjust. The truth seems to have been that there were at this time in the American Bible Society, as there were at the original controversy in 1836, Pedobaptist members who did not think the rule regarding versions wise, but agreed with the editor of the "Independent" that the duty of the society was to circulate the correct translations of the Scriptures, and that to refuse to circulate a given version, not because it was incorrect, but because it might injure the tender sensibilities of some, or have an unfavorable effect on some religious controversy, was a violation of the original constitution of the society and the solemn trusts committed to its managers. But those who held this view were not the majority, as the event proved. It would have been franker and more satisfactory had the majority pronounced its will unmistakably in the first instance, instead of giving way for the time to the minority only to reassert their sectarian prejudices in the end. But conscious insincerity and duplicity cannot with any show of justice be imputed to the Board of Managers.

The confusion of opinion became worse than ever after the failure of these overtures for a reunion, and a desire that had been for some years growing among Baptists for a final solution of the whole controversy became too strong to be resisted. There is in theory no final authority in the Baptist polity for the decision of such questions. The action of individuals and churches cannot be bound by the decisions of any body. Yet in practice the denomination has generally decided great questions of policy through a convention. While the decisions of such a body have no binding force, if the convention is so constituted as to represent the general public opinion throughout the denomination the moral effect of its decisions has always proved to be quite equal to the canon law of other religious bodies. There was a call for a Bible convention to settle this whole question, and such a convention was held at Saratoga, May 22 and 23, 1883. It was a large and representative body. The method of representation finally decided upon secured the presence of the best men, both ministers and laymen, in the denomination. A committee of seven on resolutions and other business was appointed early in the session, consisting of Thomas Armitage, Augustus H. Strong, Wayland Hoyt, Eustace C. Fitz, Henry C. Mabie, W. H. Parmly, and S. W. Duncan. This committee presented unanimously a series of resolutions which after vigorous debate were finally adopted in the following form:

WHEREAS, In the year 1833 the Baptists of America resolved "to give the heathen the pure word of God in their own languages, and to furnish their missionaries with all the means in their power to make their translation as exact a representation of the mind of the Holy Spirit as may be possible"; and,

WHEREAS, Their missionary translators were instructed "to endeavor, by earnest prayer and diligent study, to ascertain the precise meaning of the original text, and to express that meaning as exactly as the nature of the languages into which they translate the Bible will permit"; therefore,

Resolved, That this convention earnestly re-affirms these positions as sound and obligatory.

Resolved, That, as these principles are divine, it is the duty of American Baptists to circulate versions made upon these principles in all languages, so far as such versions can be procured.

Resolved, That, as there are differences of opinion in our denomination touching the several versions now existing in English, on the score of fidelity, it is the right of every Baptist to use that version which best commends its faithfulness to his conscience in the sight of God.

Resolved, While in the judgment of the convention the work of revision is not yet completed, that whatever organization or organizations shall be designated as the most desirable for the prosecution of home Bible work among American Baptists, should now circulate the commonly Received version, the new Revised version with the corrections of the American revisers incorporated in the text, and the translations of the American Bible Union, according to demand; and that all moneys specially designated for circulation of either of these versions should be faithfully appropriated in keeping with the wish of the donor.

Resolved, That in the judgment of this convention the Bible work of Baptists should be done by our two existing societies—the foreign work by the American Baptist Missionary Union, and the home work by the American Baptist Publication Society.

Resolved, That in our judgment the Missionary Union should more fully recognize the necessity of accurate translation and wide distribution of the word of God in foreign lands; that the duty of providing means for this work should be more distinctly and effectively urged by the Union upon the churches; and that the Union should employ whatever additional agencies may be required to secure this result.

Resolved, That the Publication Society should maintain a department to be designated as the Bible Department; that this department should be charged with the duty of collecting and expending funds for home Bible work; and that a special secretary of equal authority with the missionary secretary, should be appointed to take the supervision of the department.

Resolved, That as a guarantee that all the chief views current in our denomination shall be represented in the conduct of our home Bible work; and as a provision for a settlement of the questions which have arisen with regard to the administration of that work, the American and Foreign Bible Society be requested to name three persons to be voted for as managers of the Publication Society; and that upon the election of these persons as such managers, the American and Foreign Bible Society be requested, in the interest of Baptist unity, to cease active operations in the field, and to retain its legal existence no longer than is legally necessary for the custody of funds and legacies.

Resolved, That the Publication Society should maintain such intimate and close relations with the American Baptist Home Mission Society in the prosecution of Bible work, that the very large missionary force of the latter society, among people of many languages and on the frontiers of our country, may be effectively employed in the practical work of Bible distribution.

General relief was felt at this result. All the

societies concerned accepted it. The American and
Foreign Bible Society and the American Bible
Union have indeed maintained a nominal existence
since that time, but only to preserve their legal
rights to legacies, and for similar purposes. Whatever money has been received by them, or derived
from any fund in their possession, has been paid to
the American Baptist Publication Society, and been
used strictly for the purposes for which it was given.
A careful revision of the New Testament version
issued by the Bible Union has been made under the
direction of the American Baptist Publication Society by the Rev. Drs. Henry G. Weston, Alvah
Hovey, and John A. Broadus. Some difference of
opinion has developed since the Bible convention
regarding the interpretation of certain of the resolutions then adopted, but it has been a difference of
interpretation only. There has been no disposition
to revive the ancient disputes, and to fight over
again the fierce battles regarding faithful versions
and separate denominational societies. American
Baptists have been convinced that the solution
reached at Saratoga was not merely the wisest possible, but the only solution practicable; that we can
best carry on our work at home through the agency of
the American Baptist Publication Society, and that
we must carry it on abroad through the agency of
the American Baptist Missionary Union. Compared
with the years that preceded, those that have followed
the Bible convention of 1883 have been years of

profound peace. This body seemed at the time to be one of the most remarkable for weight and dignity that had ever assembled among Baptists, and its decisions were recognized, even while the deliberations were in progress, as likely to be second in importance to nothing that had ever occurred in the denomination's history. Now that a dozen years have passed there seems to be no reason to revise this contemporary impression.[1] Time has rather increased than diminished the respect that all Baptists felt from the first for this convention, both as regards the ability and moral weight of the men composing it and the importance of its decisions as affecting all our denominational interests.

---

[1] The method adopted for the representation of all shades of opinion in the denomination had much to do with making this the representative and weighty body it proved to be. The State Convention or General Association of each State, either at its annual meeting or through its Board, was requested "carefully to select and appoint delegates in the ratio of one delegate for every one thousand church-members or fraction thereof." Of course there were not wanting Baptists to object that this was a method hitherto unknown in Baptist polity, which threatened all manner of evils in future; but they failed to take account of the fact that this was an emergency that had never before occurred among Baptists, and that the evil demanded heroic measures. The fears of these brethren proved to be groundless. The precedent has never been followed, or even quoted as authority, since the convention was held.

CHAPTER XI

A COMPARATIVE STUDY OF PROGRESS

A COMPARATIVE study of Baptist progress in the Middle States during the present century cannot fail to suggest interesting lines of thought and investigation. We are confronted at the very outset of such a study, of course, by the absence of trustworthy statistics, and are compelled for a time to rely on estimates. These are not mere wild guesses, however. We have the carefully gleaned figures of Morgan Edwards, and later those of Asplund's "Registers," and these furnish us a tolerably solid starting-point; and we have semi-official figures from several sources about the number of Baptists in 1812, 1817, and other years before the publication of official statistics began. Many of the Associations began to print statistics in their Minutes long before State statistics were gathered. The Minutes of the old General Convention furnish information of no little value. After 1833 we have Allen's "Register." From all these sources it is possible to approximate very closely the numerical growth of Baptist churches.

Our point of departure must be the figures gathered by the Rev. John Asplund who, as he tells us, made a tour of the Baptist churches, visiting two hundred and fifteen of them, besides fifteen Associations, .traveling about seven thousand miles in eighteen months, chiefly on foot.[1] In the five years covered by these statistics the increase of Baptists in New York was over fifty per cent., while in the other Middle States the denomination had barely held its own. The cause of these phenomena has already been sufficiently discussed; suffice it to say that the immigration to New York during the remaining years of the eighteenth century continued in an ever-increasing current, while the other three States participated in it to a much smaller degree. For the conjectural table of 1800, as compared with 1794 and 1812, see Table I., Appendix B. In 1800, therefore, the Baptists of the Middle States were about one in every eighty-three of the population.

From 1800 to 1850 the growth of Baptists was rapid and continuous, with slight fluctuations, and in the latter year there was one Baptist to every forty-six in the population of the Middle States— certainly a most remarkable growth. This increase was largest in New Jersey, where the number of Baptists was doubled nearly three times in this half-century. New York and Pennsylvania follow close. These facts are made more impressive to the eye by the diagrams in Appendix C.

After 1850 a great change comes over the Bap-

---

[1] See Table II., Appendix B.

tists in the Middle States. With a single exception, Pennsylvania, they fail to keep pace with the proportionate increase of population, and in 1890 Baptists were only one in fifty of the people. The diagrams in Appendix C make this plainer than any figures. It becomes an interesting question to ask, What is the cause of this declension, as compared with the rapid growth of the first half of the century? There are doubtless many causes, but one was demonstrably in operation, and will alone go far to account for the observed results.

Take the State of New York, where the declension is greatest. The baptisms reported in the State Minutes in the decade from 1850 to 1860 were forty-eight thousand one hundred and fourteen; from 1860 to 1870, forty-one thousand six hundred and eighty-nine; from 1870 to 1880, fifty-one thousand nine hundred and ninety-six; from 1880 to 1890, fifty-three thousand eight hundred and twenty-two; a total of one hundred and ninety-five thousand six hundred and twenty-one. Now there were in New York in 1850 no fewer than eighty-four thousand eight hundred and twenty-one Baptists. Adding the number of baptisms we have two hundred and eighty thousand four hundred and forty-two. In 1890 there were one hundred and twenty-seven thousand five hundred and thirty-one, leaving one hundred and fifty-two thousand nine hundred and eleven to be accounted for. But one way of accounting for them is possible—at least one hundred thousand of these were dismissed by letter to other churches outside of the Middle States. It is a notorious fact, requiring no proof, that a large part of the membership of Baptist churches in all our Western centers were baptized in the East. There has been a transfusion of the best blood of churches in New York, and to a less degree of Pennsylvania and New Jersey, to the West. No wonder, after a drain so constant and so large, the churches of New York show signs of debility, and that they have failed to keep pace with the advance of population. If they could have held in their membership those who have been saved through their labors the showing would be very different.

In comparing the second half-century with the first, therefore, especially in New York, we cannot reach a fair conclusion without taking into consideration two things. Prior to 1850 there were specially favorable influences promoting the growth of Baptists, for which they were in no way responsible; such as a great immigration from New England and a marked revival spirit. All evangelical denominations more or less shared with Baptists these advantages, and experienced a somewhat similar prosperity. The most that can justly be said in praise of our fathers is that they were not slow to take advantage of these favoring circumstances, but made the most of them. Since 1850, on the other hand, circumstances have been increasingly unfavorable for all evangelical Christians.

Immigration has continued into the Middle States, but it has been an immigration from Europe of Roman Catholics, upon whom Baptists have been able to make little impression. But no other evangelical denomination has shown any greater ability to reach these immigrants. At the same time Baptists have had to contend with an emigration of their best men and women to the West. As New York profited before 1850 by New England's losses, so since that time she has been called upon to lose that the new commonwealths of the West might profit. It is just, but before we reproach ourselves overmuch for lack of diligence in the harvest field, let us remind ourselves and others that much of the wheat in our barns in a former generation we never reaped, while much that we have since reaped has gone to swell the store of others. For not a little of our earlier prosperity we deserve no special credit; for a large part of our apparent recent decline we are not to blame.

Numerical growth is, however, by no means the only or the chief test of denominational progress. Though our apparent advance during the last half-century has been slow compared with ·the previous fifty years, it does not follow that the end of the century will see Baptists of the Middle States relatively weaker than they were in 1850. There always comes a time in the growth of any organism or society when its increase in size falls off relatively or ceases absolutely; but growth does not cease, still less does decay set in. Between the years of twelve and eighteen man increases in stature with a rapidity truly wonderful; but his growth does not cease when his full stature is nearly or quite attained. Bone and sinew toughen and thicken, and the vital powers go on increasing for many years after a man's size has been reached.

We see something like this illustrated in the history of the Baptists of the Middle States. In New York, for example, the average number of members to a church in 1850 was one hundred and five; in 1895 it was one hundred and fifty-four. In Pennsylvania the average number of members to a church in 1850 was ninety; in 1895 it was one hundred and forty-three. In New Jersey, during the same period the averages have risen from one hundred and thirty-three to one hundred and eighty-two. This is denominational growth of a most solid and healthful kind, and it has not been attained by the rise of a few large city churches. New Jersey has notably few such churches, yet that is the State where the churches have the largest average membership. The facts would not be materially affected by leaving out of account altogether the largest cities in the Middle States. The growth that these figures show is due to the advance made by Baptist churches in the smaller cities and the thriving villages. Churches in the old farming communities have suffered loss since 1850, in the majority of cases, but that is because the towns themselves are suffering a loss of population. The movement of population is citywards. Since 1850 the urban population of the United States has risen from 12.49 per cent. of the entire population to 29.12. Nowhere has this tendency been more strongly felt than in the Middle States. Not only have they in New York, Brooklyn, and Philadelphia, three of the largest cities in our country, but Buffalo and Pittsburg equal a fourth, while a multitude of smaller cities dot all three States. In the decade between 1880 and 1890, 69.5 per cent. of the rural townships of New York lost population, while in Pennsylvania nine hundred and eighteen out of two thousand and seventy-five townships sustained a similar loss, and New Jersey showed a loss in one hundred and seventeen out of two hundred and fifty townships. It cannot be expected that the churches should escape the effect of a movement of population that is so profoundly affecting our whole national life. They do not escape. The rural churches have decreased, must continue to decrease, while this movement of population continues.

But this very fact lends additional importance to the work of State missions, and this is obtaining more general recognition from year to year. These country churches have been and still are the best feeders of the churches in the cities and villages. Many of them are now unable fully to support themselves, but could they have back again the strong men and women they have given up to urban churches, they would not need to ask aid. To aid them is not charity, but justice. To the obligation of the strong to help bear the burdens of the weak is in this case added the obligation of a debt, and the motive of self-interest. The city of New York is vitally interested in the maintenance of the Adirondack forests, on whose continuance depend the springs and rivulets that feed the Hudson and ultimately make of it a river on whose bosom the commerce of the world might float. In like manner our great metropolitan churches are vitally interested in the maintenance of the rural churches from which they draw so large a part of their own strength, from which come the larger part of the candidates for the ministry.

There has been a marked relative increase in the numbers and efficiency of Baptist ministers within the last forty years. In 1850 the number of Baptist churches in New York was eight hundred and eight, of ministers seven hundred and thirty-eight; in 1890 there were eight hundred and eighty-three churches and nine hundred and twenty-four ministers. The statistics of the other States show a similar condition of things—an increase of ministers more than double that of the churches. A much larger proportion of the smaller churches have pastors now than formerly, probably because of the larger means of the State missionary organization. It was not numerically possible for every Baptist church to have a pastor forty years ago—there were simply not enough ministers to go around. Now the problem is purely a financial one; every Baptist church in these four States might have a pastor to-day if it were able to support him, or if the State Convention had funds enough to supply what it lacked.

As to the efficiency of the ministry of to-day, as compared with that of a half-century ago, opinions may differ. Much depends on the point of view. Considered merely as soul winners, the ministers of 1850 were probably the superiors of their successors. God raised up these men to do a work that required to be done just then, and they did it faithfully. He made no mistake; they were exactly the men for their times. But the same God has since called other men to do a different work, and again it is quite probable that he has made no mistake. The men of to-day have had superior advantages of education and have profited by them. If they are less effective as evangelists, are they not better pastors? If their preaching converts fewer sinners, may it not edify more saints? And this last is, according to the Apostle Paul, the chief end for which the ministry was given: "And he gave some as apostles, some as evangelists, some as pastors and teachers; unto the perfecting of the saints for the work of ministration, for the building up of the body of Christ"(Eph. 4 : 11–13). Evangelism has done the churches of Christ much good, but it has done them some harm, in giving them a false standard of growth. Increase of numbers is not all of growth, nor even the chief part of it; a church may report continual annual accessions to its membership by baptism, and be growing weaker instead of stronger. In the work of edification the pastors of to-day should be more efficient than their predecessors, because they have had a training far better than was possible forty years ago.

The need of this work of edification was never so great as now. Even a hundred years ago it cost something to be a Baptist. It meant fines and imprisonments, if no worse, in several of our American States. A Baptist church in those days was pretty certain to consist only of those who knew very clearly why they were Baptists. Men do not put person and property at stake for vague and uncertain opinions; it takes clear and positive convictions as to truth and duty to bring one to that point. Even in the Middle States fifty years ago, Baptists in most communities were under a sort of social ban, were looked at askance, and nothing short of a strong conviction of duty would impel a convert to join a Baptist church. Now it costs nothing to be a Baptist; in many communities there are evident social and business advantages in being connected with a Baptist church. In comparatively few communities is the Baptist church "the leading church in town," but to be a member of a Baptist church is respectable everywhere, honorable in many communities. Multitudes therefore drift into our churches without any positive convictions of duty, knowing little of our distinctive principles. Sometimes they join a Baptist church simply as a matter of convenience; often they really join the popular pastor, not the church. Thousands of them need the edificatory work of a faithful pastor, in regard to both denominational principles and the fundamental truths of Scripture. They seem to be regenerate, but they are babes in Christ, and babes they are likely to remain unless this work is done.

The work of the Baptist young people, in their Christian Culture Courses, will do much to remedy this defect in the next generation. But, in the meantime, we have this generation to deal with, and the young people can do little to affect it. Nor will the Christian Culture Courses ever take the place of pastoral teaching. They are not intended to do such a thing; their object is to supplement, not supplant, the pulpit. The need is great for edifying preaching, for instruction in righteousness, and the ministry of to-day is better qualified for this work, so far as mental equipment is concerned, than that of any preceding generation. If it is deficient, it will be for lack of will to do the work, not for lack of ability. The signs are not few that ministers as a whole are becoming more awake to the need of this work, and are giving themselves to it with greater faithfulness year by year.

The foregoing mention of the better educational advantages enjoyed by Baptist ministers of our day naturally suggests a survey of educational progress. At the beginning of this century there was no Baptist institution of learning in the Middle States, private schools being excepted. In 1850 two institutions of collegiate grade had been founded, with one of which a theological seminary was closely connected. In the next decade our remaining institutions were established : two colleges, two theological seminaries, and eight academies. This is a very remarkable record of educational enterprise, far beyond the contemporaneous growth of the denomination in either numerical or financial strength. It denotes one of two things: either culpable previous indifference of Baptists to education, or a draft on the future which a coming generation was expected to pay at sight. The latter seems the explanation that best accords with the facts. A generation ago very inadequate ideas were prevalent regarding the endowment of an institution for the higher learning. Men with light hearts set about the founding of a "university"—they scorned such a modest title as that of "college"—with a sum that we now consider miserably inadequate for the establishment of an academy. A building and a hundred thousand dollars were considered quite a handsome beginning of such an educational enterprise. In our day one man has already given to the University of Chicago over five million dollars, and its needs are by no means yet adequately supplied. The difference in these figures is not a bad measure of the expansion of our ideas regarding education. The three "universities" established by Baptists of the Middle States are not, and probably can never become, universities; but they are excellent colleges, and the denomination is quite able so to endow and support them as to keep them in the front rank of institutions of their grade.

Our theological schools have been from the first the equals of any in the world for the purpose for which they are designed, namely, to fit men for the ministry of the Baptist churches. Their main object is not to produce great scholars, and they do not offer elaborate courses in the Oriental languages and other recondite subjects. As their resources increase they may attempt more work of this kind for the comparatively few who desire such instruction. Nevertheless, our seminaries have offered unsurpassed facilities for advanced biblical and theological training in the usual departments. The scholars who have filled their chairs have been the peers of any. There were no more learned men in biblical science (to mention only the dead) than Horatio B. Hackett, Thomas J. Conant, Asahel C. Kendrick; no theologians of their time surpassed Ezekiel G. Robinson and Ebenezer Dodge; and among the teachers of church history R. J. W. Buckland and John C. Long held no second place. Among living men other names will suggest themselves to every reader—names that stand for unsurpassed attainments, scholars of other denominations being the judges.

The weak place in our educational system, as has been intimated elsewhere, is our academies. They are the youngest of all our schools, and their importance has only of late been appreciated—is not yet fully appreciated. None of our colleges or seminaries is yet adequately endowed, if, indeed, any educational institution ever gets an endowment adequate to its needs. But relatively to the colleges and seminaries, the endowments of our academies are beggarly. There is need everywhere, but the crying need of our educational system is the generous endowment of our academies. A quarter of a million each would put them fairly on their feet and make them the equals of the best schools of their grade.

The total property of these institutions is valued at little less than nine million dollars, of which more than five millions are in productive endowments. The disparity is not great when we remember that two men are ready to invest money in bricks for one who will invest it in brains. Substantially the whole of this property has been raised by the Baptists of the Middle States since 1850, the sole exception being the value of the institutions at Hamilton at that time, which was little if any in excess of sixty thousand dollars. Certainly Baptists have no reason to feel ashamed of this record, but still less should they feel pride when they compare what has been done with that which still imperatively demands doing.

What the Baptists of the Middle States have done for denominational and general literature is also worthy of recounting. The story might be made quite brief if we were to adopt the severe rule of De Quincey and exclude from the domain of literature "all books in which the matter to be communicated is paramount to the manner or form of its communication." However well this definition may answer for that form of literature known as *belles-lettres*—literature as one of the fine arts simply—it is too narrow for practical purposes. Literature must be

> A creature not too bright or good
> For human nature's daily food,

if it is to be serviceable in this work-a-day world, and to the useful literature of their day Baptists have certainly contributed their quota. Even a *catalogue raisonné* of such books would fill more space than is available here for the purpose, but it may not be useless to indicate the character and quality, as well as the bulk, of this literature.

Denominational history, including the biographies of Baptist worthies, has naturally engaged the attention of Baptist writers to a large degree, but by no means unduly. The pioneer in this work was Morgan Edwards. Besides the volumes that were printed in his lifetime on early Baptist history in Pennsylvania and New Jersey, he left in manuscript similar "Materials towards a History of the Baptists," as he modestly called them, in the States of Rhode Island, Delaware, Virginia, the Carolinas, and Georgia. The value of these collections is inestimable; all subsequent historians have leaned upon Edwards, for a large part of colonial Baptist history would be a blank but for his diligence and accuracy. In the later collections of materials made by David Benedict, Baptists of the Middle States may claim a quasi-proprietorship, since they were published in New York. The same claim may be made on Cramp's "Baptist History," at the time of its issue by the American Baptist Publication Society by far the best book yet written on the subject, and still not without its usefulness. The larger work of Rev. Thomas Armitage, D. D., founded on later researches, at once took the place, which it still holds, as the standard work on the subject. Books less comprehensive in scope, but of high value, have been written in considerable numbers; such as the "Historical Vindications" of Sewall S. Cutting; the "Lectures on Baptist History," by William R. Williams; "The Story of the Baptists" and "Delaware Baptists," by Richard B. Cook. The work of John Dowling on "Romanism" was a contribution to ecclesiastical history (or, perhaps it should rather be said, to polemics) that had great vogue in its day.

Of biographies of the Baptist worthies of the Middle States, and of like books written by Baptists of those States, there is a great store. We may perhaps name among them the life of Francis Wayland, since not only was the book published by a New York Baptist, but one of the authors has been for a score of years a resident of Pennsylvania. Kendrick's life of Mrs. Emily C. Judson might claim a place in "literature," even under De Quincey's narrow definition, and so might Edward Judson's two biographies of his father. Other notable books of their class are James B. Taylor's "Luther Rice," Alonzo King's "George Dana Boardman," S. W. Lynd's "William Staughton," Rufus Babcock's "John M. Peck," H. Harvey's "Alfred Bennett," the life of Spencer H. Cone, by his sons, and the memoir of Kingman Nott by his brother. It is greatly to be regretted that books like these are now so entirely out of print, and for the most part known only by title, if known at all, by Baptists of the present generation.

Besides these authors of single books, there have been not a few Baptists of the Middle States who have been voluminous writers. Some names will be recalled at once by every reader. Henry C. Fish, for twenty-seven years pastor of the First Church of Newark, N. J. (now the Peddie Memorial), wrote and compiled many volumes, among which his "Repository of Pulpit Eloquence" and "Handbook of Revivals" are especially worthy of mention. Pharcellus Church, besides his journalistic and periodical writing, the bulk of which was great, found time to write at least five volumes, historical, theological, and popular. William C. Wilkinson, whose book, "The Baptist Principle," is one of the best expositions and defenses ever made of the distinctive denominational principles, is also the author of half a dozen volumes of essays and literary criticism, and of four volumes of verse of a high order: "Poems," "Webster; an Ode," "The Epic of Saul," and "The Epic of Paul."

In theological literature there are also honorable achievements to record, such as the "Systematic Theology," "Philosophy and Religion," and "The Great Poets and their Theology," of Augustus H. Strong, which have given their author an international reputation as among the foremost of American theologians. The "Systematic Theology" of Elias H. Johnson (with the appendix on "Ecclesiology," by Henry G. Weston), the posthumously published lectures on "Christian Theology" by Ezekiel G. Robinson, the "privately printed" yet semi-public lectures of George D. B. Pepper, Ebenezer Dodge, and William N. Clarke, are one and all notable contributions to the theological literature of our country. The more popular treatise on "Christian Doctrine," by J. M. Pendleton, should be mentioned here also, nor should it be forgotten that he was a voluminous and forcible writer on theological and denominational subjects for more than one generation. Of publications in what the Germans call Practical Theology there are fewer. Among them may be named Hezekiah Harvey's "The Pastor" and "The Church," Jesse B. Thomas' "The Mould of Doctrine" and "The Old Bible and the New Science," and George W. Hervey's "The Story of Baptist Missions." In Exegetical Theology Dr. Hackett's "Commentary on the Acts of the Apostles" still stands in the front rank. Dr. Kendrick's translation of Olshausen, and Dr. Bliss' translations of Lange (in the Old Testament series) are still useful books, while the former's volume on Hebrews and the latter's on Luke, are valued contributions to "The American Commentary on the New Testament." To the same work Professor William Arnold Stevens, of Rochester, contributed the volume on the minor Pauline Epistles, and is joint author, with Professor Ernest D. Burton, of Chicago, of the best English Harmony of the Gospels that has yet appeared. Dr. George W. Clark is also the author of Harmonies of the Gospels and Acts, and of Commentaries on the New Testament, books that have had a large circulation and are justly esteemed.

In the closely allied subject of philosophy there have been few notable contributions to literature made by Baptists of these States. Two books have within recent years been published that do much to redeem the previous failure of our writers to cultivate this field—the "Genetic Philosophy" of David

J. Hill, of Rochester, and "Belief in God," by Professor Schurman, of Cornell University. Whatever defects these books may be thought to possess as philosophical treatises, no one can deny their right to a place in any catalogue of literature, for their style is peculiarly limpid and graceful.

It is perhaps in journalism that most has been done for denominational progress by Baptists of the Middle States, though of course critics of the De Quincey type would be horror-stricken at the very notion of including journalism among works of literature. The first weekly newspaper established in this region was the "New York Baptist Register," the publication of which began toward the end of 1823, or early in 1824. It was printed at Utica, and edited by Elders Galusha and Willey; its circulation was small and it was not always regular in appearing. It was offered to the State Convention and accepted by them as their organ. Alexander M. Beebee was appointed editor, and Bennett and Bright, of Utica, were secured to print and mail it to subscribers. A circulation of some two thousand copies was secured quickly, and the paper soon became a power in the denomination. Mr. Beebee was an eminent Baptist layman of Central New York, an honored member of the Onondaga bar, and an accomplished writer. The paper continued with varying fortunes until 1853, when it was consolidated with the "New York Recorder"—a paper that had been begun in New York City in 1839, and had been edited by such men as Martin B. Anderson and Sewall S. Cutting. In 1855 Edward Bright bought the paper and changed its name to "The Examiner." In 1865 this paper was consolidated with the "Chronicle," which had been established in 1849, and had been edited by Jay S. Backus and Pharcellus Church.

With this same paper have been joined very recently two others that had an interesting history. In 1865 the American Baptist Publication Society began the issue of "The National Baptist," of which the successive editors were Kendall Brooks, Lemuel Moss, and H. L. Wayland. In 1882, the Society, finding the publication of the paper embarrassing, financially and otherwise, sold it to Dr. Wayland, who continued it until May, 1894, when its subscription list and good will were transferred to "The Examiner," of which Dr. Wayland became editor in 1895. For some years previous to 1857 "The American Baptist" was published as a weekly newspaper at Utica, but after that date was published in New York. In 1872 Alfred S. Patton purchased it, changed its name to the "Baptist Weekly," and continued its publication in New York. After Dr. Patton's death, in 1892, the paper was purchased by John B. Calvert, its name was changed to "The Christian Inquirer," and its character was greatly altered for the better. In March, 1895, it was purchased by "The Examiner," which for a short time thus became the only weekly Baptist newspaper published by and for the Baptists of the Middle States. In December, 1895, the publication of "The Commonwealth," was begun by the Baptists of Philadelphia and vicinity, with the aim of making a denominational paper for Pennsylvania, New Jersey, and Delaware. To indicate the future of Baptist journalism belongs to prophecy, and this book pretends to be nothing more than history.

It is entirely proper to say, however, that each of these papers has had a distinct character and individuality of its own, and each has done good service to its constituency. Baptists of the Middle States owe more than most of them will ever appreciate of their denominational progress to the excellence of their newspaper press. These papers have been the stanch friends and supporters of every good denominational enterprise, and have done more than any other one agency to promote denominational unity. They have also exerted a force not easily calculable, but certainly very powerful, in holding close to the accepted interpretations of the Scriptures those Baptists who have shown decided tendencies towards aberrations. They have therefore been a strong conservative force, such as is of the utmost value to churches whose bonds of union are so few and so slight as those that bind together the churches of the Baptist order. The extent and quality of this power were most effectively shown in the decade between 1870 and 1880, when the "open communion" controversy was raging in certain parts of the country. That the Baptists of the Middle States were less infected by the so-called "liberal" tendencies than the churches of some other States, was due in large part to the uncompromising attitude maintained by their newspapers, and especially by "The Examiner." It was charged, perhaps with a basis of justice, that the newspapers often abused their power in this and other controversies; that they sometimes attacked men quite as orthodox as their editors; that they were too domineering, and assumed too much the functions of Pope and Council. These were the defects of their qualities, and at any rate it must be admitted that they stood without wavering by what had always been the distinctive principles of the Baptist faith, and made not only a valiant and determined but successful defense against those who would abandon those principles.

The Baptists of the Middle States have had an honorable history. From the smallest of beginnings they have grown to be a great body with an influence far-reaching and deep. During much of this century they have increased twice as rapidly as the population, and they are at present fairly holding their own with the growing population, in spite of the vast influx of Roman Catholic and infidel foreigners. Their growth in intelligence has more than kept pace with their increase in numbers. Their orthodoxy of doctrine and unity of spirit are a constant cause of astonishment to other Christians. There is surely reason to believe that there is in store for them, if they are but faithful to duty and wise to avail themselves of opportunity, a future that shall surpass anything that they have yet accomplished.

APPENDIX A

The "Minutes of the Baptist Education Society" for the year 1812 contain an elaborate report by the Board on a "System of Education," from which the following extract is made, *verbatim et literatim:*

V. In relation to the studies to be pursued.
1. As to languages—
Latin.—Ross's Grammar, Beza's New Testament, *Selectæ veteri*, and *Selectæ profanis*, Cornelius Nepos, Cæsar's Commentaries, Cicero's Orations, Virgil, Horace, Young's or Ainsworth's Dictionary.

Greek—Wettenhall's Grammar, the Greek Testament, a few of the Dialogues of Lucian, or a book of Xenophon and two or three of the first books of the Iliad; Schrevelius's Lexicon and Parkhurst.

Hebrew—Lyon's or Buxtorf's Grammar, Vander Hooght's Bible, Buxtorf, Pike or Parkhurst's Lexicon.

English—Murray's and Waldo's Grammar.

2. History,
Profane—Rollin's Ancient, Goldsmith's Rome, Tytler, Snowden's America, Priestly's Charts, Kennet's Roman, Potter's Grecian Antiquities, Gray' *Memoria Technica*.

Ecclesiastical—Playfair's Chronology, Mosheim, Milnor, Hawes, Newton's First Three Centuries.

Sacred—Shuckford's Connection, Prideaux's Connection, Newton on Prophecies, Josephus or the same abridged by Dr. Crull.

Natural—Goldsmith's animated Nature.
3. Logic—Watts, and Supplement.
4. Geography and Astronomy,
General—Morse or Parish's, Keith on the Globes.
Sacred—Dr. Wells, Calmet.
Ferguson's and Bonycastle's Astronomy, Derham and Ray.
5. Mathematics—a book or two of Euclid's Elements; the six cases of right-angled trigonometry.
6. Belles Lettres and Oratory—Gibbon's Rhetoric, Blair's Belles Lettres abridged, Rollin's Belles Lettres, Witherspoon, Maury on Eloquence.
7. Natural Philosophy, a popular lecture, Ferguson, Blair.
8. Divinity—Turretin, Gill's Body of Divinity, Doddridge's Lectures, Scot's Essays, Witsius on the Covenants, Bogue, Edward's History of Redemption, Witherspoon's Lectures, Owen on Hebrews.
9. On the Composition of a sermon—Robinson's Claude, William's Christian Preacher, Mason's Student and Pastor.
10. On Criticism—Lowth's dissertation, Campbell's Dissertations and Notes, the Lectures of Michaelis.
11. Miscellaneous Reading—The Commentators generally, Gill, Henry, Doddridge, Fenelon's Dialogues on Eloquence, Burder's Oriental Customs, Blackwell's Sacred Classics, Owen on the Spirit, Cole's Sovereignty, Booth's Abbadie and Reign of Grace, Gill's Cause of God and Truth. The works of Bates, Charnack, Howe, Flavel, Watts, Toplady, Hervey, Erskine, Halyburton : Fox's Book of Martyrs, Cave's Lives of the Fathers, Middleton's Biography, Nonconformist Memorial, Johnson's Lives of the Poets, Paley's Evidences, Leland's View of Deistical Writers, West on the Resurrection, Simpson's Plea, Baxter's Reasons, Fuller's Moral Tendency, &c.

Locke's Essay on the Understanding, Paley's Natural Theology. For poetry, Milton, Young, Thompson, Pope, Cowper, Blair. The Histories of the Baptists, by Bacchus, Crosby, Ivimey, Benedict. &c., &c., &c.

APPENDIX B

STATISTICS REGARDING BAPTIST PROGRESS

TABLE I

	1800	1812
Baptists in New York	12,000	18,499
" " New Jersey	800	2,811
" " Pennsylvania	3,000	4,365
" " Delaware	400	480
Total	16,200	26,155

TABLE II

BAPTISTS IN	1790	1791	1792	1793	1794
New York	4,001	4,425	4,895	5,263	6,554
New Jersey	2,189	2,218	2,177	2,177	1,407
Pennsylvania	1,276	1,326	1,348	1,368	1,612
Delaware	457	380	382	390	385

APPENDIX B

TABLE III

The figures before 1820 are conjectural, except in the case of Delaware. The figures for 1820 are from the report of the Triennial Convention for that year.

		1800	1810	1820	1830	1840	1850	1860	1870	1880	1890
New York	Churches	......	......	362	[60,000]	736	808	836	741	878	883
	Members	[12,000]	[17,000]	31,343		79,808	84,821	94,992	101,744	127,581	114,145
New Jersey	Churches	......	......	24	63*	75	101	120	148	181	214
	Members	[800]	[1,000]	1,286	5,954*	9,322	13,517	17,595	24,508	32,931	39,529
Pennsylvania	Churches	......	......	59		241†	328	378	498	588	653 W
	Members	[3,000]	4,000]	4,998	[10,000]	20,767†	29,331	38,478	57,082	70,410	87,868
Delaware	Churches	6	6	7	9	......	1	3	5	11	13
	Members	268	509	553	546	......	352	426	......	1,924	1,783
Census Enumeration	N. Y.	589,051	959,049	1,372,111	1,918,608	2,428,921	3,097,394	3,880,735	4,382,759	5,082,871	5,997,853
	N. J.	211,149	245,562	277,426	320,823	373,306	489,555	672,035	906,096	1,131,116	1,444,933
	Penna.	602,365	810,091	1,047,507	1,348,233	1,724,033	2,311,786	2,906,215	3,521,951	4,282,891	5,258,014
	Delaware	64,273	72,674	72,749	76,748	78,085	91,532	112,216	125,015	146,608	168,493

* These are the official figures for 1834, the first official statistics printed.
† Figures for 1841, the first official statistics.

TABLE IV

EDUCATIONAL INSTITUTIONS

OF

BAPTISTS OF THE MIDDLE STATES

	Endowment.	Total Value of Property.
SEMINARIES:		
Hamilton...............	(included in	Colgate University).
Rochester...............	608,743	787,087
Crozer.....................	417,500	517,500
COLLEGES:		
Colgate...................	1,704,373	2,404,373
Rochester...............	760,237	1,280,894
Vassar.....................	1,068,000	2,172,700
Bucknell..................	400,000	650,000
Temple....................	5,000	186,000
ACADEMIC:		
Cook.......................	100,000	255,000
Marion.....................		17,000
Colgate...................	55,000	130,000
Peddie.....................	170,000	420,000
South Jersey...........	50,000	203,000
Bucknell..................	(included	above)
Keystone.................	13,300	118,300
Mt. Pleasant...........	45,000	78,000

APPENDIX C

PENNSYLVANIA

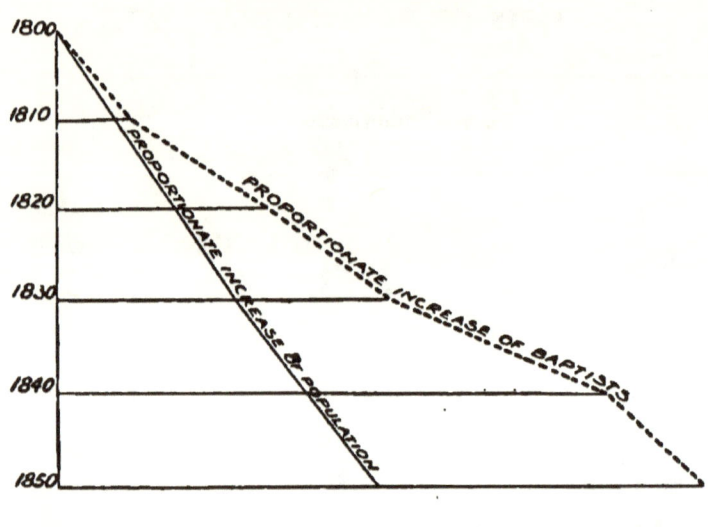

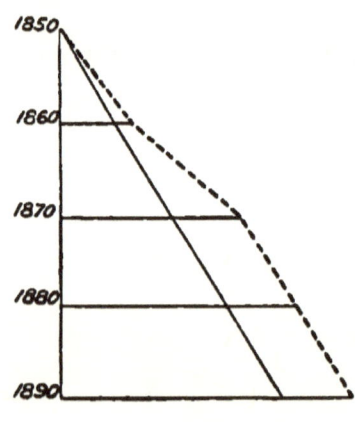

APPENDIX C

NEW YORK

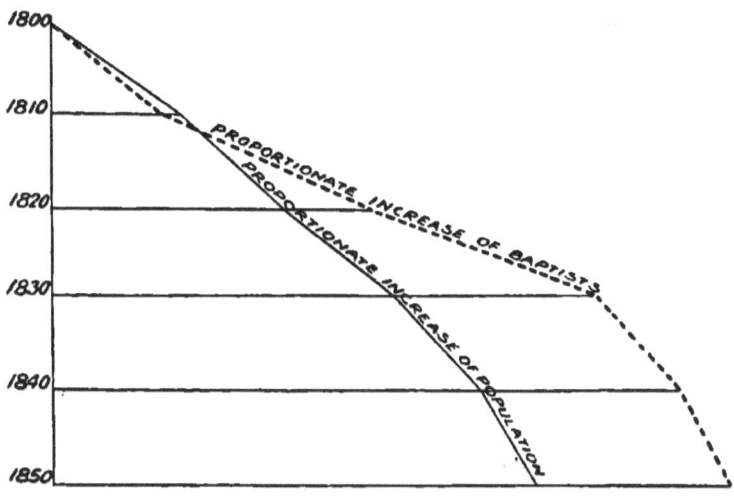

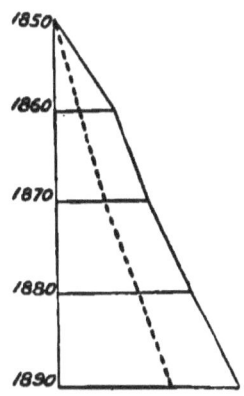

APPENDIX C

NEW JERSEY

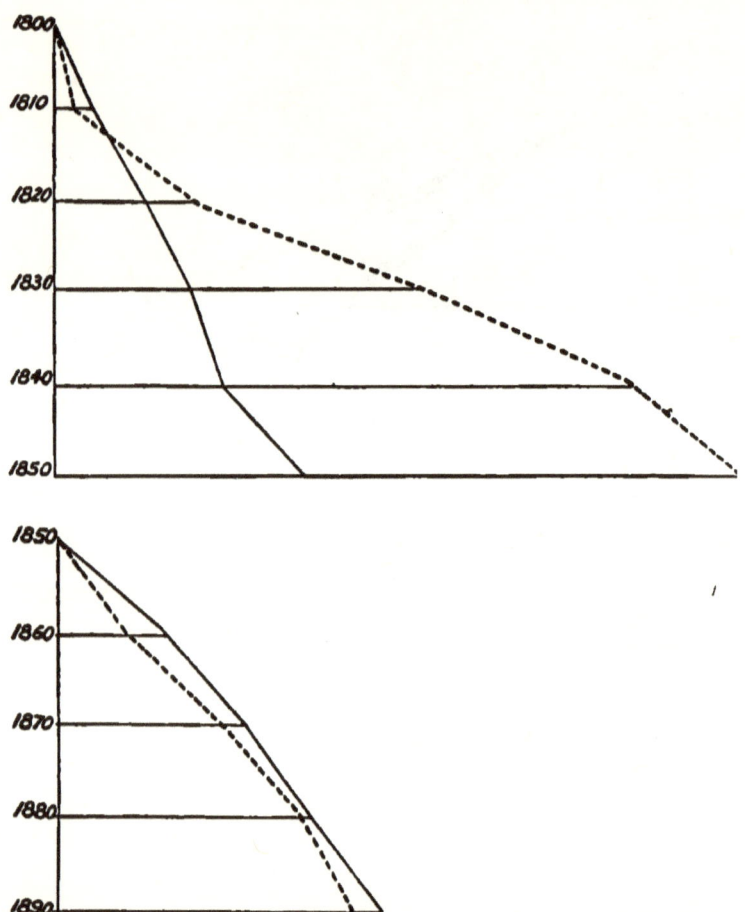

APPENDIX D

The following extract from "Half a Century's Labors in the Gospel," an autobiography of Rev. Thomas S. Sheardown (Philadelphia, 1865), will give an idea of the excitement among the churches during the Anti-Masonic agitation:

I refer now to the days of William Morgan, when the Anti-Masonic and Masonic advocates were so belligerent. While considering the matter, I reflected that wherever evil existed the only reformatory power is to be found in the gospel of God's salvation; when that is experienced, it works reform that will be permanent. I well knew that my bark was but small, and it would be safest to keep well in-shore, lest peradventure I should be swamped amid the fearful storms that were beating upon Zion. My desire was, as far as possible, to preach Jesus Christ and him crucified. For some time I met with very little opposition or trouble from either party, and thought all was going well. My aim was to run in the middle channel, and steer as clear as possible of arguments and conversations on either side. I desired to save our churches from ruin, for I thought there were good brethren on both sides of the question.

I had a preaching place in the suburbs of a little church, within the bounds of my labors. A barn was prepared on purpose for worship through the summer season, with seats for the congregation, and a stand elevated some two feet above the main level for the speaker. One Sabbath afternoon, as I was going to this station, I left my horse about a mile behind, to feed while I was preaching, and took it afoot. Up a little rise of ground in sight of the place of my appointment, I saw quite a crowd in the barn-yard. A brother was walking ahead of me a short distance; when I came up with him I said, "Why, what are all the people doing out of doors to-day?" He remarked, "You will find out, sir, that the people are not all out of doors. I presume the barn is full," and he said, I think, "you will find out what it means before you get through. If you ain't mobbed to-day, it will be a wonder to me." I inquired, "What is the matter?" "Matter enough," he said. "The Anti-Masons have found out that you are a Mason, and they are determined not to hear you preach. The Masons are here from all around to protect you, and have you preach. It is a well-known fact," he added, "that you used to attend Masonic lodges in England." "Well, what next?" "They say it can be proved that you have attended Masonic lodges in this country, and the public will put you where you ought to be." "Well, is that all?" He answered, "No. They want to know what fellowship you have for Masons who are Christians." "Anything more, sir?" "No. It will be best for you to find the other out by experience." I remarked to him, "Very well, sir. I presume there will be no trouble about this thing."

As I passed in through the people I saw there was a good deal of whispering and blinking of the eye at me. I pressed forward, and in the majesty of my religion took my stand, and laid out of my pocket, as usual, my hymn-book and Bible. There appeared to be some commotion, but not much. I remarked to them: "Now, I want to say a few words before I open religious services.

Although my congregation to-day is much larger than usual, yet I feel a peculiar satisfaction, in looking it over, that I know almost every individual present. I have preached to you in different places, and I have always had this satisfaction, that when I look upon you you always appeared as though you believed what I was telling you was the truth. I have just learned, as I was walking up the hill, that there are certain statements made relative to me—first, that I am a Mason. Now, then, I tell you candidly and honestly that I am not, nor never was, though I have wondered perhaps a thousand times why I was not, for my business life always threw me more or less amongst the Masonic fraternity. I know nothing about them in their organic or individual relations to each other. I understand it is also said to be susceptible to proof that I have attended Masonic lodges since I have been in this country. This is a grand mistake, or a palpable falsehood. As it regards there being any proof of my ever attending Masonic lodges in the Old World, I do not believe that any such proof can be brought. I have yet to find the individual on this side of the Atlantic who knew me in my own country. I am not going to deny that I ever was in Masonic lodges in that country. It was very common with the fraternity to have their lodges open on a part of St. John's Day, for all those who wished, to go in and see their tables set, and the badges, medals, regalias, pictures, etc., which adorned the walls of their dining rooms. When passing those places I have turned in with others (for hundreds often went as curiosity seekers). So that part of the story is true from my own confession, not from testimony. I have been in Masonic lodges in my own country; but never in the time of their sessions.

There is another thing you desire to know, and that is whether I have any fellowship for Masons who are Christians. My answer to that is this : I understand it to be God's work to change the heart of man and turn him from nature to grace, and if God makes Christians of Masons it would be vain for me to undertake to undo God's work, and pull down that which I am laboring so hard to build up. As it regards church fellowship for Masons, if a man has more fellowship for the Masonic fraternity than he has for the church of God, I have no fellowship for him as a Christian ; consequently my church fellowship would rest on the same base. Now I feel that I have conscientiously declared to you the whole truth, and I read in your countenances that this is an honest declaration of fact; we must believe the man. Therefore, I will now preach to you, as best I am able, without meddling with a vexed question that I know but very little about. My great object in coming among you from time to time is that I may do you good for eternity. The Lord bless you. Now we will sing " (such a hymn). My congregation was never more attentive; and I do not recollect that from that time onward I ever was called on publicly to say pro or con upon that subject (pp. 117-120).

APPENDIX E

The following anecdote regarding Elder Bennett, one of many such, seems to be worth rescuing from its undeserved oblivion. It is from the autobiography of Sheardown:

On one occasion the Association met in the town of Prattsburg. They had what is termed a log meeting house, far too small to hold the hundreds of people who had come together, and we repaired to the woods. I was invited to preach the first day. Elder Alfred Bennett (so widely known and so much beloved by the churches, not only as a pastor, but also as a missionary agent) being present, I invited him to pray before sermon. The sky had been lowering, and there were indications of rain. The thunder muttered upon the distant hills. The good man when in prayer appeared to be talking with God face to face. He said: "Now, Lord, thou knowest all about us, in what a helpless state we are. We have no shelter to flee to. We are here to worship thee. And now do not let it rain upon us and scatter us; for what should we do?" The thunder appeared to come nearer by—the blue-winged lightnings scathed the brow of heaven—everybody was looking for a severe drenching—but, to the utter astonishment, perhaps, of all present, there was not enough rain fell to cause a man to put his coat on (for scores were in their shirt-sleeves), while the rain continued to pour down all around us, sometimes within a quarter or a half a mile of the place where we were gathered. It was proverbial for many years, in that region of country, that Elder Bennett kept back the rain by prayer (p. 123).

APPENDIX F

By an inadvertence in the numbering of the pages, not enough space was available for the author to say in the Preface all that he desired to say. The following paragraphs should be read in connection with, and as a part of, the Preface:

For all matters of consequence the authority is indicated in footnotes. These have been made as few as possible; it would have been more easy to double their number and length, but the constant danger has been that the notes might become so voluminous as to swallow up the text. In all cases the most accessible edition has been chosen for reference. For example, the references to Backus are to the Newton reprint of 1871, and those to Benedict are to the one-volume edition of 1848, instead of, in either case, the rare first editions so dear (in every sense of the word) to the bibliophile.

Fitting acknowledgment should here be made to those who have aided so courteously, often at no small trouble to themselves, to make the history accurate and full. A list of all to whom application has been made for help would fill at least a page; and not one case is recalled in which aid has been refused or grudgingly given. In particular, thanks are due to Mr. Henry E. Lincoln, for many years the librarian of the American Baptist Historical Society, who was unwearied in his efforts to place at the author's disposal the treasures of a once invaluable collection of Baptist documents, and whose special

APPENDIX F

knowledge of Baptist literature has been of utmost service. Grateful mention should also be made of the courtesy of Prof. Ralph W. Thomas, of Hamilton, N. Y., curator of the Colgate Historical Collection, now the most valuable library of Baptist literature in the world, and to become more and more valuable to all Baptist historians, through the wise liberality of its founder, as the years pass by. Great help has also been derived from the valuable collection of books, pamphlets, and MSS., many of them extremely rare, bequeathed to Crozer Theological Seminary by the late Horatio Gates Jones. This includes what is now probably the only complete set of the "Materials" of Morgan Edwards (but a small portion of which was ever printed), without which so large a part of early Baptist history would be a blank. Friends all over the country have given or loaned copies of valuable documents, rare books, tracts, Minutes, etc., and to one and all the author returns his most hearty and sincere thanks.

INDEX

Academic education, 208, 212, 253, 320.
Adams, John Q., and Masonry, 195.
Anointing the sick, 67.
Anti-Masonry: origin, 194; becomes a political issue, 196; effect of on Baptist churches, 197.
Anxious seat, 153.
Asplund, "Register," 309.
Associations: Effect on Baptist progress, 86; first in England, 87; errors of English, 94; common principles of, 100; missionary operations of, 145.
Associations, New York: Canisteo, 118; Cattaraugus, 118; Chemung, 118, 136, 204; Chenango, 117; Cortland, 117; Franklin, 117; Holland Purchase, 139; Madison, 117; Mohawk, 117; Oneida, 117; Ontario, 118; Seneca, 118; Steuben, 118; Wayne, 118; Worcester, 117; Yates, 118.
Associations, Pennsylvania: Abington, 137; Beaver, 138, 191; Centre, 138; Clarion, 139; French Creek, 138; Monongahela, 139; Pittsburg, 139; Redstone, 138, 191.
Associations, New Jersey: Central, 139; East, 160; West, 159: Sussex, 160.
Associations, other States: Charleston, 95; Congaree (Bethel), 96, 98; Delaware, 84; Dover, 191; Kehukee, 97; Ketockton, 98; Mahoning, 185, 191; Rapi-

dan, 98; Sandy Creek, 96; Warren, 97.
Authors, Baptist, 323, *seq.*

Baptism: for remission of sins, 189; trine immersion, 73.
Baptists. New York: first mention of, 81; first congregation, 23, 25; and Governor Burnet, 23; First church, 28; difficulty in finding, 29; later history of, in New York City, 166 168; Calvinistic, 37; Arminian, 54; in Eastern New York, 36, *seq.;* of Dutchess County, 27, 33; pioneers in Central New York, 111; comparative growth, 310, 312. Pennsylvania: first, 59; after Revolution, 74; statistics of Edwards, 75; growth after 1800, 134, *seq.;* relation to New York, 136; in Philadelphia, 169, 174. New Jersey: first churches, 42; "Old School," 47; mixed communion, 51; Tunkers, 52; Rogerines, 53; Arminians and Calvinists, 54. Delaware: Welsh Tract, 65, 85, 90, 93; other churches, 82, *seq.;* in Wilmington, 83; many become "Old School," 84; antimission, or "Old School," 47, 103, 203; alleged decline of, 205; Arminian, 54; begin to decline, 92; Calvinistic, 37; ascendency of, 93; general, in England, 94; golden age of, 113; Rogerine, 53.
Baptists, Seventh-day: in New

351

Jersey, 52, 53; in Pennsylvania, 65, 68, 71; and literature, 323, seq.; and evangelism of the West, 145; and journalism, 285, 328; seq.; Separates, 98, 115; Welsh, influence of, 93.

Baptist colleges: Brown University, 91, 93, 209-212; Colgate University, 221, seq.; Bucknell, origin, 247; later growth, 249-251; Columbian University, origin, 216-218; relation to Hamilton, 222; University of Rochester, 222-227, 231-238; Vassar, 251, seq.

Baptist academies: Hopewell, 208; other early, 212; Colgate, 227; others in Middle States, 213.

Baptist theological schools: why founded, 213; Staughton's private, 214; Newton, 248; Hamilton, 221; Rochester, 234; Crozer, 242-247; present condition, 321.

Baptist preachers in the West, 145.

Baptist societies. General Convention: organization, 102; domestic missions, 104; representative character, 146; educational enterprise, 216. Home Mission, origin and history, 147, seq. Publication: origin as Tract Society, 258; removal to Philadelphia, 259; first publications, 261; Arch street building, 263; later history, 264; its expansion, 265-269; and the young people's work, 281-285; changes its name, 298; ·ible work, 307. Lake Missionary, 105, 121. Young People's: early, 269; Christian Endeavor, 262; denominational, 275, seq.; Loyalist movement, 277; Baptist unions, 279, seq. Education, early, 213. New York Baptist, 218. New York Baptist Union, 234. City Mission, New York, 167.

Baptist laymen: Anderson, Martin B., 147, 235-238, 300; Beebee, A. M., 106, 328; Bishop, Nathan, 147, 300; Bowne, John, 17, 42; Brown, Nicholas, 212; Bucknell, Wm., 247, 248, 249, 251; Colgate, Wm., 106, 147, 230, 287, 293, 295; Colgate, Samuel, 231; Colgate, James B., 227, 231; Crozer, John P., 147, 241, seq., 248; Dodge, Jeremiah, 27; Hart, John, 48, 95; Holmes, John, 62, 63; Miller, Wm., 194, 198-200; Olmstead, Jonathan, 115, 219, 230; Payne, Samuel, 115, 218; Raymond, John H., 223, 252; Stout family, 42, 46; Vassar, Matthew, 251.

Baptist ministers: patriots in the Revolution, 79, seq.; Armitage, Thomas, 304, 324; Baker, Nathan, 121, 123; Baker, Elijah, 82; Benedict, James, 34; Benedict, David, 34, 36, 39, 46; Bennett, Alfred, 123, 130, seq., 196; Brown, J. Newton, 134; Bright, Edward, 165, 300, 329; Calvert, John B., 165, 329; Chaplin, Jeremiah, 219; Cone, Spencer H., 173, 287, 292; Conant, Thomas J., 234, 321; Davis, Noah, 257; Dodge, E., 229, 321; Dongan, Thomas, 59; Eaton, Isaac, 48, 208; Eaton, George W., 229; Edwards, Morgan, 29, 43, 77, seq., 94, 207, 309, 323; Eyres, Nicholas, 22, 23, 24, 25; Feeks, Robert, 27; Foster, Benjamin, 32; Gano, John, 29, 31, 32, 47, 91, 95, 208; Galusha, Elon, 106, 133; Going, J., 147; Griffith B., 263; Griffiths, Thomas, 66; Harris, J. H., 250; Haskall, Daniel, 106, 219, 229; Haynes, S., 106; Hill, David J., 237, 249, 327; Holcombe, H., 171; Hosmer, A., 110, 121, 123; Hoyt, Wayland, 283, 304; Hovey, Alvah, 307; Hughes,

INDEX 353

Philip, 82, 83; Jones, Samuel, 42, 76, 209; Jones, Jenkins, 63; Jones, H. G., 61; Judson, Adoniram, 101, 182, 287; Knapp, Jacob, 154; Keach, Elias, 59-62, 92; Killingworth, Thomas, 54; Knollys, Hanserd, 45; Kendrick, A. C., 233, 321, 325; Kendrick, N., 106, 219, 221, 228; Kincaid, Eugenio, 139, 220, 248; Lawton, John, 111, 123, 136; Luce, Matthias, 187; Maclay, Archibald, 106, 215, 287; Malcom, Howard, 218, 249; Manning, James, 17, 93, 208, 210; Morgan, Abel, 42, 65; Miller, Benjamin, 49; Nobel, Abel, 65; Osgood, Howard, 246, 300; Parkinson, William, 173; Peck, John, 106, 123, seq.; Pepper, G. D. B., 246; Rauschenbusch, A., 241; Rice, Luther, 101, 102, 105, 216, 259; Rhodes, William, 26; Robinson, Ezekiel G., 239, 321; Rogers, William, 77; Root, P. P., 111, 136, 219; Smiley, Thomas, 74; Smith, Hezekiah, 47, 91, 208; Somers, Charles G., 106, 215, 287, 293; Staughton, William, 77, 214, 242; Stearns, Shubael, 96; Stamford, John, 212, 215, 258; Strong, A. H., 239, 301; Swan, Jabez, 154; Taylor, Stephen W., 228, 248; Taylor, James M., 252; Van Osdel, O. W., 277; Watts, John, 63, 76; Wade, Jonathan, 220; Weston, Henry G., 246, 307; Wickenden, William, 19, 22, 26; Wightman, Valentine, 22, 26; Williams, John, 215; Williams, Roger, 58; Williams, William R., 324.

Bible, versions of: Judson's, 228; Pearce and Yates, 289, 293; Missionary, 293; English, 294; Bible Union, 296.

Bible societies. British and Foreign: organized, 286; policy on versions, 289. American: founded, 287; grants to Baptists, 288; decision on versions, 289; protests of Baptists, 290; change in by-laws, 299; final action, 302. American and Foreign: origin, 292; action on English versions, 294. American Bible Union: formed, 295; achievements, 296; attempts at union with other societies, 297 seq.

Buffalo: settled, 119; Baptist church organized in, 133.

Burnett, Governor, 23.

Butternuts, settlement at, 34.

Campbell, Alexander, 176, 177, 180, 184, 186, etc.

Campbell, Thomas, 176, 181.

Christian Endeavor, origin of, 272.

Clark, Francis E., 272.

Confession, Philadelphia, 91.

Controversies: on removal of Hamilton institutions, 223-27; with Campbellites, 190, seq.; with Masons, 196; with Millerites, 202; on Young People's work, 275, seq.; with American Bible Society, 289, seq.; on Bible translations, 294, seq.

Conventions: General Baptist, 102, 104, 216, 292; character of State, 108. New York State: origin, 105, 106; early missions, 120-134; later growth, 162-165. Pennsylvania: origin, 107; missionary activity, 139-142. New Jersey: 162-162. Albany, educational, 225; Philadelphia Bible, 292; Saratoga, Bible, 304; B. Y. P. U. A., Chicago, 283.

Churches, New York: Bottskill, 33; Brooklyn (First), 27; Buffalo (First), 133; Burlington, 110; Butternuts, 110; Calvary,

x

168; Carmel, 33; Chester, 37; Charleston, 110; Dover Furnace, 33; Edmeston, 110; Fairfield and Palatine, 110; Franklin, 110; Fishkill, 27, 33; Hamilton, 115, 116; Hartwick, 110; Kortwright, 110; Morris, 35; New York (First), 28, 90, 168; New Berlin, 110; Northeast, 33; Otego, 110; Otsego, 110; Oyster Bay, 26; Pawling, 33; Pleasant Valley, 33; Richfield, 110; Rochester (First), 133; Springfield, 110; Stamford, 33; Warwick, 33; Wellsburg, 35; White Creek, 33.

Churches, New Jersey: revivals among, 150; Burlington, 88; Cape May, 49; Cohansey, 45, 61, 88, 90; Hopewell, 46; Middletown, 42, 55, 90; Morristown, 49; Piscataway, 44, 90; Salem, 51, 88; Scotch Plains, 28, 49; Seventh-day, 52; Tunker, 52; Wantage, 50.

Churches, Pennsylvania: Brush Run, 179; Chemung, 74; Cold Spring, 59; Great Valley, 68; Hilltown, 69; Little Muncy, 136; Marcus Hook, 69; Montgomery, 68; Mt. Pleasant, 137; New Britain, 69; Palmyra, 137; Pennepek, 60, 66, 88, 89; Philadelphia (First), 62, 171-174; Roxborough, 69; Shamokin, 136; Southampton, 69; Wellsburg, 185; White Deer Valley, 74; White Deer, 136.

Churches, Delaware: Bethel, 83; Bryn Zion, 82; Cowmarsh, 82; Gravelly Branch, 83; Mispillion, 83; Sounds, 82; Welsh Tract, 65, 85, 90, 93; First Wilmington, 83, 85; Second Wilmington, 84.

Christian Culture Courses, 285, 319.

Delaware Baptists in 1791, 85.

Disciples: origin of, 176, *seq.*; excluded from Baptist churches, 91; cause of growth, 192, 193.
Dover Association, action on Disciples, 191.

Ephrata colony, 71.
Evangelism and preaching, 156.

Finney, Charles G.: his revivals, 151; new measures of, 152.
Friends, yearly meetings, 87.
Fulton Street prayer meeting, 157

Goetwasser, Rev. Ernest, 15.
Great awakening, 96, 149.

Hines, Rev. J. B., 200.
Hodgson, Robert, 15.
Hudson discovers New Netherlands, 9.
Hunter, Governor, 22.

Independence of churches, 94.
Indians, work among, 162.

James II. charter, 21.
Jefferson, Thomas, 143.
Jews, disfranchised in Pennsylvania, 58.

Keifft, Wm., 12.
Keith and the Keithians, 64, 65, 69.

Laying on of hands, 62.
Louisiana purchase, 143.
Loyalists, 277.
Lutherans persecuted, 13.

Michælius, Rev. Jonas, 11.
Miller, Wm., 194, 198-200.
Millerism: origin of, 197; progress of, 201; effect of, on Baptists, 202.
Mormonism, rise of, 175.
Morris, Robert, and the Holland Purchase, 119.

INDEX

New Amsterdam: settlement, 10; first pastor in, 11.
New Jersey: early history of, 38, *seq.;* revivals in, 150.
"New Lights"; see "Separates."

Otsego Association: organization of, 110; strict rules of admission in, 116; area of, 117; its fruitfulness, 118.

Pennsylvania: why settled, 10; and religious liberty, 56.
Persecutions: of Goetwasser and Hodgson, 15; in New Jersey, 41; of Baptists in Massachusetts, 114; of John Bowne, 17; see Religious liberty.
Philadelphia Association: origin of, 88-90; Confession of Faith, 91; great influence of, 93; refuses to become a court, 94; promotes formation of other Associations, 97, *seq.;* missionary efforts of, 135; its decrease in membership, 169; disunion in, 171; educational work of, 209.
Philadelphia, First Church: origin of, 62; controversy in, 171-174; and Dr. Staughton, 204.
Population, movements of: from New England to New York, 113, *seq.;* into Western New York, 119, *seq.;* into Pennsylvania, 134, *seq.;* across the Alleghenies, 142, *seq.,* 311; in New York City, 168; toward the cities, 315.

Raikes, Robert, not a Baptist, 255.
Reformed Church: its ministers intolerant, 15; and the Dutch, 11, 16, 18.
Religious liberty: and the Dutch, 11, 16, 18; and the English, 20; in New Jersey, 39, *seq.;* in Rhode Island, 40; denied in Newark, 41; in Pennsylvania, 56-58; petition to Continental Congress for, 80; see Persecutions.
Revivals: notable, 86; in New England, 96, 149; at Hamilton, 116; Finney's, 151; in the West, 149; in Pennsylvania, 150; effect on church growth, 158-160.
Rogerines, 53.
Ruling elders, 61, 62.

Sandamanian sect, 178.
Separates: in Virginia, 98, 99; and missions, 103; in New York, 115.
Seventh-day Baptists: in New Jersey, 52, 53; in Pennsylvania, 65, 68, 71.
Scott, Walter, 189.
Spiritualism, rise of, 175.
Spruce Street Church, Philadelphia, 173.
Stuyvesant, Peter: character of, 12; and the Lutherans, 13.
Sunday-schools: earliest, 255; rapid progress, 256; literature for, 257.

Tunkers: in New Jersey, 52; in Pennsylvania, 70, *seq.;* theology and practice, 72.

Virginia, settlers of, 10.

Washington, opinion of Baptist chaplains, 30.
West India Company: formed, 10; on persecution, 14; proclamation of liberty, 16.
Wild Yankees, 74.

www.ingramcontent.com/pod-product-compliance
Lightning Source LLC
Chambersburg PA
CBHW030252240426
43673CB00040B/954